An Unexpected Journey
Kiersten Hall

with Forewords by
Kimberly Dawn & Lisa Ann

An Unexpected Journey

Kiersten Hall

For My Person, F.D.N.

An unplanned book for an unplanned relationship
that was but wasn't, and is always and forever.

www.foxpointepublishing.com/author-kiersten-hall

Library of Congress Cataloging-in-Publication Data
HALL, KIERSTEN, author.
FARR, CHELSEA, designer.
AN UNEXPECTED JOURNEY / KIERSTEN HALL. – First edition.
Summary: An unplanned book for an unplanned
relationship that was and is, always and forever.

Hardcover ISBN 979-8-9952827-4-7 / Softcover ISBN 979-8-995282-75-4
[1. Autobiography – Memoir. 2. Relationship – Romance.
3. Mind, Body, Spirit – General.]
Library of Congress Control Number: 2026938274
First printing June 2026

Table of Contents

A Message to Readers i
Foreword by Kimberly Dawn v
Foreword by Lisa Anne vii
Prologue xi
Chapter 1 1
Chapter 2 5
Chapter 3 9
Chapter 4 12
Chapter 5 18
Chapter 6 26
Chapter 7 33
Chapter 8 36
Chapter 9 42
Chapter 10 51
Chapter 11 73
Chapter 12 81
Chapter 13 89
Chapter 14 100
Chapter 15 105
Chapter 16 123
Chapter 17 130

Journal Entries
    from November 19, 2024 &
    March 11, 2025 - March 31, 2026 137
Epilogue - written on March 31, 2026 271
April 2026
    Journal Entries 276
Fred's Thoughts on April 21, 2026 284
Acknowledgments 289
About the Author 291

Throughout this book, you'll see *(video)* after paragraphs, every so often. You can use this QR Code to access the playlist for *An Unexpected Journey* on my YouTube Channel, www.youtube.com/@wyrdnwylde, to see the corresponding event/situation.

A Message to Readers

Thank you for choosing to read this memoir. I wasn't planning on writing a book about my travels; I had actually started a YouTube Channel instead. I thought it would be much more fun to record the adventures I go on rather than write about them. For example, recording and watching a museum visit is more fun than reading about it over a couple of chapters.

So, with my YouTube Channel set up, all my "needed" necessities shoved into the back of my midsize SUV, a promise to my twelve-year-old self, and an unhealthy lack of fear of the unknown, I set off down the road with no idea what would happen.

My three main objectives were:

- Never see a snowbank ever again for the rest of my life, or have to live in sub-zero temps, or deal with black ice, or blizzards, or… You get the point.
- Live an adventurous life—something different from the first fifty-four years on this planet.
- Sit in a lawn chair and watch lizards jump on and off rocks in the desert.

The above three points are what my first fifty-four years of life had boiled down to: No icy winters or cold temps, adventure, lizards on rocks, and a lawn chair for comfort.

Simple and stupid, and it worked for me.

Well, what is that phrase about making plans and the universe laughs? Mmm hmm…

I met a man.

I knew I'd most likely meet new people during my travels, but meeting a romantic interest wasn't on that carefully crafted BINGO Card.

Throughout this book, you'll read all about him, how we met, our time spent together and apart, and serendipitously together again, as well as my thoughts on the biggest adventure, to date, that I have experienced.

I'd like to add and stress that even after the death of this gentleman, whom I had befriended, I was only journaling about my experiences for myself. Actually, this was the first time in my entire life I had ever journaled or kept a diary; I've never had the discipline to write each day… until this unexpected journey began.

Anyway, I started journaling my experiences with him after his death. Yes, you read that correctly—after his death, as well as jotting down the experiences with him while he was still physically in this realm. My goal was to keep these notes for myself so I wouldn't forget any of them. My end-all was never to publish a book. However, he had different plans. Again, you read that correctly. This book is Fred's idea—and you read that correctly, too.

I have been journaling since March 12, 2025—the day he died—and for this book, I will include all experiences through March 31, 2026. He has lit a fire under my derriere, which you will read about further along in this book. I told him that I would finish writing in March of 2026, with a hopeful release on what would have been his sixty-fourth birthday, June 25, 2026. Typically, writing a book and all of the other processes of getting a book to market take a lot longer than a few months, but he's on a mission, and I'm in the office pulling ten- to twelve-hour days to get this done for him.

My other conundrum was that I wasn't comfortable slapping a price tag on it; I didn't want to "cheapen" or disrespect Fred, or our relationship. He, however, has made it clear that this book needs to be written and sold to the masses as soon as possible. Again, you read that correctly, and you'll find out how he expressed his urgency further in the book.

I'll also add that although I began documenting this experience in March 2025, I didn't begin writing the beginning chapters of the book until early February 2026, after receiving my latest homework assignment to write this memoir.

Noteworthy: These are solely my memories, my views, opinions, and experiences with Fred. I have not spoken with anyone in his family or any of his friends.

Because this is a compilation of several notes and documents, there are some repeats. However, the repeats contain different information and were most likely placed to support the story being told at that time. The *Journal Entries* section of the book, covering events from March 12, 2025, through March 31, 2026, lays them out chronologically. (The decision to include the April 2026 occurrences was made because the book was still being compiled then, and some of those activities are included in the manuscript.)

I'll add that there are tidbits of thoughts I noted in the middle of the night after waking up unexpectedly. Going through those entries now, after some time has passed, I wasn't always sure what I meant at 3:33 a.m. that particular day, so I left the tidbit. I might actually remember what it means in the future.

Interestingly, though, as you read this book, you'll recognize why things happened the way they did: the culmination of events, the answers to lingering questions, etc. It's been a unique learning experience for me, cementing that old adage, "Everything happens for a reason." And yes, it does.

You will also notice that this book isn't written in a traditional/typical story form per se, but more along the lines of a "documented" story, and is very conversational as if we were all sitting around having tea. So, the layout and "vibe" are intentional.

I wrote this from a first-person perspective, and there is some swearing, some references to sexual angst, some broken thoughts, a lot of laughter, and a bit of crying. Essentially, the reader will go on this unexpected journey with me.

Lastly, for people in his family or friend circle, I don't use their names since they have no idea about this book's creation; instead, I use descriptors when possible. There is one person, however, from Fred's life whom I list as "L.M."—her initials. I don't know her personally, nor have I ever spoken to her, but I feel she should be mentioned because her name comes up both before and after his death.

With all that being said, both Fred and I hope you enjoy this book as well as the experiences we have shared thus far, and that we (hopefully) will continue to share in the future.

Foreword by Kimberly Dawn

written on March 30, 2026

The deepest loves carry the greatest losses. Love can lift us to unimaginable heights, and when it is taken from us, it can send us plummeting into the lowest valleys. Words left unsaid, moments never shared, and unfinished business can make the absence feel unbearably sharp.

When I learned of Kiersten's loss, it was early in my own journey of self-discovery and spiritual exploration. I was still learning how to honor the gift I have—the ability to receive and share messages beyond the physical—and how to navigate the responsibility that comes with it. This gift is sacred and never casual; it calls for care, respect, and discernment.

Part of the reason I felt compelled to share and approach Kiersten is that knowing that there is an existence beyond physical death carries with it a quiet sense of duty; to help others navigate grief by offering moments of connection, comfort, and closure that might otherwise feel unattainable.

In Kiersten's case, I knew her well enough to reach out. I was confident that this gift had a purpose, and keeping it to myself would have been a disservice. If I could provide even a small measure of comfort, clarity, or closure within her grief, it was not only an opportunity—but a responsibility—to do so.

Over the months that followed, I witnessed a quiet, profound process unfold. This book is the story of how she navigated love and loss, and how, even in the most raw and vulnerable moments, connection—whether emotional, spiritual, or unseen—can provide support and healing. My role was never to define her experience or take her grief from her, but to honor it and hold space while she found her own path forward.

Grief is deeply personal. Each of us experiences it differently, and there is no universal roadmap. Yet one truth has become clear to me through both personal experience and quiet observation: nothing in this world truly ceases to exist—it simply changes form. We understand this through the natural laws that govern the physical world, where matter is never destroyed, only transformed. In my own experiences surrounding death, I have come to witness it not as an ending, but as a transition. The physical body may no longer remain, but the essence—the soul, the energy, the love—does not disappear. It continues, unchanged in its presence, even if it is experienced differently. Nothing has been lost, only transformed.

For many, this continued connection is not always experienced through words, but through moments—subtle, meaningful synchronicities that seem to arrive at just the right time: a song, a symbol, a memory, or an unexplainable sense of presence. Many people recognize these moments instinctively, feeling them as messages or signs in their own quiet way.

It is an honor to witness this transition, just as welcoming a new life into the world is precious. I share this not to convince, but to consider. Sometimes, even the possibility of continued connection can soften the edges of grief and allow space for healing in ways we might not expect.

I offer these words not as a claim to knowing all the answers, but as an invitation to approach this book with an open heart. Allow it to meet you where you are. Perhaps it will offer reflection, comfort, or even a sense of connection to your own experiences of love, loss, and the transformations that follow.

- Kimberly Dawn
KimberlyDawn@dandelionwise.com

written on April 25, 2026

Have you ever met someone and immediately felt as though you had known them forever? As a retired, full-time RV traveler, I have met many people all across the country. In most cases, my friendship with those people has been limited to our shared time and place. When I met Kiersten, however, our friendship was instantaneous and felt as deep as one nurtured for years.

We had spent time together, but the catalyst behind our friendship became very clear only after I helped Kiersten move to another location. During our drive across the Arizona desert, Kiersten began to share the story of the tremendous loss she experienced when her "person" passed away. She had shared bits and pieces of their relationship in the past, but never to this extent.

Although their time together had been short, it was apparent that his effect on her was life-changing. Her emotions were raw and unfiltered as she spoke about him, and the depth of her grief was palpable. I was very relaxed, lounging in the passenger seat of Kiersten's car on our trip back to Phoenix. My eyes were closed, and as I listened to the cadence of her voice and the hum of the tires on the pavement, I was transported in a way I had never experienced before. I was able to give her the answer to her most pressing question: *Why did he leave her so soon?* Then I told her she needed to write this book because Fred told me their future depended on it.

I never met Fred, had never seen a picture of him, and yet, in my mind's eye, I could "see" him. I described to her what he looked like: a big man with silver hair, twinkling eyes, and a dimpled smile. I told her what he was wearing: a black leather jacket, dark sunglasses, black boots. She confirmed to me that I was, in fact, seeing Fred. With that confirmation, the floodgates were opened! A vibration of energy coursed through my body, starting at my toes and surging to the crown of my head. My heart was racing; I began sweating even though the car's cabin was not warm, and, although my eyes were closed, I became hyper-aware of the energy surrounding me.

I only remember disjointed snippets of the conversation that occurred next. Key phrases stand out, yet the surrounding context remains cloudy. I remember Fred showing me Kiersten in the future. She was sitting at a table, signing copies of this book, while a particular man observed the signing. I could see that Kiersten and this gentleman had met briefly, but didn't really know each other. I also knew that this man was "Fred." Not the physical Fred whom Kiersten had known, but Fred's soul in a different package. (I shared more details with Kiersten during the channeling and in the initial draft of this Foreword, but decided to omit those specifics for safety and privacy.)

I then turned to Kiersten and told her, in a voice she described as being much lower in timbre than my usual speaking voice, that she needed to write this book, that the book was the key to Fred returning to her in this lifetime. She momentarily took her eyes off the road, looked at me incredulously, and asked, "Well, how in the hell is that gonna happen?!" Chuckling, I told her in my normal voice that I had no clue, but that Fred would come back to her in THIS lifetime.

I told her Fred was showing me that their story would serve as a beacon of light and hope to anyone struggling with the darkness of loneliness, by demonstrating that true love transcends time and space and that there is more out there than the here and now. Again, I told her she needed to write the book. She argued that, while she had always planned to write about their story, she never wanted to publish it or profit from their extraordinary relationship. I looked directly at her and reiterated in that same low timbre, "Write the book!"

At some point during our ride, Kiersten revealed the name she had chosen for their story. I remember repeating the title back to her in that low timbre, slowly enunciating each word as though I were contemplating its appropriateness. "An unexpected……..journey. I like it." I can assure you that this is not the way I would normally react or speak. I tend to be a bit "over the top" with my praise and enthusiasm when I like something.

Fred also shared with me that he had not told Kiersten he was dying because her heart could not have handled it. That is also why he has not communicated with her directly. As for the answer to her most pressing question, Fred explained to me why his time with her had been so brief. "You aren't patient," he said. Fred's spirit knew that Kiersten needed this brief interlude with him so he could show her the path to their pre-destined future. Kiersten was becoming disillusioned about where she perceived her life was heading and was impatient for something better, something more. His brief visit was meant to get her back on the track that would reunite them as this life intended.

Fred continued to communicate with me and through me for the remainder of our ride, and has visited me a couple of times since then. The first time was when I was talking to Kiersten one afternoon about writing this Foreword and told her I would welcome a visit from Fred so he could light a fire under me to get this written piece done. While he had been turning her solar light on and off as we talked, she asked him to come visit me. Within a minute of that request, a strong wind pushed off the side of her RV. A minute later, a strong gust shook my RV on a day that had been, and continued to be, calm. Wind is just one of the ways Fred makes his presence known.

On a different day, when I was supposed to be finishing the Foreword I had started writing, I was playing a game on my phone instead, and it froze. No matter what I did to fix the issue, I couldn't get the phone to unfreeze.

So, I finished writing and sent my contribution for this book to Kiersten. Completing that task unfroze my phone, and I went back to my game. I later found out from her that a few minutes before my phone froze, she had asked Fred to "remind me" to finish the Foreword she'd been waiting on.

A couple of weeks ago, Kiersten visited me for the weekend, and that first evening, Fred made his presence known with a couple of bumps to the RV. I witnessed, first-hand, the flickering lights and his penchant for playing with the car stereo. It was off, then suddenly turned on at a high volume, surprising everyone in the car. Fred is very much still here.

In fact, just this morning when Kiersten asked me to expand on my experiences with Fred, I got that same surge of energy, even stronger this time, and have worked nonstop ever since. Fred helped me remember some of the specifics I had forgotten when he was talking to Kiersten through me.

It is my hope that these insights help you in understanding how extraordinary these events have been. You now have in your hands the story of a love so profound it defies logical explanation and a connection so deep it spans lifetimes. Regardless of what you believe to be true about the human soul, you owe it to yourself to open your mind and experience what true love really is.

- Lisa Anne

Prologue

Around 1981, I was an inquisitive kid who spent much of my time alone, entertaining myself with anything I could read: Books, of course, but also maps, encyclopedias, the dictionary, newspapers, magazines, brochures, the VCR manual (although I never bothered to reset the clock)—you name it, and I probably read it. I also had an old Rand McNally mapbook in my room, along with old AAA maps/travel books, and a globe. From this wealth of information, I made lists of grand plans for what I would do when I got older and was no longer living in my parents' house.

One day, while my parents watched football in the family den, I sat in my bedroom making another one of my lists; this one covered all the traveling I intended to do as an adult. I figured that if, in my early twenties and after college, I got out on the road and lived in each of the fifty states for at least one year, I could really soak up the experiences each state offered, and I'd have something to do through my early seventies. It sounded like a good plan to me. So, I excitedly waited for the commercial break, then shared my latest "grand master plan" with my parents.

The first thing they asked was when I planned to get married. I replied that I wasn't that interested—the traveling sounded like a lot more fun. Then one of them asked when I was planning to have kids, and at that time (the age of twelve), I told them that kids weren't necessarily on my list of things to do, but if I changed my mind, I would just head over to a sperm bank and get that taken care of. (With the lack of the internet in the early eighties, and my age, I really have no idea where I got "sperm bank" from, but that was my backup plan should I decide that I needed their services—and I do remember telling my parents that idea.)

Needless to say, that was not what my parents were interested in hearing, especially my dad, and that original exciting conversation went down the tubes quickly.

Fast-forward to the age of sixteen, and I procured myself a "mandatory" boyfriend. I graduated high school at the age of seventeen, eventually moved in with said mandatory boyfriend, and then married the mandatory boyfriend when I was twenty-one. All the while, though, I yearned to travel and had not forgotten my grand master plan to live in each state for at least a year.

In my early twenties, realizing that my life was heading down a predestined detour scripted by others, I set a plan to spend at least six months in each state. As my detoured life settled in with the mandatory husband who only believed he (and me) should live in Minnesota and nowhere else on the entire planet, as well as children, businesses, everyday responsibilities, etc., the list of states started narrowing; which states could I skip and still not miss the entire idea of living in various locations? Or which states could I visit over a handful of months and still get the full experience? I had lived in Minnesota since 1975, and before that, in Southern California. So, I figured I had those locations out of the way, and there was no way on this green Earth I would want to be in Alaska for the winter, so I could combine that state with others over the course of a year to still get the "full" travel experience. I was still making plans, though they were constantly reshaped to appease others' expectations for how I should live my life.

Fast forward again to 2006, at the age of thirty-seven, I had concluded that the mandatory husband who only wanted to live in Minnesota, along with all the other issues that came with that mandatory marriage, was really not what I was looking for in life. Regarding our four children (and myself), the environment we were living in was not the type of life I wanted for all of us.

I remember looking out the north-facing kitchen window on a cold, gray September day in 2006, running through a mental calendar and thinking about the fact that my youngest would graduate high school in 2020. If I could just make it to June of 2020, I could become a "snowbird" and/or move completely in the winter of 2020/21. My other mission was to never, ever, ever see another Minnesota winter or live through another polar vortex after the kids got out of high school.

Needless to say, no one could have predicted what happened to the world in 2020 and 2021, especially fourteen years earlier, while looking out the kitchen window wistfully thinking about the future.

I will also add that I did get four wonderful kids out of my marriage—really, the only four good things to happen during that twenty-one-year mandatory detour from the life I was planning to live. All of them are still an integral part of my life, and, as my daughter once put it perfectly, I "gave birth to my four best friends." That statement still holds today, and I'm sure it will continue to hold for the rest of my life. I'm quite happy about that, too.

Getting through 2020/21 and spending a few more years in Minnesota while the last of my children finished up college, I found that the summer of 2023 had rolled around and that the youngest two had informed me they were moving to the next town over, closer to their workplace. It made sense, especially with the distance and winter driving.

But upon agreeing with their plans, it occurred to me that now was the time that I had planned for in 1981 and again in 2006. Now was the time to throw all sensible reasoning to the wind, and to sell/throw away/give away/store all of my belongings from the last fifty-four years of my life. I needed to get in the car and leave before the first hint of frozen water fell from the sky in 2023. It was now or never to finally live out my "inner-twelve-year-old's grand master plan," which I had come up with in 1981!

In 2020, when my youngest had graduated high school with a drive-through ceremony since no one could be within six feet of each other, I had started looking through YouTube and other online videos with a more serious attention span since I knew in a couple of years the kids would be out of school and out in the world, on their own. Mom would no longer be needed for daily activities or for a place to live. The time for me to also "fly the coop" was getting closer by the month.

It still shocked me, though, when my kids told me they were planning on moving in July of 2023. They had a couple of friends they were going to move out with in September 2023. I had sales events lined up for myself through mid-November and was actually planning on a possible surgery at the end of November 2023. But when they told me their timeline, and I remembered my plan to be out of Minnesota before the first trace of frozen water fell from the sky, I bumped up the move-out date by two months, from December 31, 2023, to October 31, 2023. It was a lot of packing, storing, giving away, and throwing away all of my belongings accumulated over fifty-four years. I also had to juggle my scheduled weekend events and weeklong sales events, e.g., exhibiting at state fairs in the Midwest. I canceled my surgery until further notice, and I still haven't done it. With the weight loss since leaving Minnesota, it's no longer really needed.

In early 2023, I had started a YouTube Channel for fun—figuring I would get used to producing videos to document the upcoming travels that I already was scheduled for, and prepping myself for the time I finally would get to "run away from home" and start the life my twelve-year-old self had suggested back in 1981.

Although the idea of monetizing my YouTube Channel was (and still is) a pipe dream, I wanted to document everything I saw and did so that I could look back on the memories later in life. Or, if I no longer knew what was going on, I could watch the videos and think, "The nice lady on the TV show looks like she's having fun," and wonder who she was. (Again, I was pre-planning for the future.) I also made the channel for my mom and all four of my kids; they could keep tabs on me and make sure I wasn't getting into too much trouble as I roamed across the world, wherever the wind took me.

When I finally did get out on the road, I had six published books. People who knew me asked when the first book about my nomadic life and experiences would come out. I had absolutely no plans to write about my travels—I wanted it all documented on the YouTube Channel that I had been filling with videos. As far as I was concerned, a travel video was much more exciting to watch than reading about a travel experience in a book over a chapter or two.

So, yes. This book was never on any grand master list I had ever put together. It certainly wasn't on my horizon of things to do. It was simply never planned.

But then again, what happened to me in the desert was never planned, either. And certainly never fathomed. The popular saying "I didn't think this would be on my 2023 Bingo Card" would be an understatement.

What happened? I found love. True love. A real love that I had grown to believe corporate America capitalized on over the first fifty-four years of my life. A tagline that sold more greeting cards and boxes of chocolates for birthdays, weddings, holidays, and courtship to the rose-colored-glasses crew. This belief of "true love" was merely to sell romance movies and books to the gullible. Over the first fifty-four years of my life, without experiencing what I did in the Sonoran Desert during the 2023/24 season, I had become cynical and jaded with all matters of "romantic" love. I'm not saying that tongue-in-cheek, either. I truly thought it was all a sham, based on my experiences over the first fifty-four years of my life.

The person who made this indelible mark on my existence, who gave me this profound experience… He is the one making this book a reality by haranguing me darn near every day to finish it.

Originally, after a heartbreaking and devastating situation in March of 2025, which you'll read about later in this book, I started keeping a journal. I'll add in here, I have never been good at keeping a journal—ever—but I started one and kept up with it for this significant person in my life.

Writing has always been my therapy and, at times, a cathartic experience. This entire situation, before/during/after and ongoing, has been (to date) the pinnacle of all events in my life—or at least under the header of romantic love experienced. This whole thing has been a doozy and continues to be, so I have relegated myself to writing this story that both Fred and I believe needs to be told.

I left Minnesota on November 19, 2023. It was a sunny day, fifty degrees, and not a cloud in the sky; almost as if Minnesota was taunting me. "Are you sure you want to leave? You can always stay…"

While saying goodbye and hugging my two younger sons and my future daughter-in-law, my third child/second son took my phone and told me he was going to set something up in my car. He told me that when I start my car, I should hit play on my phone. He had lined up the orchestral version of the theme song for the movie *Indiana Jones*, and the music filled my car.

My kids "got" me. They understood my drive and passion to get out on the open road. They had only been hearing about my open-road adventure plans their entire lives. The significance of the theme song was that, throughout their lives, whenever I took them on road trips, we'd all hum (obnoxiously, at the top of our lungs) the *Indiana Jones* theme song as we pulled away from the driveway.

Being hellbent on getting out of there before I changed my mind, or the weather got bad, or the car broke down, or some other doomsday thing happened that would keep me there, I drove down I-90 out of Rochester,

MN, made a short stop at my storage unit in Austin, MN, to pick up all of my camping gear plus anything else I could use—all shoved into the back of my car, and then headed south on I-35 to Iowa.

Once I got to Iowa, I actually felt I was making progress; I was finally leaving Minnesota permanently, after arriving in 1975. I was free! OMG, I was finally FREE!!!! It was a lovely, sunny, and somewhat warm day, and I was leaving! There was no blizzard, no ice on the road, my car was working as it should, and I was LEAVING!!! My 1981 and 2006 plans were in motion! With a permagrin, I drove to Missouri for my first night of officially living in my car.

Yes, I moved out of a perfectly fine, livable house with three bedrooms, two baths, full laundry, a heated attached garage, a beautiful backyard, and an HOA, and moved into the back of my seventy-two-cubic-foot midsize SUV. I was so desperate to get out, I literally moved into and lived out of the trunk of my car.

And I was happy!

Chapter 1

Sunday, November 19, 2023. Sunny, fifty degrees, not a cloud in the sky—a beautiful fall day in Minnesota. It was as if the state was tempting me to stay. But it wasn't going to happen. I was finally (*finally*!!!) leaving Minnesota with no idea when I'd be back. *(video)*

When I crossed into Iowa, my inner twelve-year-old's excitement was amped up. I was in a different state! I was out of Minne'snow'ta! The roads were dry and clear, and there was no bad weather in the forecast that day. I was headed to Colorado on my way to my final destination, Quartzsite, AZ. A place I had been "studying up on" while pre-planning my great and inevitable escape.

My first night was spent in my car (now "home" until further notice) at a truck stop in Bethany, MO. It was a truck stop where I had stayed before during my years of traveling for my sales job. The next day, I drove through Kansas and spent my second night at a truck stop in Burlington, CO, where it started to snow. I knew that weather system would be part of my drive, but I was fine with it because I was no longer in Minnesota. I was heading south—that's all that mattered.

The third day of traveling had me arriving at my daughter's and son-in-law's place in Denver, CO. The plan was to couch-surf at their house until the Monday after Thanksgiving (which happened a couple of days after I had arrived), when I would start on the final leg of my trip to Quartzsite, AZ.

However, I didn't get on the road until the afternoon of Tuesday, November 28th. My daughter had the twenty-seventh off from work, and I wanted one more day with her, so I stayed. I didn't have anywhere crucial to be at any specific time. Quartzsite wouldn't care if I was a day late, plus I knew no one down there, so I stayed in Denver for one more day.

With many hugs and kisses from both my daughter and my grandpuppy (my son-in-law was at work), and assurances that if it all goes to hell quickly, I can always move in with my kids in Denver, and we'll never speak of the time that mom tried to "run away from home"—I got into my over-packed, midsize SUV and drove south on I-25 toward New Mexico.

I had been as far south as Pueblo, so the scenery I was driving through was "old hat" to me. Nothing too exciting. Pretty, but "been there, done that." However, once I got past Pueblo, my inner twelve-year-old's sense of wonder with my traveling to-do list in hand, showed up! Every turn in the road, every vista, every building, every tree, every bird flying, every bug that slammed into my windshield—I was absolutely excited and thrilled, although I'm sure the bugs that hit the windshield weren't that happy. Everything and anything excited me. I was free and flying high!

On the evening of the twenty-eighth, I arrived in Las Vegas, NM. I had no idea there was a Las Vegas, NM, but there I was at another truck stop along I-25, happy as could be, nestled into my new home on wheels for the night.

The next day, I got up and made it to Camp Verde, AZ. I headed west on I-40 off of I-25. I did stop in Holbrook and make a short, excited video about the scenery, my excitement about the whole situation, and the great unknown. I completely forgot to stop in Winslow, AZ, to take a picture on their famous corner ("Take It Easy" by the Eagles), and one of these days, I'll make it back up there to get that task done. *(video)*

On Thursday, November 30th, before heading south out of Camp Verde along I-17 between Flagstaff and Phoenix, I arranged my car the best I could. It had become a repository for all the things I thought I would need, and all the things my kids thought I would need while living in my car in the Sonoran Desert. It was a disaster, and I needed to get it organized. The way it looked, there was no way I'd be able to get into the back that night and go to sleep. *(video)*

After organizing the car, I stopped in Anthem, AZ, and went grocery shopping (keeping in mind that I only had a twenty-quart Coleman cooler for a refrigerator and a large plastic tote for a pantry). Packed and ready to go, I headed west on Carefree Highway (a perfect initial theme for this book), then further west on Hwy 60 through Wickenburg.

I remember driving through the little towns along Hwy 60, seeing the various RV resorts, and wondering when I'd get an RV. Or better yet, would

I be able to afford one? Or have I just relegated myself to living in the back of my midsize SUV for the rest of my life?

There were some things—a lot of things—I hadn't planned on, figuring it would all "work out."

Along with the RV resorts, I was taking in all of the scenery. The Saguaros, the vistas, the mesas, the completely different "everything" from Minnesota and the Midwest that I had just been in a week earlier, with absolutely no plans of going back anytime soon.

I arrived at Quartzsite around 3:30 p.m. on November 30th. Everything looked just as it had in the thousands of videos I had watched over the past few years, preparing myself for the great exodus I would make as soon as my youngest kids told me they were going to make me an official empty-nester.

I drove straight to the La Posa South LTVA (Long-Term Visitors Area), one of my purposes being to visit The Lit Cactus. Aside from getting the heck out of cold and snow, my life up to that point had been stagnant… predictable… for the most part, utterly boring. Not that visiting a location on a map named for putting a solar spotlight on a Saguaro Cactus was my end-all in life, but it was something I had never done or experienced, so I was excited. It was something new! The unknown!!! And I was on board for… whatever happened.

I got out to the LTVA, paid my permit fee, and found a spot in the middle of nowhere, but still close to where The Lit Cactus was marked on the map. I got out of the car, looked around, and was told by a guy sitting in his lawn chair a few hundred feet away that I had twenty-five minutes before sunset and that it would be pitch dark afterward.

Okay! Twenty-five minutes to get my car organized and ready for me to sleep in it that night—in the trunk area rather than leaning the driver's side seat back as I usually did. I hadn't had much to eat that day, and needed to get acquainted with my new kitchen—figuring out where things were, finding my camping equipment that had bowls and utensils… I was quickly realizing that my organizational efforts from that morning weren't done correctly.

The sun was setting, it was getting colder out, and I needed to put on warmer clothes, but I had to dig for those. I found some salsa and chips, but had no idea where my camping dishes were. I spent as much time as I could in my lawn chair, outside of my car, before finally crawling into the back hatch of my Nissan Murano.

Sitting crooked and cramped in the trunk of my car, I ate my "dinner" in the light of a small flashlight I found, held the chip bag in my lap, and balanced the salsa container's lid on the plastic tote (my makeshift pantry) as a bowl, wondering if I had lost my mind. It wasn't a full-on panic attack, but I was certainly questioning my sanity and intelligence. After an hour of insane laughter and doing my best to avoid a salsa mess over everything I currently owned within my car, parked in the middle of nowhere, I fell asleep for twelve hours, from 6:00 p.m. to 6:00 a.m. *(video)*

Little did I know that the person who would get me to write this book was a couple of days away from leaving Overton, NV. A mere six days after I arrived in Quartzsite, AZ, I would meet my soulmate, and my life would change for the better, the worse, the unknown, and the uncertainty of it all. At that time, though, my main (and only) goal was to avoid a salsa mess in the trunk of the car I was now inhabiting.

Chapter 2

December 1, 2023:

The first morning after darn near twelve hours of sleep. Up with the sun… and my bladder. Time to start my new reality: sitting up as much as possible, doing my best to put on clothes while seated in a cramped space, bending into interesting yoga positions to open the Murano's back hatch without it snapping shut and breaking the ankle of whatever foot I used to kick it open, scooting to the edge of the car to put on my shoes, and then getting out to straighten myself and walk to the nearest vault toilet—all with a full bladder and limited time. Clearly, I needed to start pre-planning for some of the daily situations I would face. The days of getting out of bed and walking into the master bathroom were over, and I had no option of returning to that routine, either. *(video)*

Over the course of that first day, sitting out on what could best be described as the surface of the moon, with some shrubbery and occasional short, sand-blasted trees, the full, glaring realization of *OMG! What have I done this time?* came into a clear and sharply-edged reality. The saving grace, though, was that I knew that if this adventure failed, I could remake myself as I had in the past when I came out of divorce and other family situations that called for such a remedy.

Once I got past the first few hours of that morning filled with surveying my surrounding moonscape, I busied myself with errands. I had signed myself up for a mail service and was expecting a variety of items that day. Unfortunately, not everything I ordered—including a rooftop carrier for my car—showed up. The delivery date had been rescheduled to two days later. That meant shoving all of my stuff and me into the car each night. Sigh…

The most I remember about my first full day in Quartzsite, besides hearing that part of my deliveries was delayed, was sitting in my lawn chair and really questioning my life choices up to that point. My goal was always to "sit in a lawn chair and watch lizards jump on and off rocks." Simple and to the point; just let me sit and zone out. But on that first day, although I did sit in my lawn chair, I substituted the lizard-and-rocks schtick for existential dread and life-choice questions. I was, however, determined to make a go of it and deal with whatever came my way. Hopefully more positive than not, too.

December 3, 2023:

Three days into the adventure, the rest of my deliveries had shown up at the mailbox around 2:00 p.m. I drove into town, picked up those items, and stopped for some food (the chips-and-salsa combo can only placate for so long for dinner every night).

On my way back out to my site, I passed a converted shuttle bus with Minnesota plates. That was essentially what I was looking for: a school bus or a shuttle bus. In the past, I have gutted and rebuilt homes, so I was looking forward to doing that with my residence on wheels. For now, though, I was going to be happy in my car with my personal belongings shoved into a rooftop cargo carrier.

It turned out the shuttle bus driver parked near me at the La Posa South LTVA, and, seeing that I was not having success attaching my recently delivered rooftop carrier to the car, she came over and offered help.

Turns out she was from Central Minnesota and was in her second year of full-time travel. She was a few years younger than me, and to begin with, seemed friendly enough.

After a little time spent helping me with various tasks around my campsite, she left to go into town to attend a Singles Event at a local restaurant. I stayed behind to eat my cold dinner and putz with other items on my to-do list before I fell asleep again at 7:00 p.m. (Getting up with the sun at 5:30 a.m., lots of fresh air, sunshine, and way too much anxiety will tend to put a person in bed by 7:00 p.m., especially when it's pitch dark because the sun disappeared behind a mountain range).

December 4, 2023:

My new Minnesota acquaintance popped back over for a visit and told me that although she didn't meet any men at the Singles' Event, she had met another woman from Minnesota who was camped out in the same LTVA. They had talked about getting together to make a "Minnesota Camp" and had invited me. It sounded good to me—the more the merrier, as far as I was concerned. The number of people I now knew in Quartzsite could be counted on two hands: these two women from Minnesota, the three people at the mailbox place, and the cashier at one of the grocery stores in town. My social circle was expanding!

This new person showed up in her Jeep, picked up the one I had met the day before, and they were off to scout out new locations for us to establish the "Tribe of Minnesota women who wanted nothing to do with Minnesota winters." When they left, I started tearing down everything I had just put up in and around my camp area, in an effort to be ready when they returned with the coordinates for a new spot.

It didn't take long for them to return. They had found a location only a couple of hundred yards from where I had originally parked. We moved everything over—arranged our vehicles—me in my car, the first acquaintance in her shuttle bus, and the most recent person, in her C-Class camper.

That day was spent getting to know each other, building a campfire, and making plans to expand the group and offer events to others in the Quartzsite area. Sounded like fun to me, but I also had work to do; I purposely made it so that as long as I have a computer and an internet signal, I can work anywhere—even hanging out of the back of my Nissan Murano in the middle of the Sonoran Desert.

One of the planned events was to host a movie every Wednesday evening, at 6:00 p.m., for anyone who wanted to stop by. Someone had a projector and planned to hook it up to a Bluetooth speaker, and I had suggested hanging a flat bed sheet off the side of the shuttle bus for the screen.

That night, before the person in the C-Class camper went to sleep, she posted on several Quartzsite Facebook pages that our camp, just east of The Lit Cactus area, was going to start hosting these movie nights, and the first movie to be shown was going to be *Elf* that Wednesday, December 6, 2023.

What she hadn't told either the shuttle-bus-woman or me was that she posted the event with the information: *Three single women from Minnesota are hosting a movie night on Wednesday evenings, and single men are encouraged to attend.* Then she gave the coordinates, the event date and time, and the movie name. I didn't learn about this wording until a week or so later.

December 5, 2023:

Preparations were underway for the camp, which was on track to become one of Quartzsite's social meccas. While all of that was going on, I was busy working. At the time, I was an insurance agent busy with fourth-quarter open enrollments, and I was also working in the publishing business with my daughter, handling year-end paperwork, holiday sales, etc. I was too busy to be hassling with buying party supplies and beer, and hanging bed sheets on the side of shuttle buses, among other things.

Chapter 3

December 6, 2023:

The day went along as usual—all work for me while hanging out of the back hatch of the Murano. Light day drinking and last-minute arrangements filled the schedules of my newly acquired friend group/campmates from Minnesota.

At 4:30 p.m., I put away my computer for the day, cut my hotspot connection, made sure I looked somewhat human, pulled my lawn chair over to the "audience seating area" off the side of the shuttle bus, and found something quick to eat in my plastic tote pantry out of the back of my car.

At 5:30 p.m., the movie-going attendees started arriving. Four trucks, initially, to be precise. The other two women and I stood up and got ready to greet everyone showing up for the movie.

Of the four trucks that pulled up and parked, the one that caught and held my attention, for whatever reason, was a cranberry-colored Ford F-150. From what I can remember, I instantly honed in on that truck and waited for the driver to get out. In my peripheral vision, I saw other vehicles parking and people getting out and walking toward my two campmates, but I was locked on that one particular truck from the moment it arrived.

When the driver got out, he only looked in my direction and started beelining toward me. I'm sure I had a smile on my face, but it was more of a curious expression—a *why am I so wrapped up with the driver of this specific vehicle?* smile. He was smiling as he approached, too, but when he was roughly thirty feet away, he broke into an ear-to-ear grin, and I was absolutely dumbstruck. My peripheral vision had all but disappeared, leaving me in absolute tunnel vision. I had a damn good-looking, tall, and well-built male walking toward me with a big ol' grin.

Oh, boy!

After a quick internal self-doubting process of why this handsome man was beelining toward me, he got within five feet of me, and out of habit, I said, "Hi." And he said, "Hi, my name is Fred, and I have a motorcycle." And we stood there for a couple of seconds, smiling at each other. At this point, I remember thinking he was going to lose interest and walk away, realizing he'd made a mistake by talking to me, but he stayed standing in front of me.

I remember the introductions—names, where we were from, the places we had been, and how long we had been traveling. I learned about the videos he made and posted on Facebook under the #WFN hashtag, and I let him know I had started a YouTube Channel to document and share my travels. I took a stab at guessing what the *WFN* meant after he had told me his name, and while I slowly offered up my guess, his eyes sparkled, and his smile became warmer and more involved while leaning back, waiting for my complete guess, "Where's Fred… Nass?" He laughed and corrected me to "Where's Fred Now?" We spoke to each other in our own little bubble of mutual fascination for a couple of minutes, which seemed longer—in a good way—and I didn't want it to end. By that point, I couldn't have cared less about the movie.

My conscience kicked back in, though, and reminded me that if we were hosting a get-together, I needed to be a gracious hostess and talk to everyone, not just this extremely handsome guy. So, I wished him fun that evening, during a lull in the conversation, and then peeled off to the right. He took the obvious cue and walked over to the others who had arrived while we were immersed in our little world of permagrins and topical chit-chat.

However, instead of greeting other people, I quickly walked back to my car. I hid on the other side, pretending to be busy with whatever, asking myself, *What the hell was that???* At the same time, my "inner monologue" stated the obvious: *Holy schnikeys, he's handsome!,* and I peeked at him through my car windows. I had never, ever had that experience with a person, much less a man, in my life. Sure, I've been attracted to men my entire life, but I've never been in a state where tunnel vision set in and the rest of the world dissolved into nothingness. I had read those words before and heard of that situation in movies, but in the "real world" I lived in, that nonsense didn't happen.

After a couple of minutes of futzing around on the other side of my car, I reappeared with a new bottle of water (I needed to look like I was doing something other than freaking out) and walked back toward the group.

Conversations with anyone else there didn't amount to much. I greeted others but never hopped into any other conversations, which was fine. I was too busy internally over-analyzing what had just transpired between this guy named Fred from the southwest corner of North Dakota and me. And besides the little bubble of permagrin fascination between the two of us, *what was this concentration I had experienced from the moment his truck rolled up and was parked? Why did I focus on that one vehicle specifically? Why did I get tunnel vision with this guy approaching me? Why did the world (sights, noises, the breeze, the birds, traffic, everything in the surrounding area) fall off to the side and go completely still and quiet? What in the actual hell???* And lastly, I reminded myself of my decades-long plan: To avoid cold winters and sit in a lawn chair, watching lizards jump on and off rocks. That was it. That was all that was planned on my immediate calendar of life. And then, at 5:30 p.m. MST on December 6, 2023, I experienced tunnel vision for a guy from North Dakota.

To make matters worse, when I got back to the group of people congregating for the movie, I saw him (naturally) talking with other people—women, in particular—and my mind instantly switched to a light shade of jealousy and the desire to be talking to him again in our little conversation bubble. Even typing this, that memory brings back that feeling of, *Hmmm, how do I start talking to him again and lead the conversation back to a permagrin fascination?*

I kept myself from looking like an utter fool, though. I quickly busied myself with other things—helping to make sure everything was set up and working. But it was very obvious to me that it wasn't me talking to him—it was other women. Although none of that should have mattered, my "conniving" female instincts were considering going into overdrive for max attention from this man.

I'll add that throughout the entire movie, I could feel his presence two rows behind me to the right. Afterward, everyone sat around the campfire and got to know one another. We looked at each other over the fire and exchanged smiles, but I was still busy inside my head, asking a lot of questions. While I'm writing this, I don't remember us talking the rest of that evening.

Chapter 4

In the days after we met, Fred made an effort to stop by every other day, if not every day, for at least the campfire. He enjoyed the group's company, and I enjoyed the multiple unsuccessful attempts to keep from staring at him, still wondering what was going on. (I'll be the first to admit that I'm a little dense.)

He caught me staring at him many times. I was not as sneaky as I had hoped. He'd give me one of his signature smiles, and I would either smile back or pretend I didn't see him; it all depended on where I was in the internal narrative running through my mind. A lot of that narrative was peppered with questions and phrases such as: *What the hell is happening? Why is that guy smiling at me? Am I staring at him? Oh, gawd, I am staring at him! Why did he beeline toward me and talk to me first? When will he talk to me again? Should I make an effort to move closer to him around the fire? Should I talk to him now? I bet he has a girlfriend. Does he have kids? What's his story? Where has he traveled?*, etc., and so on.

I embarrassingly carried on this way for at least a week. I'm sure he thought there was something wrong with me, but he did continue to stare and smile at me, too. Perhaps he found me entertaining with my awkward social skills?

Of the times we spent together, or I should say, sitting next to each other at the various events at The Lit Cactus (where he'd most often make a concerted effort to place his chair next to mine, and we would talk), they'd have a fifty-fifty firewood fundraiser (half the pot went to buying more firewood, and whoever had the winning ticket would win the other half of the pot). So, he bought me some tickets for the fifty-fifty drawing, and I promised to split the money with him if I were lucky enough to win. I didn't win the money, but I got to sit next to him. That was the better "win" as far as I was concerned.

On one of those evenings, The Lit Cactus was also hosting a fundraiser for the group, and one of the organizers had made zipper pulls with little charms: a cactus, a camp sign, and a lantern. They were also offering large stickers featuring the group, and, in passing, I said I'd chase them down later to get both the sticker and the zipper pull. He asked why I didn't just buy those items then, and I told him that I generally didn't carry cash while wandering around in the desert.

After a few minutes, he disappeared and then came back with one of the zipper pulls and a sticker. I thanked him and told him I'd pay him back, but he said it wasn't necessary, and then added, playfully, that I was *indebted to him* moving forward. Not knowing what *indebted* meant to him, I found $6.00 in cash at the bottom of my purse a few days later and paid him back. To this date, I still have that zipper pull on my purse and the sticker on the back of my RV.

A couple of days after we met, we became Facebook Friends, and a couple of days after that, with an excited smile, he asked if I had looked through all of his pictures and watched all of his posted videos yet. I told him the truth, "No, not yet. I'm busy with end-of-year work stuff." The excited look on his face dissolved. That's when I realized he had (most likely) already watched and learned everything about me, and I had just let him down with my truth and busy calendar. So, that night and on, I watched as many videos of his as I could before falling asleep in the back of my Murano, and I looked at all of his pictures, and made one specific assumption that would plague our relationship for the next fifteen months. From the pictures and his Facebook posts with friends, I surmised that he had a girlfriend who wasn't yet retired and lived in South Dakota. This led me to back off on any plans to see where a friendlier relationship with him could go; he was "off the market." His status said *Single*, but the ever-so-wise me thought I knew the truth.

At the end of that initial phase of "getting to know you by Facebook stalking," which both of us did to each other, non-stop, for the entirety of our relationship—and we were both very good at it—I noticed he stopped liking every one of my posts cold turkey. There used to be a thumbs-up or a heart on everything I posted since meeting him, then nothing.

I knew he was still stalking me only because when we spoke around campfires or at The Lit Cactus events, and I brought something up, he'd chime in with comments only someone who knew what was going on would make.

He was also one of the first people, if not the first, to hop on any of my Live Facebook videos. He may not have figured it out, but the Facebook videos will show you who is watching during the stream or afterward. That's another way I tracked him; he was usually on within two minutes of me going live, at any time of day. Would that qualify as cyber-stalking, in a roundabout way?

I have a habit of talking with my mom at least once, if not twice, a week. Of course, Fred came up in those conversations, and even my mom was suggesting I "move things along with Fred." I told her that he was a taken man, or at the very least in some kind of relationship, based on what I had gathered from his Facebook page. She played the Devil's advocate and asked me all sorts of questions regarding this possible relationship—seeing if there was any type of relationship "crack" I could get into to confirm whether or not it was a real relationship, or... I told her that unless Fred said something, or "came clean" about his current relationship status, I was going to let it be. The ball was in Fred's court; if he was interested in seeing where things went with me, I needed his input. If no input or differing information were given, I'd have my answer. He's a nice guy (with a questionable relationship status, though it's listed as "single" on Facebook), so he'd be off my radar as a possible love interest.

Again, though, I was out in the desert with the main goal of watching lizards jump on and off rocks with no snowbank in sight. That was my goal. My goal was *not* to find a man to fret over and place myself in a season of mental gymnastics over whether a male liked me or not. I had lizards and cacti to watch. And Arizona sunsets.

Of course, that stated conviction only proved that I had been thinking about him nonstop since he got out of his truck on Wednesday, December 6th, and made a beeline for me. *NOT THAT I WAS THINKING ABOUT ANY MAN WHILE I WAS OUT IN THE DESERT SEARCHING FOR LIZARDS JUMPING ON AND OFF ROCKS.* I want to make that clear.

But I will admit that after initially meeting him, I quickly started looking forward to Fred showing up at the campfires and any other gatherings, every day. It never failed; he'd show up, and I still remember the feeling of happiness, comfort, and the inner relaxation of having him present, whether we spoke or not. More often than not, it was the two of us sitting around the fire—closer to each other with each fire, and both of us doing our best not to get caught staring at each other.

Again, this whole cat-and-mouse game had to be played out smoothly. And at that time, I knew I was playing it smoothly because he wasn't on the market romantically, yet I enjoyed his personality. It wasn't lost on me that my heart and subconscious were conspiring against my mind and logical side. As for him playing it smoothly, at that time, I was getting mixed messages all over the place: *Did he like me, like me? Or was he a social butterfly, friendly with everyone, and did that personality often get misconstrued? Or???*

I later found out what was going on, but until then, we couldn't read each other's intentions. In hindsight, we both excelled at being two grown-ass adults who didn't communicate clearly and made a lot of assumptions. And that will all be explained later, too.

In that second week, he came up to me while I was sitting in the back of my car, working, and asked if I wanted to go into town with him for a beer and to watch a game at a local bar. I remember he looked shy as he walked up, his hands in his pockets, peeking at me while mostly looking at the ground. The only thing missing from his body language was him shuffling the rocks on the ground with his feet.

I know I smiled, but I'm sure I gave him a look of, *Huh?* followed by telling him I was busy working. He nodded with a defeated look and said, "Oh, you're not in the same place I am," then added that I was not yet retired; I was still working. I did clarify that, as a business owner, I write my own calendar, but I was already busy that day and probably wouldn't be the best company to watch football with, since I'm unable to wrap my mind around that game. But maybe in the future, with enough lead time, I could hang out with him. And so, he wandered away.

Again, I sat there wondering what in the world that was all about—especially since I had already assumed him to be a taken man, but dismissed it as "whatever" and went back to work.

Around this time, he made the first of two or three invitations for me to visit him at his campsite. A thoughtful invitation, each time, but—as far as I was concerned—he had a relationship going and one: I wasn't going to get involved in a relationship between two people. And two: he had already mentioned this person a couple of times around the nightly group campfire, and with everything on Facebook—as far as I was concerned, he was taken, regardless of what he either said or inferred. Of course, he didn't strike me as someone who would cheat on someone else, and he didn't seem poly to me, and I wasn't going to jump into someone's open relationship… All of that sounded like a hassle that I wanted no part of.

Remember: Lizards, rocks, cacti, sunsets, and no snowbanks… That was why I was where I was.

A couple of invitations to visit his camp had been made. Under all of the things I had assumed, along with the basics: *I know the grass in my non-existent desert yard better than I know this guy*, and *stranger-danger*, and again, not getting involved with someone who is/may be involved with someone else, I politely declined each time.

I also didn't know where he was camped. Anytime the subject had been brought up, either personally with those invites I declined, or when the group was sitting around a campfire, he always swung his arm in a general direction with, "My campsite is over there." ("Over there" around here looks a lot like every other "over there" out here, too.) But in one of those group conversations, he narrowed down the direction and said he was near the Magic Circle—the clothing optional part of the La Posa South LTVA.

So, on one of those rare days when I could no longer sit at my desk, and I thought, *Let's try that thing called "exercise" again*, I ventured out according to Google Maps, in search of the labyrinth that was noted to be right next to the Magic Circle.

Hmm… I'll take a walk under the guise of "exercise" and… if I happen to bump into him… well, what a coincidence! Imagine that! Such a small world!

So, I crawled out of the back of my car and started walking south. Again, still no idea where he was. I had never seen his setup, but he did say he had a toy hauler. I knew what his truck looked like, and he said he always sat outside. So, if I happen to amble by and he notices, my "color me surprised" plan would work.

I finally found the labyrinth, and I saw one site that might have been his setup, but a voice in my head said "no," so I kept walking. I definitely didn't want to end up on a real stranger's doorstep.

It wouldn't be until the following November that I found out where he camped, and I'll explain all of that then in the story.

Chapter 5

By the middle of December, the assumed hierarchy and overall attitudes among my campmates had taken shape. The first woman I met on the shuttle bus became the sidekick of the woman with the C-Class camper. Since the development of our little camp area, two other women arrived and became fast friends with those two; one was a retired nurse from upstate New York, and the other was a traveling nurse working in the Phoenix area but hailed from South Carolina.

Although I hung out with them, and anyone else who showed up—Fred included—around the near-nightly campfires, my overall characteristics did not include day-drinking, daily Tinder checks to see who the evening entertainment would be and where (your camper or mine?), getting utterly smashed, and flashing any guy who was nearby. I didn't "fall in line" and lodge my head up the butt of the woman with the C-Class camper like the rest of the women did. The pecking order had been decided, and I was in a completely different barnyard, in a different state. I had matured past the seventh-grade mentality, where these women still lived with a heaping dose of the *Mean Girls* schtick.

Although I knew they wouldn't have cared if I had disappeared, I remained cordial around the nightly campfires, and with the people who attended, Fred included. But in any given year, December was the end of the fourth quarter for my insurance business and my personal businesses. I wasn't being unfriendly on purpose; I was simply very busy.

On a group outing to a local bar earlier in December without Fred, I revealed that my last relationship ended in 2019 and that there had been no "action" since then. I was fine with that since I had more work than I knew what to do with, and that occupied my time. Upon hearing this juicy little tidbit, the four women I had eventually dubbed the "mean girls" all decided they would set me up that season to break the dry run I had been experiencing—their mission solely for their entertainment; it had nothing to do with my well-being. I told them it wasn't necessary, but they had their little nugget of harassing fun and ran with it. Again, whatever. I had better things to do over in the "land of adults."

Whether it was around the nightly fires or at camp when no one was around, darn near every day, these women would tease me about random men who had attended the various events and campfires at our campsite. I shot down every one of them. Over the years, I had become proficient at resisting others' attempts to get me to do things solely for their benefit. Again, I had matured in ways some people hadn't.

One of the names brought up, of course, after all other possibilities had been suggested, was Fred. That stirred something in me—a defensiveness that he shouldn't be involved in any of this crass behavior these women were exhibiting. Out of respect for Fred, I shot those suggestions down, too, with probably more emphasis than I did for any of the other suggested men.

I'll add now, after thinking about all of this, and while writing this part of the book: Did those women see something with Fred and me that neither of us saw? Or, more pointedly, something I didn't see? If so, that doesn't excuse them for being heartless and condescending in how they delivered any talking point to me, but it certainly makes me wonder.

For December 2023 and into January 2024, when they did bother to talk to me, and believing Fred was a taken man and thus off my radar, I reiterated to these women that I had high standards for potential mates—however long they may stick around—and that my life and the lives of those they suggested were not in existence for their shallow forms of entertainment. Their answer to that statement, and every variation of it, was that I needed to lower my standards. I laughed at their solution every time.

Christmas in the desert came and went. The nightly and sometimes daytime campfires came and went, and although I'd catch him staring at me across the campfire, I stuck with my assumption of him being off the market, so I never instigated anything. My campmates were still immature, condescending seventh-grade girls, even though their ages ranged from the mid forties to the mid sixties.

December 27, 2023:

That morning, I made a move: I established a connection with him (beyond sitting around a campfire, occasionally talking and sneaking looks at each other). I first texted him, then I called him, then I messaged him again.

My car was having battery issues. Mainly, the Murano was not built to live in the desert with its back hatch open nonstop, while the driver sat in the trunk and conducted business off the top of a plastic pantry-tote lid, serving as her office desk.

I called him and asked if he could jump my car so I could get to the store to pick up a new battery. He answered, and I played it as cool as I could, and I didn't faint from massive nervousness. After the short and awkward phone call, I realized that in my anxiety-filled mind, I forgot to pinpoint a time that he'd be stopping by, so I sent him a DM through Facebook, and he answered right away:

Fred Nass

You're friends on Facebook
Lives in Rhame, North Dakota
Former Technician at USDA-NRCS

View profile

DEC 27, 2023 AT 9:15 AM

When he arrived promptly, he and I stood side by side, looking at the engine compartment of my car. I was over the moon to be standing next to him, talking to him, back in a little bubble with him. If there had been more time and I hadn't had a lot to do, I wouldn't have put it past me to sabotage a lot of things under the hood of my car if he'd come back over to talk with me. I could play the automotive ditz really well for a little attention.

Somewhere along the line, a "field trip" to the Desert Bar & Nellie E. Saloon outside of Parker, AZ, was planned for December 30th. You can only get out there in off-road vehicles or well-built, sturdy trucks that don't shrink at the idea of driving on unmaintained roads through mountains. Fred volunteered to drive people out during the planning conversation. I asked if I could ride out with him, and he confirmed that it would work.

December 30, 2023:

The morning of the planned field trip arrived, Fred showed up, and we all got organized into the vehicles we'd be riding in. He was quiet, and I wasn't sure how to read his demeanor. I may have overanalyzed him ad nauseam… and may have thought about him more than lizards jumping on and off rocks, too. I also had to admit to myself that I potentially had one helluva crush on him. It was growing by the day, which really had me in an inner turmoil because, as far as I knew, he had a significant other he was keeping quiet about. (Oh, the convoluted stories an overactive imagination can come up with!)

While people were figuring out where to sit, I asked to sit up in the front passenger seat because my legs don't bend very well anymore, and squishing into the back seat with two other people and my legs bent would be extremely uncomfortable. Everyone was fine with that, and I climbed in.

All the way out to the bar, a little over an hour's drive, Fred was—for the most part—quiet. The chatty people were in the backseat, and I added to the conversation every so often. I'll add, though, that if those three in the backseat hadn't spoken, I would have completely forgotten they were in the truck altogether. I spent the ride to and from the bar in my little happy bubble of being with Fred, BUT remembered that it was only fleeting because he was a taken man, according to what I had surmised from his Facebook photos, videos, and posts a week or two prior. *(video)*

With all of that integrity I live by and the high standards I have for not only the men I might involve myself with but also for my personal charac-ter, I chose to honor whatever relationship he had with the woman pictured on his Facebook page. I looked at it as if I were in a situation with him and wasn't yet retired. While he wintered in Arizona, I wouldn't want another woman moving on him, although I know most others wouldn't limit them-selves. I couldn't, in good conscience, take advantage of or be involved with someone who had someone at home.

At the Desert Bar, Fred kept to himself, often surfing his phone, although there wasn't much of a signal out there. He drank his beers and listened to the music. I, on the other hand, after getting a basket of ribs and fries, was told by the "mean girls" that I couldn't sit with them, even though countless seats were open. So I went to the table where Fred was sitting and asked if I could sit down. He motioned to a chair and nodded. I sat down, began eating, and talked with the other guys at the table since Fred didn't seem to want to talk and was busy on his phone.

The field trip participants took a group picture in front of the stage, the day wrapped up, and everyone began to leave. However, the retired nurse in her mid-sixties, who was in the truck with us on the way out to the bar, decided to leave without telling us.

She had found two unknown drunks to ride back to Quartzsite with, leaving the rest of us out there until closing time, wondering where in the hell she went. No one knew.

The bar finally kicked us out and told us to get off the mountain before nightfall, and so we left. Once out on the main road, I called the others in the group to see if she had caught a ride with them. Instead of any sane answer, I got my butt chewed off because we supposedly had left her there, although she was nowhere to be seen.

Turned out she—according to her own account—"had a free spirit experience and went home with two guys she had met there." Besides my displeasure with the whole thing, I strongly suggested that she apologize to everyone who was in the truck; all four of us who had scoured the entire place for her, so we didn't leave her there. She answered with, "I don't owe anyone an apology." (According to Fred, later that evening, she simply muttered, "Sorry," as she walked past him.)

December 31, 2023:

The morning of New Year's Eve arrived, and as we sat around the morning campfire—Fred wasn't there—the "mean girls" pounced again with the ever-looming deadline of me getting together with a guy—any guy—so they could hit their self-imposed goalpost they had set up a couple of weeks earlier. Clearly, their intentions were disingenuous at the beginning of December. By the morning of December 31st, they were downright condescending, and they had no problem showing it.

Between the day before, when they witnessed me sitting next to Fred at the Desert Bar, and our inability to stop staring at each other over the past few weeks… Now that I'm typing all of this, I'll answer my own earlier question of, Did they see something we didn't? Or at the very least, did everyone see something I didn't? "Yes," on that last question.

But back to the campfire that morning, sitting around with the group sans Fred, the mid-sixties retired nurse gave me the snarkiest look while everyone else discussed my potential mating behavior and said, "If you don't make a move on Fred, I'll take him myself."

I answered that I didn't believe that either Fred nor I were put on this Earth for her amusement, or for the amusement of anyone else. She looked at me, and I looked at her. She with a look of condescension, and me with a look of "try me," hiding the real look of, *Why am I so concerned with this guy, his character,* and *OMG! Do I really like him that much?*

Damn it! I was out here to watch lizards jump on and off rocks, and I was failing at that simple task.

With a little over six hours left of 2023, I was sitting by myself waiting for the New Year's Eve activities to start at The Lit Cactus. Fred came up from behind me, set up his lawn chair next to me, sat down, gave me a string of green LED solar lights, and asked me to get them situated in/on the stocking cap he was wearing. I said, "Sure," turned to face him, reached up for his hat, and then realized I should probably stand up to get this job done. But even standing, I found it difficult to keep the lights in place and told him so. He told me he had a remedy for the problem, excused himself, and went back to his truck. Within five minutes, he was back to sitting next to me, holding a container of safety pins. He told me he had everything in his truck. Clearly…

I stood back up and started fashioning how I was going to pin these lights into his hat. He held the container of safety pins, and I told him to sit still. I unrolled the brim, tucked the light strand into it, and then it was time to pin it altogether. I opened up one safety pin and aimed for the side of his head, and then stopped—suggesting that he take off the hat but keep it stretched out with his hands to accommodate the circumference of his cranium. I told him I didn't want to stab him, and he agreed that he didn't want to be stabbed, either.

He took off his hat, keeping his hands inside to make sure he could put the finished decoration back on his head. I sat back down, leaned over a bit, and pinned the light strand into his hat and rolled the brim back up. He put it on his head, and then I asked if I could take a picture with him, and he agreed. This is the only picture of us together I have, and it's the one on the dedication page, and back cover of this book.

We spent a bit more time talking and watching the group activities unfold around the large bonfire and in the general area. Eventually, he excused himself and began taking photos and videos of the evening's activities from different angles. I sat for a bit longer, then started wandering for different camera angles, and such. I did catch him aiming his camera at me a few times, and I will admit I felt uncomfortable because (let's say it altogether)... I thought he was a taken man and didn't want to encroach on anything he might have been doing with another woman. As I mentioned earlier, I wouldn't have liked someone moving on my partner, so I minded my manners and respected this person, whom I assumed was in a relationship with him. It was strange to spend so much time apart, but people have strange relationships.

Of the time we spent in Quartzsite in December 2023, he has quite a few videos and pictures of me on his Facebook page. Needless to say, I'm now thrilled and thankful that he took those pictures/videos and posted them. Most of those have me sitting right next to him, too.

Around 11:45 p.m.-ish, I no longer saw him and figured he had gone home. I stuck around for the mandatory countdown, then went back to my car and crawled in for the night, and for the year of 2023.

Chapter 6

January 1, 2024:

Mid-morning at the community camp, a handful of us gathered around a campfire. That morning, I was a person or two to his left, and when he scanned for one of his #WFN Facebook video posts, I waved overeagerly.

It was at that time, too, that he told everyone he'd be pulling out of Quartzsite the next day and heading down to Yuma for January. People chided him with the old line of, "You'll miss us, so you'll come back." But he persisted and said he'd be gone for the rest of the season—wouldn't be back until November/December of 2024.

Upon hearing this news, my heart sank. But because my heart sank, I told myself it would be good for me, so I didn't spend time worrying about what a taken man thought of me and could get back to important things like searching for lizards that jumped on and off rocks.

I will add that the ambiance at the camp where I was parked had also become very unfriendly. Clearly, there was no room for adults in the "daycare of bad decisions." I had some peripheral friends outside the group, mainly men—actually, typing this now, all men—just men—less BS. Besides Fred, the other guys I hung out with were younger than me; most of them reminded me of my kids.

Anyway, when Fred said he was going to leave on the second, my heart sank, regardless of what my logical brain suggested I should feel.

January 2 - 5, 2024:

I worked out of the back of my car and did my best to ignore my camp-mates. They didn't seem too bothered with me being busy, either.

Back on December 26th, I had made a windshield appointment with a glass company in Yuma for Monday, January 8th. At the time I made that appointment, I had no idea that Fred was leaving right after New Year's Day. On Wednesday, January 3rd, after a good thirty-six-hour absence of what had become my "Daily Fred Fix," I sent him a text. I didn't know what kind of response I would get, if any. But I thought I would try… For what reason? I wasn't sure, because he was a taken man, but I sure liked hanging out with him, so… I hit "Send" and waited with excitement, apprehension, and the general thought of, *What are you doing?* along with the other thought of *What's your end-all game plan here?* I didn't have answers for either of those questions.

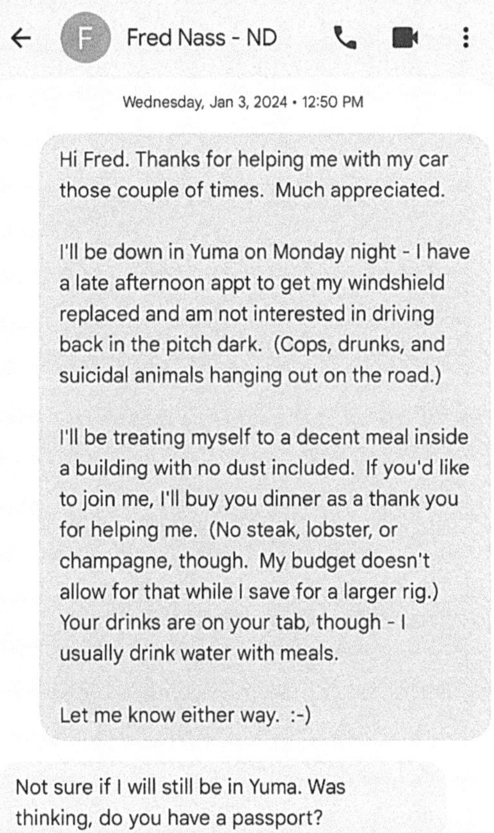

  Fred Nass - ND  

I do have a passport but am not planning on going to Mexico this year. Not going in a car, and haven't scheduled into my calendar. Will only be in Yuma overnight.

If not this time, I'm sure we'll bump into each other again. Thank you for the jumps, though. :-)

For Mexico, I park in the USA side and walk about 300 feet and bingo, Mexico. What time is your appointment?

4pm at Safelight.

I was planning on doing the date museum tour on Tuesday morning before heading back.

Just thinking, if you come early we could walk into Mexico and have lunch. Los Algodones business start closing about 4.

If you pay (I'm assuming they need pesos???) I can pay you back in USD.

No pesos, all us money. It's quite on experience. The only thing that has price is the restaurant. All the street venders barter. It's there cultural. You end up paying 50/70 % of what is is first asked.

Wednesday, Jan 3, 2024 • 5:17 PM

You guys still having a movie?

Nope

Possibly tomorrow night.

I'm in town, though. Nothing for me to do out there while it's raining. And my camp mates seem to forget I'm out there and don't bother inviting me into their RVs when they're day drinking. So, to avoid a repeat of the last time it rained, I left for the day.

A weird dynamic out there...

Whatever...

Your trip to Yuma, just a bad battery or something else?

Yesterday was the battery. Monday is the windshield. Hit with a rock in KS when I was getting down here.

And if the battery holds, everything should be good - knock on wood.

Glad it was just a battery

Yep

And I will admit that I, too, can be a condescending and snarky bitch. I had thought of and toyed with the idea that if I did have lunch with Fred and could bring it up somehow in conversation—maybe have it tagged on Facebook where all of us were in the same group —I could shove the nose of the retired nurse into it all… But do that nonchalantly so as not to offend this guy about whom I had no business having romantic ideas, because he was a taken man.

Oh, the simplicity of a lizard on a rock…

Great laid plans… What's that one saying about great plans?

January 6, 2024:

The day began quietly until the retired nurse decided she was upset that I was sitting in her lawn chair because someone was sitting in my lawn chair, while she was sitting in a lawn chair that belonged to someone else… If you can follow that, and the absurdity of it all.

The conversation, with its constant barbs, began while others around the fire watched. She wanted me to get out of her chair, and I told her she was fine since she was already sitting, and someone else was in my chair.

She persisted, and I told her to chill out. She balked at my eating a banana while sitting in her chair. I told her I wouldn't let the banana touch her chair. She was being a petty bully, and I was using chilled-out logic.

Eventually, I got up to make a bathroom run and quickly forgot about the banana peel I had set on the ground near the chair leg (it wasn't touching the chair). When I got back to my campsite, I found the banana peel on the ground behind my car, with a smear of banana on the back window. She sure showed me!

So, to make sure the rest of the world was clear on the lawn chair's ownership, and all things "flying banana peels," I posted on Facebook with a picture of the banana peel on the ground behind my car—without tagging her, but she definitely saw it:

> *A petulant sixty-five-year-old, retired nurse,*
> *just threw this banana peel at the back of my*
> *car to protest me sitting in her lawn chair when*

someone was sitting in my lawn chair, and she
was sitting in someone else's lawn chair…

Of course, that post lit up with laughing emojis and other comments and GIFs. However, she saw it and stomped over to the "C-Class bitch," and before you know it, I was officially kicked out. I was told they were going to the bar, and when they got back in two hours, I was to be gone.

So be it.

Later that night, as I sat in the back of my car, I texted Fred:

Saturday, Jan 6, 2024 • 8:40 PM

Hi Fred. Two things:

1. What's the plan for Monday?
2. I've been kicked off the island of the mean girls because I'm not cool enough. (Whatever) Can I camp near you? It doesn't have to be right next door, and you're not responsible for my entertainment. Just thought it would be nice to be near someone I know.   If not, that's fine, too.

Let me know -
Kiersten :)

Sure, it's a LVTA with only garbage, no water or dump. We do have dump next door at a gas station, and water for a price. Not sure what the rules are, if you need to be self contained or not? There is a 14 day on the east side of town, or one about 1/2 mile north of me just on the north side of the interstate. Just thinking, could park next to me and if you get questioned, we are together. Might be here of a week or two. What are your plans n

 Fred Nass - ND 

Sure. I can come down in Monday and stay. Will need to pack up and such, so if I'm staying down there, we can always do lunch on a different day.

My only plan is to avoid any snowbanks. So, anything is good. ;-)

Thanks for helping me out. Much appreciated.

I buy my own water, don't need dumping, and can throw garbage where it's available.

Ps. Your new haircut looks good.

I'm going to sleep now. Chat later.

Thank you again.

Don't worry about me and lunch and stuff. You get your self to a happy place. Later....

Thanks

Chapter 7

January 7, 2024:

I woke up to a hailstorm. It was hailing in the desert, because of course it was.

Late December into January was cold and rainy, and now it was hailing. It was cold and miserable, and I was looking forward to my new sunny location. Fred had told me that Yuma is touted as one of the sunniest cities in the U.S., if not the sunniest, and it was always seven to ten degrees warmer in Yuma than in Quartzsite. Looking at the weather and radar on my phone, I could see that he was telling the truth.

I got my car organized and drove into town to get a decent breakfast—preferably something warm. While I was there, I looked at the forecast for Quartzsite again, scrolled south to check the weather forecast in Yuma one more time, then texted Fred.

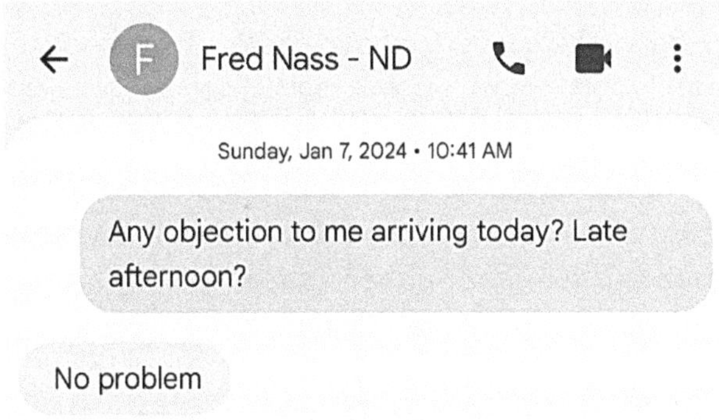

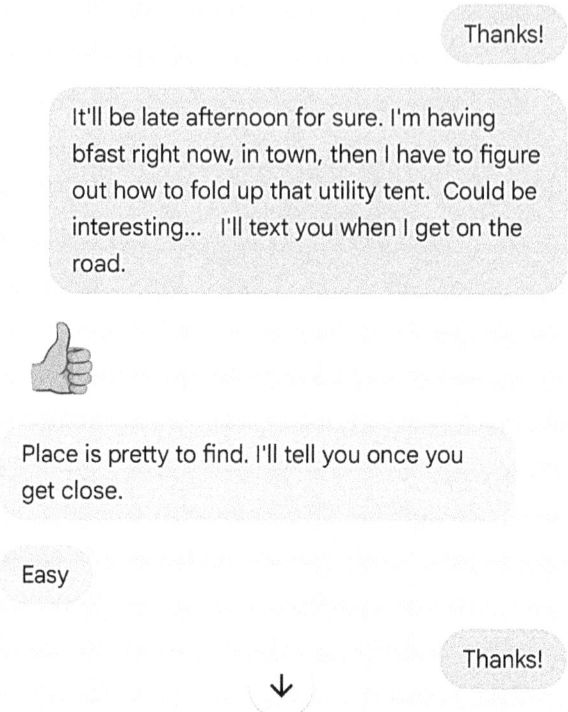

I wrapped up my breakfast, got back to my campsite in the desert, and packed up as quickly as I could for two reasons: I was giddy to see Fred again, and I wanted to get everything into the car before the next thunderstorm began. I'll add that I wasn't being neat about it, either. Everything was thrown into the back hatch, and the doors bumped shut to make sure they locked.

I drove back down the very road I had driven in on thirty-nine days prior: the La Posa South LTVA driveway. My car was no longer neatly packed and perfectly "Tetris-ed" together. It was now a mishmash of disorganization—I could barely see out of any windows—and I was off on my next adventure with the only other person I knew in the entire Sonoran Desert. In reality, I didn't know him all that well, either, but he gave off a good vibe, and I figured if my new plan didn't work, I would simply drive away.

I was also doing my heart good—I could really feel myself slipping into a mental funk without seeing him every day at the camp. He was gone, and I didn't know if I'd ever see him again. So, when he agreed that I could come down and camp with him, my heart was aflutter even though I had convinced myself he was a taken man. I may not have been able to pair up with him, but he was still a good guy—from what I could tell. He seemed able to put up with me, and he wasn't hard to look at; maybe too easy, in fact.

At the intersection of Hwy 95, instead of turning right to go into Quartzsite, I turned left and headed south for the next part of my unexpected journey.

Chapter 8

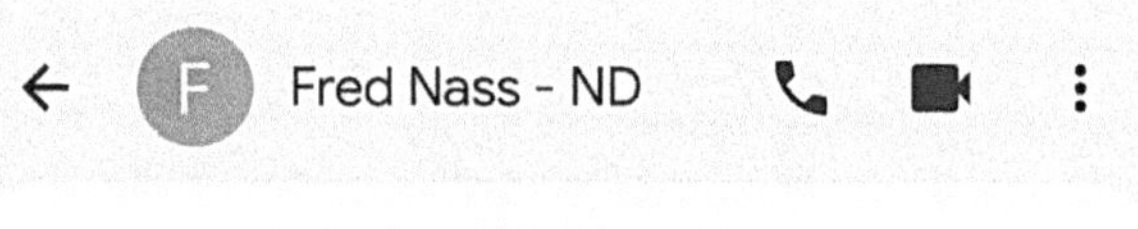

Sunday, Jan 7, 2024 • 12:34 PM

I'm on the road. Please send directions.

Go west on interstate into California. About 8 miles west of Yuma you will hit an agricultural inspection station. You my get stopped or not. All my crossing I've only been stopping twice. Anyway, go though the station and take to next exit, about 1/2 mile. Then left, south over interstate and you will see the LVTA. Let me know when you leave Yuma or so, I will meet you in the parking lot.

Sunday, Jan 7, 2024 • 1:42 PM

What's the address of the Ltva?

Don't know. Let me see if I can find it.

601 sidewinder rd. N. Winterhaven ca

What do they ask when you get stopped? Obviously, I'm not human trafficking or carrying people from other countries.

If you have any grapefruit, don't want to transfer any bugs

Okay

Ate all the grapefruit, already. I'm going to get gas before moving on..

I've been thought this port over 50 time. When I was stopped it was 3 years ago. I will bet you will just get the wave though.

Okay

I'm leaving the east side of Yuma now.

I'm guessing about 20 miles to Here. I'll head out in 25 minutes to meet you

15 not 25

What a difference a couple of weeks can make when accepting invitations to campsites belonging to people you don't know very well…

Arriving at the campsite, I got out of my car and surveyed the area, instantly finding a circle of rocks on the ground—a fire ring that someone had once used—and pointed it out. "We can have campfires!"

He then told me that he generally doesn't build campfires when he's by himself. So, I told him that was no longer the case and that we should definitely have campfires. As many as possible, in fact.

With campfire scheduling out of the way, he suggested that I park my car perpendicular to his trailer to protect myself from the wind that kicked up to the west over the Imperial Sand Dunes. I could put my "bathroom" (a tent for a portable toilet and extra stuff) between the trailer and the car. He then took some ratchet straps out of the back of his truck and secured my tent to the tongue of his trailer. (He had put some pre-planning thought into this setup.)

After I set up on my end, I asked him if I could work in his trailer on the days I needed to get some stuff done (January wasn't nearly as busy work-wise as December). He told me there was no room for me to sit and work in his rig. Although I said I understood, he motioned for me to follow him, and he opened the door. I peeked in, and there was definitely no room, as it was sparsely decorated—his recliner was darn near the only thing in there except for the kitchen, fridge, and bathroom, since it was a toy hauler. Not that I was looking for "proof," but I appreciated that he was willing to back up his story about not having room, rather than possibly leading me to believe he was only saying that to keep me out of his domain.

Once situated, he asked if I wanted to go for a tour of the area and Yuma. I said, "Sure," and off we went.

He first took me down to the All-American Canal along the southern border, south of the Pilot Knob LTVA. Then he drove me through Winterhaven, CA, on the way to Yuma. He pointed out some store locations, one of the libraries right off the highway where I could do computer work, a couple of his favorite bars, the shopping areas, a couple of movie theaters he frequented on days that weren't that sunny, and downtown Yuma. I know we picked up some firewood, and I'm sure we picked up something for dinner on the way back to the campsite. *(video)*

I'll add that after I arrived, for the first day, I had a hard time looking at him. I was experiencing extreme shyness. Me, of all people, being "shy." I can't even remember the last time that happened… maybe (literally) half a century ago? I had no problem looking at him in Quartzsite, even with other people around. Still, now in this one-on-one situation, my heart was aflutter (even though I thought he was taken), and I had questions about what he thought of me and whether I meant anything to him beyond a person he met in the desert who was now a campmate.

Note: In the short amount of time I spent with him in January and into February, I quickly picked up on his "tell" of either being nervous, unsure, or embarrassed, depending on the subject matter at hand, and/or if I was delivering another compliment: he'd resituate himself in his chair, or he'd change his position if he were standing. I suppose that could be a subconscious way of "changing one's perspective"—getting a different angle on things, for example. Needless to say, he kept shifting around me a lot between my constant compliments and his uncertainty about the situation with me as a campmate. I, of course, simply had my idiotic permagrin on. I'm afraid I failed to be subtle around him in that regard.

That night was our first campfire with just the two of us. He had taken his above-ground firepit out of his trailer and told me he was happy to have campfire company. It's amazing how fast six hours can go when you are locked in a permagrin, nonstop conversation bubble with a handsome man.

By the time the fire was going, though, he realized what was happening/could happen/the optics of our set-up, and he started getting cold feet… nervous cold feet. Plus, it's really hard not to get caught staring at the only other person across the fire from you, eight feet away.

I can't remember what we were talking about initially. Still, after an hour or so, he began bringing up reasons why we really shouldn't be camping together. He was distancing himself from whatever was happening out on the barren land just south of Hwy 8 through Southern California.

His first comment in what would be a barrage of reasons I shouldn't bother with him was, "I hate people." He puffed up his chest, sat up a bit straighter in his chair, and steadied himself, waiting for some type of blowback on that comment. Instead, I let out a little laugh and continued looking at him without saying anything.

Realizing I wasn't going to respond to that, his second reason for me not to hang out with him was, "I'm not smart."

I looked directly at him over the fire, from eight feet away, smiled, and confidently said, "If I didn't think you were intelligent, I wouldn't be sitting here right now."

He shifted in his lawn chair.

After a moment, he came up with the next reason why I shouldn't bother spending time with him. "I don't talk right."

Not breaking my gaze on him, I continued to smile and confidently said, "I can understand you just fine."

He again resituated his pose in his lawn chair.

Finding little success with those excuses, he then—and I forget the exact wording, but something along the lines of—told me he believed younger generations/people in general should have to work for a living. We were talking about a mutual acquaintance out of Quartzsite who was in his early to mid twenties, fully into the nomadic lifestyle, and busking wherever he could to make some money.

Along with wholeheartedly agreeing, I also defended our mutual acquaintance, noting that he was living his life and doing the best he could with what he had, including his musical talents. I also reminded him that he and the other person were on personal journeys, and that judgment was unnecessary.

Once again, he resituated himself and admitted that I had a point.

Then we sat in silence, across from each other—occasional glances, but mostly staring into the flames.

After a bit, Fred decided the fire needed some more logs. He got up, walked to the pile of wood behind him, and as he was about to lean down to pick up a couple of pieces, he looked at me over his left shoulder and said, "Well, I guess we should talk about L.M.," then he bent down to get the wood. After the two seconds it took to pick up the wood and face me again, he saw that I was waiting for him to continue (I was finally going to get the lowdown on that entire situation, and figured even if they had whatever they had going on, we could still be friends because he seemed like a chill guy). In the blink of an eye, he lost the fortitude to tell me anything; he started talking about a completely different subject.

Good that I didn't need to hear the inevitable letdown, but bad because I still didn't know where I stood in this *whatever I was detecting… I mean, I'm not dead yet*, situation.

Another note: I always gave him the time to tell me whatever he wanted to, whenever he wanted to, throughout the entire time I knew him, and, for the most part, still do.

That night, like all of the following nights, carried on with the two of us locked in a permagrin conversation bubble filled with constant laughter, stories of family and childhood to that very moment in time around the fire, questions about everything and anything, dreams along with the plans to make those dreams come true, and celestial suppositions as we stared out into the fascinating universe above us.

Chapter 9

I'll clear this up right now. I'm not a morning person. In fact, my motto on all of that is: "A bad day starts with an alarm clock."

I'm seriously not a morning person—at the very least, let's start the day when there are two digits on the clock. 10:00 a.m. would work best for me, bare bones. With that being said, around 7:15 a.m. the next morning—my first full day of being Fred's campmate—I got a knock on the window with a follow-up of, "Do you want to come sit outside with me?"

First off, I don't know what planet I'm on in the morning. I also don't have the bandwidth to contemplate sitting outside at an early hour, let alone wonder why in the world someone would make that choice.

But to make a good impression, and of course to begin another perma-grin day, I told him I'd be right out. I kicked open the back hatch of my SUV and ambled out in all my morning glory: messy hair, pajamas, eyes half-shut behind dark sunglasses, an unhealthy pallor, and a good percentage of my brain still sleeping.

I set up a lawn chair next to the metal folding table he had set next to his chair, dropped myself into it, and stared at the southern border in silence. He found it amusing and regaled me with stories of waking up at 5:30 a.m. every morning for thirty-five years while working for the USDA. In a deadpan morning voice, I congratulated him and then took another fifteen minutes or so to come online, with most of my cognitive functions intact.

After that day, though, I made a concerted effort to get up and out of my car every morning to sit with him. I amended my belief of "a bad day starts with an alarm clock" to "a bad day starts with an alarm clock unless Fred is involved." If Fred was in the picture, the alarm was set the night before, with great anticipation of being with him again in six or seven hours, and my eyes would spring open with full brain function, usually thirty minutes to an hour before the alarm would go off. I'd literally lie in the back of the car, watching the clock. At 7:00 a.m., I'd kick the back hatch open, get myself out, and try to look somewhat decent—all things considered, since it was still technically way too early in my world—then set myself up in a lawn chair. There were a handful of mornings when I'd be outside first.

Over the next five weeks of camping with him, we easily fell into a daily routine: sitting together in the morning and doing something together during the day, unless I had some work to do, in which case we did our own things. We would have dinner at the campsite or out at a local restaurant, and darn near every night—unless the weather was not ideal or he didn't feel good— we sat around a campfire in our bubble of permagrin conversations.

Aside from the morning rituals—listening to the Yuma radio station that informed snowbirds of local happenings, watching the sun crest over the eastern mountains, and observing our surroundings (Mexico to the south, the Imperial Sand Dunes to the west, and more mountains to the north)— we had conversations about the day's plans mixed with long stretches of comfortable quiet.

I'm one of those people who says "thank you" when someone does something for me, or gives me something, along with "please" and "you're welcome," as basic manners dictate. Fred did so many nice things for me— even mundane things like setting up my lawn chair or starting the evening fire. I kept thanking him, and he kept blushing and fidgeting in response to every compliment or expression of gratitude I offered.

I'd also compliment him on everything: his ability to fix things and get things done, his ideas, his accomplishments past and present, and, of course, everything about him. This caused him to fidget endlessly, whether he was sitting or standing (his "tell" of when he was embarrassed or didn't know how to handle a compliment).* I tried to keep the compliments about him and his attractiveness to a minimum, though. I didn't want to give him the wrong idea since he was (in my mind) in a relationship with someone else. Of course, now, I kick myself whenever I think about how I played the whole situation.

Without reliving and writing about our day-to-day activities, I'll touch on some of the highlights that stand out to me:

Los Algodones:

My very first time in Mexico was with Fred, who took me to lunch, and we wandered around Los Algodones. This was early on during our time together; the follow-up to my original offer to take him to lunch for helping me with my car issues. After a few hours there, we stopped at the Quechan Casino in Winterhaven, CA. We had stopped at the casino on the way back to our campsite for drinks, a light dinner, and to play on some of the machines. He won, I lost. He smiled about his good luck, and I still had my idiotic permagrin on even though I had just lost $20. I was simply happy to be with him. *(video)*

Whiskey Road Saloon in Yuma:

We were out at the Pilot Knob LTVA for three weeks, and on those three Mondays, we found ourselves either driving to this bar together or meeting up there after spending the day apart. Both of us were good at identifying songs from a couple of notes. I'm not entirely sure he won any of the games, but on our first night, I won four games and received four free drink tokens. I picked up one more free drink token because I knew some random trivia about Pee Wee Herman. I kept two of the tokens and gave three to Fred, who used one that night, and kept the other two for the next evening we

---

*Eventually, to warn him of impending compliments—so he could either get a headstart on blushing and fidgeting, or brace himself, I began pre-empting each one with, "Not to blow sunshine up your arse, but…"

were there. Besides the Monday evenings, we stopped out there a couple more times over those three weeks in Yuma.

Speaking of Whiskey Road Saloon, the first night we went there, he walked in front of me, opened the door, and went in. Then I got up to the door, opened it, and went in. That stood out to me in the "manner-verse" I seem to find myself in quite often. When I got inside and sat down with him, I mentioned holding the door open when someone was following him inside. From that point on, he always opened the door and held it for me. Even if I opened the door for him, he'd refuse to enter first and insist that I walk in first while he held the door. Again, something that I noticed and had stuck with me. Might be small and inconsequential to most, but it stood out to me, which, of course, earned him another "thank you," causing him to fidget.

One time we went, I met him there and came up from behind him as he sat at the high-top table, waiting for me. He was looking at something on his phone, which was sitting on the table to his right. I came up on that side, happened to glance at what he was doing, and saw his phone. I blurted out, "What are you looking at?" and he quickly shut down his phone with an embarrassed look. I won't say anything more, but it was pretty funny. His expression showed he was mortified. I was laughing.

We did frequent that establishment more than any other place in Yuma over those three weeks. One of those evenings, we were talking about height, and I told him that I bet he is assumed by most to be scary with his stature of six-foot-five in height, but I saw him as more of a "big teddy bear." He leaned back in his chair with a hearty laugh. What I didn't tell him then, that I do now, is that he had a sweet face with sweet eyes. Where some may have been afraid, I felt very safe.

The Yuma Marketplace:

We stopped out at the Yuma Marketplace a couple of times to "peruse"— his idea, not mine. I'm not a shopper, and for the most part, neither was he from what I saw when we spent time together, but he did like to wander and peruse. *(video)*

Cocopah Racetrack:

When I first got out to Pilot Knob, my social media logarithms started showing me local interests, one of which was the Cocopah Racetrack. Being a diehard for anything involving cars and other vehicles (racing—cars, sleds, bikes, as well as drag racing, demolition derbies, tractor pulls, etc.), I was all over this idea. I shared the idea of going to the track with Fred. Surprised that I was interested in all of that, and hearing my stories of past excursions to these types of events, we set January 12, 2024, to attend the Winter Nationals at Cocopah.

As we were walking up to the ticket booth, he told me he gets the Senior Discount since people assume he's older because of his gray hair. He was rather amused with that, too, and flashed me one of his smiles—a version of his sneaky/tricky smile, then bought his ticket for $12.00. When it was my turn to buy my ticket, I was charged $15.00, and while I was standing there, he walked up the path to the track and turned back to give me his sneaky "I-tricked-them-again" smile. I can still see him glancing over his left shoulder, looking like he was a kid who successfully stole cookies out of the cookie jar.

We sat in the top row of the stands, using the concrete wall as a backrest. He had brought a blanket to sit on, whereas I hadn't. When the sun went down and the air cooled, I pulled my hands into the sleeves of my hoodie and pulled up the hood. Noticing this, he offered to share his blanket with me. He stood up, pulled the blanket off the bleacher, and covered both of our laps with it. Not being the biggest blanket, I had to scoot closer to him (cue the permagrin). Shortly after that, though, he decided he really didn't want to sit on a cold bleacher, so he went out to his truck to grab another blanket. We spent the rest of the time sitting together on one blanket, covered with another. I also showed him how to do a Facebook Live video that evening. *(video)*

After the racetrack, he drove us over to Whiskey Road Saloon on the way back to camp. We went in for a couple of drinks, and a trio was playing that night. He sat in a corner seat at the bar, and I sat next to him. I faced the stage, and to my right, he was leaning back against the bar, facing me.

Oh, boy!

It took every ounce of control to ignore his body language and the energy radiating from him—he had those come-hither, let's-take-this-further, bedroom eyes on. I would glance to the right, and there he was, smiling at me with a sly, suggestive smile. The whole right side of me was toasty. Oy! I would smile politely and make a brief comment about the band, then turn to look at the stage again, all the while feeling his gaze burn into the right side of my head. (Damn my integrity!) We were there for a couple of hours, and then we went back to camp.

Side note:

Reliving these memories, I really wish I had been better prepared with either a GoPro strapped to the top of my head or a hidden camera somewhere on me to save all of these interactions and adventures with him. Of course, I know I kept him entertained by my quirkiness, but if I had had a camera strapped to me, that probably would have been a deal-breaker.

Movie Theaters:

Going to the movies was reserved for rainy, windy, and/or cold days. Both of us liked the matinee prices, too, so if it was a movie day, dinner at a restaurant was usually on the docket for later. I'll add that he'd buy the seat right next to me, but in the theater, after realizing there were all these empty seats around us, he'd fidget and then move to the next seat. Again, the optics, I would imagine. Plus, at matinees, there was usually plenty of room, or we were the only ones in the theater.

I know we went to three movies during our weeks together, but I only remember the second one—*The Beekeeper*. We were looking through the movie offerings on his phone, and when I saw that Jason Statham was in it, I unilaterally decided that was the movie we would see that afternoon. Overall, it was a great movie and well told. But the reason this particular movie stands out to me is what happened next: I had to pick up some stuff at the store.

On his Facebook page, he had made it a tradition to log in and share his movie reviews with his followers. So, when we got to Walmart, he said he would stay in the truck while I went in to pick up what I needed. While I was in the store, he went on Facebook and made a live movie review video, claiming he was at the laundromat. Toward the end of the video, his eyes darted to the right, and then, all of a sudden, he announced he had to get off the video to take his clothes out of the dryer.

In reality, I was coming back out of the store and walking toward where he was parked. He needed to get off his video quickly because I was about to get into the truck. I'm still laughing to this day about his sudden excitement to go "pull his clothes out of the dryer." For further proof that he was not at the laundromat but was actually sitting in a Walmart parking lot waiting for me to finish my shopping, you can see rather large vehicles driving by out his back window, along with what looks to be one of the shopping cart corrals. The laundromat parking lots in Yuma aren't large enough to accommodate larger vehicles, and none of them have shopping cart corrals. I still laugh at his attempt at sneakiness to this day; seriously, who gets that excited to pull their clothes out of the dryer?

Harbor Freight, Walmart, and various grocery stores:
We did a lot of errands together, and every day shopping was one of them. A trip to Harbor Freight was always a welcome jaunt, and that happened a few times. But the trips to the grocery stores and Walmart evolved for us. At the beginning, when we were hanging out, it was separate carts, and we'd go our own ways with a plan to meet back up at the truck. By the third trip into town for supplies, I had pulled out a cart, and he skipped doing the same. I figured he was only getting a couple of items and didn't need one. Walking further into the store, though, he didn't peel off and go his own way. Instead, he started adding his stuff to my cart, and we walked through the aisles together. Again, that wouldn't be a big deal to most, and in the grand scheme of things, it doesn't make a twit of difference. But the fact that he was getting more comfortable with me and including me in his life was a big deal for me.

With all our adventures and hanging out together, I kept in mind that he was a taken man and I was simply enjoying his company. Sure, it was full of mixed signals; sometimes I could tell he really liked me, liked me. But at other times, I observed a kind of dismissal that left me feeling like the little sister of the annoying kid down the street. The signals were all over the place with him, and he could/would change his energy at any moment. It was interesting to keep pace with him. The overarching feeling I had was that of an idiotic schoolgirl with a major crush, but it wasn't attainable because I thought he was in a relationship. And I'm sure, he, following my mixed signals, was matching/keeping up with my hesitancy and such. We were two adults who couldn't get our communication together. He had major health issues that were stunting his future, and I was the presumptuous other half who never got clarification on the situation and was happy to hang out with him. Typically, if someone dismisses me or a communication issue isn't resolved, I don't hang around. But with him, exceptions could be made—similar to waking up way too early to sit in the morning cold and watch a ball of fire rise over a mountain.

Restaurants:

He was definitely a "foodie," which I appreciated. His diet didn't consist of only cheeseburgers and beer, although there were a few cheeseburgers and a lot of beer.

Whenever we went to a restaurant, we would always be engrossed in conversation and spend hours there. Great conversations, and as usual for me, the world melted away. It was just us, at the table, talking and eating, and often laughing. He had a great laugh.

As a matter of fact, I have often said that when I was with him, there could be bombs dropping behind me on one side and over the other shoulder, a monster could be running at me with a *Sharknado* flying by, and I wouldn't flinch or notice, for that matter. I was focused on Fred. I felt safe with him. That was it; if Fred was next to me, I was good.

It never failed: whenever we were together somewhere, and someone else spoke to us, people would ask how long we had been together and/or married. Fred would automatically blush and shift positions (his "tell"), and I would pipe up and say that we had met a little over a month ago. That would certainly stump people, and a few added that by looking at us, they definitely didn't expect that answer.

Candy Stores:

My gosh, I had found someone who liked going to candy stores! We went to candy stores in Mexico, Yuma, and El Centro. A serious match made in heaven! However, he went to these places not so much for himself as to pick up some candy his friend liked, and would buy it for him as a thank-you for picking up the mail and watching his house when he traveled. I believe the purchase was candied almonds or spice-dusted almonds, or... He had told me, and I may have even seen the bag, but I was busy being the proverbial "kid in a candy store" on a sugar high.

We visited several other places, but the above were the highlights or the circumstances that stood out to me. Fred always mentioned bringing me to one of his favorite dive bars in Yuma, Red's Birdcage, but that never happened. I'll have to stop out there one of these days, when I can bring myself to go to Yuma* again.

―――――――――

*He passed away at the Yuma Hospital. In the last year, I've only had to drive through there once, and when I did, I kept my eyes focused on the road and my mind as blank as I could; no memories, no nothing.

<h1 style="text-align:center">Chapter 10</h1>

Aside from all the places we went, the crown jewel of it all was the campfires and conversations we had.

One of our first conversations over our first campfire, he asked me again if I had finally figured out that I wasn't like the previous women I had been camping with?

I acknowledged that it was downhill from the get-go once the pecking order had been decided, and I was nowhere near that barnyard. He told me that the C-Class female was jealous of me. I asked him about what? He didn't elaborate too much, but figured it out when he gave her a ride to Blythe, CA, to pick up her car from a mechanic; from what she said, he decided she was jealous of me. Still not sure of the exact reason, and for the most part, I really don't care.

Aside from telling me she was jealous, for whatever reason, I then asked him if she said anything else about me. I had told these women early on some info about me that could be considered "salacious" about my history, although it really isn't, but people build things up in their minds. Anyway, I asked him what else may have been mentioned, and he fidgeted in his chair. I knew he had been told something from that response. So, I asked him more pointedly about a certain subject, and, like a kid unable to hide a big secret, he answered with as much bluster as he could, "I have absolutely no idea what you're talking about." I nodded, but I was laughing inside, and it took him a bit of time to be able to look at me again. I also had my answer: she did, indeed, tell him this convoluted, personally deemed salacious info about me.

Regarding the other women in the "mean girls" group, he asked if something was wrong with the one who lived in the renovated shuttle bus and dutifully did whatever the C-Class camper woman told her to. I asked, as in how? And he said she was always sitting and smiling, and that she generally didn't say anything; she just sat there with her dog, smiling. I told him that she follows orders and is high most of the time.

As for the sixty-five-year-old nurse who threw a banana peel at my car and threatened to make a move on Fred herself if I didn't take care of business, he said he got a bad vibe from her; that she radiated negative energy to him.

Additionally, I shared with him what she had challenged me about. He shook his head and said nothing would have happened with her—he wasn't interested. Then he told me that on New Year's Eve, he was walking back to the party from his truck, and she passed him on her way to her RV. She asked him to walk with her, so he turned around and obliged. He said she was quiet. When they got to the RV, she went in, and he stood outside. Not once did she say anything, and she never came out of her rig, so he turned around and went back to the party, leaving her alone in the RV. (That was her attempt at closing the challenge she threatened me with.) She's also the one who, the day before, had a moment of being a "free spirit" on the trip to the Desert Bar and didn't bother telling any of us, but wound up giving Fred a short, flimsy apology. He wasn't impressed with her.

One of the first evenings after becoming Fred's campmate, while getting ready for our nightly campfire and chatting, we talked about our upcoming trip to Mexico, and he coached me on what the street vendors would ask. I should say "no, thank you," or, if I do stop and engage, I should be ready for a lot of negotiating. He also told me about the other businesses in Los Algodones as well as the restaurant where we'd be having lunch. Fred then added that, on his first trip across the border, outside the pharmacy, one of the employees offered him a sample of Viagra. Even though he had refused, they pressed it into his hand, and he wound up taking it home. So, at that point, he stood right in front of me and, on a lark, told me it was in his trailer. Then, with an unsure but hopeful, what-the-hell smile, he asks, "Should we try out the blue pill?"

I don't remember exactly what I said, but I know I had to fight every ounce of myself to take him up on the idea, believing he was already in a relationship I didn't want to intrude on. So, I'm sure I smiled and said something—I really don't remember the exact words, but the little blue pill remained inside his toy hauler.

I still feel bad to this day, and I have apologized countless times, but between my love-swooning gazes and all that embarrassing stuff, I shot him down with his blue-pill offer. In reality, his heart wouldn't have been able to take the stress; he was getting mixed messages from me, and I was getting mixed and omitted messages from him. To this day, I still kick myself for the lack of communication between us. For two people who could talk about anything and everything, there was still one topic on which neither of us could convey feelings.

Early on, he had told me that he'd rather people-watch than start a conversation. But if someone started talking to him, he'd carry the conversation easily.* And he did. I had no problem starting; he jumped in, and we talked for hours, nonstop. Of our conversations around campfires, the following points/subjects/conversations are what stood out to me:

Fred told me that he never makes a promise he didn't intend to keep. At the time, I thought that was very impressive; I appreciate people who do what they say and say what they do. After his passing, that phrase, about his promises, became very important. More on that further into the book.

A couple of days after arriving at Pilot Knob, I told him I needed a massage and was researching respectable massage businesses in Yuma that emphasized professionalism. He asked why, and I told him I was a sucker for a good massage. He fidgeted in his chair. Then, to tease him further, I asked if he had ever had a professional massage, and he immediately answered with a definitive "no," sounding as if I had offended him. I then pushed it further and asked why he wouldn't want a stranger slathering and rubbing his naked body with warm oil? He fidgeted a lot in his chair after

---

*I'll point out that when I was driving Lisa (one of the people who wrote a Foreword) back to Phoenix, while she was beginning to channel Fred and telling me messages, I told her what Fred told me about conversations: that he wouldn't start them, but he would carry the conversation. When I got to the second half of that sentence, she said the "but he would carry the conversation" right along with me. She had never heard that sentence before, and she wouldn't know what I was going to say, but she spoke in tandem with me, word for word. I knew at that moment that I was talking directly to Fred in that car as he channeled through Lisa in my passenger's seat.

that comment. I let him sit there and stew in that thought while I watched him with a sly, amused smile.

That same evening, we both retreated to our own vehicles; he in his trailer, and me in the back of my car. Before climbing in, though, the moon was full, and I took a picture of our two empty chairs around his firepit with smoldering embers, then posted it on Facebook. Almost immediately, one of our mutual friends replied, suggesting that the picture gives off a romantic night-for-two vibe. As much as I would have preferred to agree with her and play into it with a suggestive answer, I knew the guy in the trailer right next to me had himself a girlfriend (from what I had surmised) and didn't want to offend him and ultimately shut down our friendship. So, I replied along the lines of that wasn't the case—just two friends. I know he read that line that night before he went to sleep. I misread everything. It takes two people, and better communication between them would have helped.

I'll add that there was one other (short) conversation about various people's likes and dislikes of the boudoir variety, and I don't remember how it was brought up. Still, it sure got him fidgeting—actually squirming—in his chair. I wrapped up that short conversation with, "Everyone has their own kink," and with that line, he nearly fell off his chair. I can still see him, and I'm still laughing. This is where I really wish I had that GoPro strapped to my head to catch all of these moments.

On one evening, I plopped into my lawn chair and, with an exasperated voice, said a line I've been saying for as long as I can remember (and something my kids and I have had as part of our vernacular). Upon sitting, I asked, "Oh… You know what I mean?" And Fred instantly responded with a "no." I asked what the "no" was for, and he repeated my question. I laughed and said that it's part of my everyday speech, and really, the best answer is, "Yeah, I know what you mean." He looked at me, confused, and I suggested that I would say it again, and then all he had to do was answer with, "Yeah, I know what you mean." So, I repeated the question, and he nodded and repeated the best answer. Over the time spent together, whenever I said it out of habit, he'd answer the question with the appropriate answer and a nod of agreement.

When I arrived at Pilot Knob, I only had a few pieces of firewood to contribute to our planned nightly campfires, and he had a few pieces, himself. I had said we needed to take some time to find firewood in Yuma, and he quickly took out his phone and started searching. (He was always ready to look something up on his phone.)

A day or two later, when I had been at the library all day, I picked up some dinner for us and got back out to the campsite. When I arrived, Fred started the fire. We ate and talked, and when he put the last log on the fire, I commented again that we really need to schedule a trip to find firewood.

He unexpectedly got up, walked over to his truck, turned around, and looked at me with one of his smiles and asked me to come over to the truck. When I was standing next to him, he rolled back the cover to reveal that his entire truck bed, side to side and from bottom to top, was filled with firewood. I was floored! "Where in the world did you get all of this wood?"

With a big smile and a proud look, he told me he cleaned out three firewood resellers, driving all over Yuma that day to do so.

First off, getting firewood in the desert is not an easy feat. Secondly, it's really expensive because it's brought in from northern Arizona—supply and demand, along with a captive audience that wants campfires. The firewood in southern Arizona is not cheap.

The cost, plus the fact that he spent nearly five hours finding these places and loading the wood into the back—that's impressive! And was very much appreciated. He got several big "thank you"s, and true to form, fidgeted in his lawn chair each time.

During a conversation regarding how much of certain products you can bring over the border in thirty days (they track this at the border, too), he told me about a bottle of unopened Tequila he'd been carrying around for years in his toy hauler. I suggested we open it, but he refused, saying it was for a special occasion. I queried, and he didn't say. At least not that I can remember. I never did see it, and I don't know if he ever opened it.

Fred told me about his various health issues and what he'd been through in the past with all of them. He noted that he had had a heart attack at the age of thirty-nine and wound up getting a pacemaker. It was also new to me that pacemakers transmit stress levels and other information to the doctor's office. That conversation led to a subject he brought up on his own accord; after some time spent with a woman one night, his doctor called in a panic the next morning about the "off the chart" readings that were being transmitted the night before—worried that something medically detrimental was happening. Of course, that situation had caught him with his pants down, literally. We laughed and continued our conversation, and I didn't ask any more questions because I felt it wasn't my place and wasn't any of my business.

But a couple of days later, around a campfire, he suddenly brought up that issue again: "You know, my heart can't take a lot of banging around." I acknowledged and agreed. I understood what he was saying, but I was unclear why he kept repeating this fact. Over the time we spent together, he brought this fact up with nearly the same delivery line, out of thin air, almost ten times that I can remember. The last time he repeated that line was in mid-November 2024. Each time, though, I only nodded and didn't put more effort into that possible conversation because why would I? It was not my business; he was involved with someone else as far as I knew, and he never came clean about what was going on in his life. As far as I knew, he had a "very good friend" who was female. Based on pictures and various Facebook posts, the logical conclusion was that he was "taken," and I wasn't interested in anything beyond friendship, while harboring a secret lust for this person who was already in a relationship.

Because of my opinions and beliefs regarding that whole situation, whenever he would pull this line out of thin air—either during a conversation or during a quiet time between the two of us—my expression and/or response, or lack thereof, would always make him look like he was wondering if I was picking up on what he was laying down, or look at me incredulously as if I were "out to lunch," and that announcement would hang in the air between us. After he delivered that line each time and let it sit between us for about seven seconds, he would change the conversation to something completely different, ending that almost-subject for the rest of the day.

He did ask me about my relationships, and I had filled him in, and of course, talked about my kids as any proud mom would. Not too much, but he had a good grasp on how cool I thought my kids were.

He also asked why I wasn't involved with someone at that time. I gave him the abridged version of my relationship history: that being out on the road, living my own life, was more important to me than being stuck in a snowbank, waiting to die, and forced to stay somewhere because I was tethered to a guy who liked Minnesota. I had already done the "mandatory marriage thing" and was good with where I was at in life.

I also told him that more often than not, men didn't really talk to me. By the look on his face, he was surprised. I continued by pointing out that men will either talk to me only when they're looking for some action, avoid me altogether, or approach me to say derogatory things. I told him that if that was all there was for an offering, I was good with being alone.

I asked him about his past jobs, including his more recent one with the USDA, and he sat up a bit straighter, took on a more formal tone, and opened up about all he did and his various experiences. Besides having him explain the solar and water systems, and other topics, I asked him about those surveying tripods—how they work and the information one can glean from them. I also asked him to explain the geological survey caps, showing him a picture of one I had taken in Grand Marais, MN, back in 2019.

I was enraptured by everything he had to say, especially when he discussed science and provided explanations for things I knew but lacked essential information on. He filled all of that in for me, and I listened intently, my attention peppered with thoughts of how intelligent and handsome I found him.

I also asked him to explain football to me since he watched it constantly and had played in the past. He broke it down so I could finally understand it (the "downs" thing confused me—and he made it make sense). After that, at various times, I began asking him if he wanted to go to the bar to watch football.

Regarding our conversations (and I laugh at this because I still talk to him)—I mentioned that my daughter told me I talk a lot, and that's why I'm so successful in sales: people buy stuff from me to get me to shut up. Without missing a beat, he agreed with, "Yeah, I can barely get in a word edge-wise." Then he gave one of his smiles and readjusted his position in his lawn chair. I laughed and agreed. Nowadays, with him no longer in this physical plane, I let him know that, *yes, I do talk a lot, and even in death, you can't get rid of me*. So, really, the joke is on him.

I told him about my time growing up on a dairy farm in New York Mills, MN, and he said he knew exactly where that town was located. I told him that I spent the better part of a year, about a decade earlier, helping a neighbor milk cows because of their health issues. Not only was he surprised to hear that I did that, but he was also amused that I was going on about the parlor system in the dairy industry versus how cows were milked in the seventies when we lived in Mills.

He told me he once had a ferret. I forgot its name, but I told him my ferret's name was "Spanky." He liked cats, and I liked dogs. We talked about the flora and fauna of Arizona and the Southwest, as well as the area's geology. We shared places that we've been and where we'd still like to go. We talked about UFOs, the weather, military planes, classic cars, field crops, and history… You name it, we probably talked about it.

We talked about fishing and how it would be fun to get some poles and find a spot along the Colorado River; he was so invested in the idea that he pulled out his phone and started researching nearby fishing excursions. I told him I'd like to go deep-sea fishing, and he told me about his fishing trips in Alaska.

He told me about his first trip to Florida—it sounded like maybe his only trip to Florida, since he said he preferred the western half of the US rather than the eastern side. But he went out there for business with his first job out of college, and wound up putting over 2,900 miles on the rental car in a week. I asked him if he ever stopped and got out of the car. He also mentioned that he went to New Orleans to help with cleanup and infrastructure after Hurricane Katrina.

We talked about travel, both business and personal. We shared experiences with family, co-workers, and friends. I had once asked him what he thought his friends would say about him if asked. With one of his great smiles, he leaned back with a hearty laugh and said he had no idea what any of them would say. I told him I bet they would say he was a great guy and always willing to help, based simply on what I had seen and picked up on so far. He got quiet, and I noticed him blush and fidget.

We talked about our experiences with county and state fairs: My experience as a vendor, his experience serving on the Bowman County Fair Board, and his various contacts at the North Dakota State Fair. I had mentioned that I was considering vending at the ND State Fair in Minot in 2022, and he asked who I had been talking to. Turns out it was the same person who offered him free concert tickets that season. I forgot the band he saw, but when he was talking about it, I was internally kicking myself for not getting up there that year. I might have had the opportunity to meet him then, rather than 1 ½ years later in Arizona (my goal was more time with him, with no specific endgame). Unfortunately, that summer was already filled with other commitments, and the ND State Fair would have overlapped with them.

Actually, bringing that fair up for 2022, reminded me of how I had hoped to get to Quartzsite for December 2022 and January 2023 with the main goal of visiting The Lit Cactus, getting the feeling of the town and attending the Big Tent RV Show; doing a couple of months of boondocking in my car to see if my "grand master plan" was really what I wanted to do before getting rid of the house and all that came with that upheaval. But, as usual, work showed up and took over my calendar.

2020/21 winter wasn't going to work because the world was still closed and I had oodles of work to do. The 2021/22 winter wasn't going to happen because of the world opening back up, and my calendar filled with work immediately. The 2022/23 winter was on the table as an option to skip out of Minnesota for a few months to get away from the cold and snow, and to check if I *really, really, really* wanted to get on the road full-time. I already knew the answer, but I thought a few months in Arizona during the winter wouldn't hurt; it was legitimate and appropriate research for my future when I officially became an empty-nester. But, true to tradition, my calendar filled up, and that was that. Of course, realizing that Fred had been spending his winters in Quartzsite since 2020/21, and spending time at The Lit Cactus, I once again kicked myself for letting work take over my life. I could have met an awesome guy from North Dakota in Arizona sooner rather than later in 2023. Back to the "shoulda, woulda, coulda"—the 20/20 hindsight theory.

He told me about Cando, gave me the address of his family farm, and told me I could stop and boondock there with him if I ever found myself in that area. He also told me exactly where he lived in Rhame and extended the same invitation. I thanked him and told him I'd keep those offers in mind.

We talked about how we each learned about Quartzsite and what drew him back each year, and why I would return for another season. I'm not sure where or when I got the idea to go to Quartzsite. I'm going to guess I learned about it through one of those YouTube videos I took copious notes on, back in 2020. Being that I'm all about maps—every type of map—I started looking at various points of interest in and around Quartzsite, followed up with checking out the videos that corresponded to those places, etc.

I'll add in here that when Fred and I first met, I was carrying on about maps for some reason—maybe future travel routes? He said he had a few books that I might be interested in and dug them out of his truck. One was for open BLM camping throughout the US, another for State Forests, and the last for Corps of Engineer land available for boondocking, too. I looked through them briefly, then pulled up Amazon while still standing in front of him and ordered them on the spot, thanking him for the information. When we were camping together over the next month or so, he would often find me poring through those books with great fascination—usually for hours. I still use them to this day, and I go into panic mode when I put them in a "safe place" in here.

Before buying my RV, I had mentioned that my birthday was coming up in mid-February and that I was thinking of going to Palm Springs and taking the Aerial Tramway to the top of San Joaquin Mountain for a birthday dinner. I offered that I'd pay for his ticket and dinner if he drove. He sat there silently for a moment, and then quietly said that he had dress pants in his trailer and that we could go. I showed him YouTube videos of that location, and he seemed excited. But between buying my RV, believing I had to be in Quartzsite while the rig was being worked on, the camp host telling me I had to move if I wasn't self-contained, and the various times he made me feel like a nuisance, it didn't happen. I wish it had, though—I think he would have had fun.

We would often talk about childhood and experiences through adulthood, as well as past and current relationships, including romantic ones. After he told me about some of his past girlfriends and situations, I asked if he had ever been married. He told me no, and I asked why. His answer was quiet and shy, unsure if he should even say it, but something along the lines of, "I never found a woman I could fall in love with." I thought that was noble and was happy to hear that he thought highly of himself and wouldn't settle into a relationship just because it was expected of him. I appreciated his open candor and his own self-respect.

Throughout our conversations, especially those about personal/romantic relationships, he made astute observations about the world of love and pairings, which revealed that I was dealing with a true human rather than the "everyday" man, if that makes sense. Fred had depth and was okay with showing it, or at least showed it to me. He told me that men of his generation and older generations were raised to be quiet and unemotional, and that men spoke with (generally) no hidden agenda. He added that most of the time, interactions with men were surface-level; they rarely picked up on nuances and conversational cues that could suggest an alternative meaning. Thinking about that now leads me to believe he wanted me to tell him everything directly. I did tell him up to a point, but I omitted my suspicions and assumptions about his relationship with someone else. However, to my credit, he never came clean about it, never corrected/clarified, never… nothing. So again, what was I to believe?

His last question to me about potential relationships was: "How do you flirt with men?" I told him I hadn't done that in so long that I'd most likely forgotten. I do know, though, that I get awkward where most people think I'm strange and wind up leaving me alone.

I did ask him what he was looking for in a woman to fall in love with, and he shrugged, looked at the ground, shuffled rocks around with his feet, and fidgeted in his lawn chair before giving me the quiet "I dunno" answer.

We talked about our parents, siblings, extended family, family situations, and expectations—past, present, and future. Work, co-workers, various situations, and other random stories also made their way into our nonstop conversations. In reality, we covered a fair share of what we were all about. Talking with each other wasn't hard for either of us.

One conversation covered religious/spiritual beliefs. He said he was raised ELCA Lutheran, but didn't practice/focus on it. Then it was my turn. I grew up ELCA, too, but then I told him everything about my adult spiritual beliefs, which I had had since I was about five years old, but kept to myself. He did another one of his chair fidgets, but I also got the vibe of curiosity. Fortunately, he didn't run for the hills and tell me to go away when he heard my thoughts.

When I brought up my interests in astrology, divination, and tarot*, he claimed he didn't believe in all of that stuff and fidgeted in his chair again. I described his sun sign, Cancer, to him, and I could tell I was pinpointing his traits perfectly, and he knew it. I'd say a good percentage of him was interested, especially since he claimed to read people's energy and vibes when he met them. He knew what I was talking about, although he quickly jumped in and told me he didn't believe in that stuff. Typing this out now, he had the same tone and quick retort that he did when he told me he had no idea what I was talking about when I asked him if the "C-Class bitch" told him anything about me on the drive to Blythe, CA, to pick up her car a month earlier. I tell you, he sure dominates the metaphysical realm now.

We were great at being friends, buds, campmates. We had that down pat. Every so often, though, I caught a glimmer of him being interested in

------

*Throughout this book, you'll read about me learning/studying tarot. I use the terms "learning" and "studying" loosely. My goal was to learn and master something that had confused me while growing up. The choice was between calculus and tarot. I chose tarot, thinking that would be more fun. I'm beginning to see I should have chosen calculus.

me as more than friends, but as quickly as it appeared, it disappeared, and we were back to being platonic friends. Occasionally, he would get quiet, and I felt like the little sister nuisance to the annoying kid down the street. In reality, he had me from one end of the emotional spectrum to the other. For the most part, he liked me. We were buds. Sometimes there'd be a glimmer of attraction, and a few times I got the feeling I was overstaying my welcome.

Around twenty days after I got to Yuma, I had been lazily searching for an RV or a bus to live in and move out of the trunk of my car. It just happened that the very RV I'm currently sitting in, popped up on Facebook Marketplace, and I got a hold of the owner right away. Made arrangements to drive back up to Quartzsite to check it out the next day.

Fred knew I needed and wanted to move out of the Murano into something bigger, and he knew I was looking. The evening of the day I found the RV, we were sitting around the fire—and I will say, as time went by, our chairs tended to move closer to each other. We were no longer directly across the fire from each other. We weren't bumped up against each other, but we weren't on polar opposite sides, either.

Fred had gotten up to get another log or two for the fire, and as he walked to the pile of wood behind his chair, I told him I had found an RV and was going up to Quartzite the next day to check it out. He stopped midstep, literally spun around, and asked, "You're leaving?" (I still feel bad remembering his sad voice when he heard my announcement.)

As soon as he said it, he realized the disappointment and desperation in his voice and instantly course-corrected with another question about my plans for the next day. I don't remember what it was, but I had definitely thrown a monkey wrench into his new daily life of having a campmate.

I told him I was going up there to take a look. I had arranged for someone to come look it over while I met with the owner. I told him I'd be back that night in time for dinner; I didn't want to be up there for any longer than I needed to be. The Big Tent RV Show was happening then, and there's a reason I enjoy sitting out in the middle of nowhere, by myself. Plus, the option of spending time with Fred versus sitting in Quartzsite by myself... That decision wasn't hard.

Before leaving Quartzsite, I posted a picture of myself posing with the new-to-me RV on social media, so Fred knew right away what was happening before I returned to our campsite that evening.

When I got back, we went out for a celebratory dinner for me finding somewhere to live other than the trunk of my car before going back to camp for our nightly campfire. I told him that the RV was having some work done before it could be pulled from the previous owner's property. New batteries, steering assembly, etc.—this is not exactly a *new* RV, but it was a good deal and allowed me to stop sitting in my car to work, and sleeping in my car… I could stand up, had somewhere to hide from inclement weather, could cook in it, and had indoor plumbing!!! He knew I was happy to be moving into a bigger space—and a couple of times, he marveled at how I was living in my car, so it was a needed purchase.

In the time that the RV was being worked on—new batteries, steering linkage, tires, brakes, etc.—a money pit—we had moved from the Pilot Knob LTVA, over to the Old Fogey Hot Springs LTVA just east of Holtville, CA.

I remember packing up with him on that sunny morning, the day we moved. While he was getting the inside of his trailer together, I quickly drove over to Yuma, filled up the gas tank, and then drove back the eight miles into California, where gas prices are generally higher. Sometimes it's a $4 difference, so it's definitely worth the sixteen-mile round trip. After I got back, he needed a little help with the back door of his trailer while he was loading his bike and a couple of other things, and then we set off for the next destination, which he frequented each winter.

I found it amusing as we were driving toward Holtville; I was following a guy I had known for less than two months, farther into California. Again, up to this point, the only people I knew were Fred, the women who were still living in seventh grade, and a few stragglers who sat by their campfires back in Quartzsite. Well, I also now knew the guy who sold me the RV and the mechanic who looked it over before I bought it. That was it, and "jaded and cynical me" was willingly putting my safety and trust into the hands of a guy I only knew for maybe fifty days? This was very unlike me to do with anyone. But Fred? He was quickly becoming "home" to me.

We pulled into the Holtville LTVA, and he stopped, got out, and came back to my car to tell me to look for a spot that I might think would be a good place for us. I was thrilled to hear that he was interested in being in a spot with me. I know we had been right next to each other at Pilot Knob, but as I said, sometimes I got the feeling of being the little sister of that nuisance kid down the street, and then sometimes he was looking at me with bedroom eyes. Throughout all of it, he never clarified his situation of having a "very good friend," but we were friends and vibed well as campmates.

I followed his truck and trailer all the way back to the end of the park, where he jumped out again to ask if I had seen anything. When I didn't have a preference for what I saw, he said he might have found one.

He picked a great spot and told me to pull my car in first, then he would back his trailer in. He'd park his truck in front of the trailer, and his bike in front of my car. Again, he had put some thought into this.

I had helped him back his trailer in, right up against the scrub brush on the driver's side, leaving enough room for us to have a courtyard to share. He strung lights in the tall bush that secluded us from passersby. He pulled out his above-ground fire pit again, the lawn chairs went up, and the spotlights were positioned to keep nighttime critters out from underneath the vehicles. We certainly had no problem setting up our area so we could spend time together. I also helped him put up his ten-by-ten canopy, and with that, we had a nice space between my car and his trailer. Very cozy and mostly secluded with killer views of an unobstructed nightly sunset, and I was very much in heaven!

After setting up, he took me to the hot springs and started walking down the hill. I was wearing old prescription glasses that did great for seeing long distances, but at close distances, I couldn't see diddly-squat. Plus, it was that golden twilight hour where it's extremely hard to see anything. I asked him to help me down the hill, and he didn't take it seriously until he turned around and saw me still standing at the top, beckoning him to come back up and give me his arm for help. Had it been sunnier without that twilight haze and coloring outside, I would have made it just fine down the hill by myself. But nature allowed us to be closer to each other—the closest we had been up to that point.

He gave me his arm and, carefully, with trepidation and some distance between us, started to lead me. But I figured if I was going down, he was coming with me. I grasped more of his arm and pulled us closer together. I couldn't see anything but golden light; I couldn't tell where the brown dirt on the hill began and where the golden light ended, so I couldn't see the hill's grade. Again, if I was going to fall, he was coming with me. With his arm offered cautiously, I easily picked up on how nervous he was to have me so close. We got down to the spring, he showed me everything around that area, and then we went out for dinner. It really was nice to have a foodie to hang with—again, someone who was into more cuisines than just fast food.

The next morning, instead of being bundled up and watching the sun come up over the Pilot Knob Hill that divides Arizona, California, and Mexico, it was on the docket to now be in a bathing suit with a towel and Crocs on, ready to be in the truck by 7:15 a.m.

I had gotten used to getting up and sitting outside in the warmth of the sun, wrapped in a blanket with my pajamas underneath, maybe even a hoodie, socks, and slippers on. But to be yanked out of my car into a forty-degree morning wearing a bathing suit and Crocs, and holding a towel? That was pure insanity. When it's still hazy, and the sun is barely up, and it's cold, this is why I left for warmer climates in the winter. Forty and fifty degrees are not the temperatures to be standing around wearing only a bathing suit, especially after crawling out of a warm bed.

BUT Fred was part of the equation, which meant every morning I dutifully set my alarm clock, kicked open my back hatch at 7:00 a.m., and crawled out, doing my best not to tumble and hit the ground. I ambled to my bathroom tent, located on the passenger side of my vehicle—the side opposite our shared courtyard. I changed out of my warm pajamas (I tried to change in my car, but the lack of space meant I could only put on socks, and even that was cumbersome) and into a cold bathing suit.

We would also hit the hot springs in the evening. On one of those evenings before heading out to the hot springs (we were parked far enough back in the LTVA that we had to drive up to the hot springs area), I had gone around to the other side of my car to where my bathroom tent and makeshift changing area were to get my bathing suit on.

My makeshift changing area had a tarp wrapped around each side of the shower tent, and if I parked my car within three feet of the tent, I could tie the tarps to the roof rack, giving me a changing area outside the small bathroom tent. Although I bought the larger 4 x 4 tent, it didn't seem very spacious inside, so I used the space between the tent and my car. I could also open my back passenger door to access the inside of my car to pull out clothes and such.

Anyway, I was getting myself into my bathing suit while he was inside his trailer changing. I just happened to glance into the car through one of the small back windows of the Murano and saw him sitting on his trailer step, exhaling, quietly clapping his hands together, and then looking off to the side—like he was avoiding something. I realized what he saw—me topless while changing into my bathing suit.

I didn't say anything to him when I came around and got into the truck to go. But one time, when he ran into town for something, and I was left at the campsite, I sat on his step and looked through the back window to confirm what he had seen, and sure enough, he had gotten a little show from me. He never brought it up, and neither did I, but I sure found it amusing.

Speaking of that, the first Saturday we were out at Old Fogey Hot Springs, we spent the day sitting outside and soaking up sunshine. So, instead of doing the whole bra thing—ask any woman, and they'll tell you it's not their favorite thing to wear—I put on a loose-fitting tank top (I had lost eighty-five pounds between leaving Minnesota a few months before, to when I was sitting in Southern California with him). The temperature that day was also in the nineties. So, to wear a bra for no good reason was stupid, in my mind.

I had put on one of my now-too-big tank tops and sat out in our little courtyard. I figured he was probably familiar with the female body, so it wasn't a big thing for me to go braless. Plus, I didn't want to sit there and sweat all day just because I was with a man.

I had brought up being hungry and dug through my pantry tote and pulled out a can of beef stew, and figured I'd start a fire to warm it up. Instead, he disappeared into his trailer and came back out with a tabletop grill for me to use.

I was sitting with my back against his toy hauler, right next to the door. So, when he came out with the grill in his hands, he asked me to help pull out its legs so he could set it down on the table under the canopy. He stood next to me while I was helping, and when I looked up at him to tell him it was good to go, he had a sheepish smile on his face, looking straight down the front of my shirt. Mmm hmm. He got another show. I didn't mind—I found his reaction rather amusing.

One morning, we were out at the springs when a young family with one kid got into the tub I was soaking in, and I started talking to them. I asked them if their three-year-old enjoyed reading and found out that, in fact, the little girl did. I offered them a couple of my children's books if I saw them later in the day, after sitting in the hot springs. They told me they were in a converted skoolie up at the front of the LTVA, and I made arrangements to meet them after getting dressed back at camp.

I can't remember where we were going, but I grabbed one of each of my children's books and asked Fred to stop at their campsite on the way out of the area. Fred saw the books and was curious, but didn't ask. I showed him where this family was parked, and he drove me over there. I dug through my purse, grabbed my "signing pen" (I'm picky with pens), jumped out, and walked over to the family. I was about twenty feet away from Fred, who was still sitting in the truck; he had turned off the engine, not knowing how long this would take.

He witnessed me talking to both parents and their kid, then taking out my perfect book-signing pen and signing each paperback on their outside table, giving the first one to the excited three-year-old, then the remaining two to the parents. He also witnessed them give me three $20 bills; I refused, but they insisted. Fred then saw everyone at that campsite, excited, and the family thanking and waving to me as I walked back to the truck. I got in, and Fred looked impressed, so I pointed out how I had just made $60 in cash within ten minutes.

Lastly, one of the early evenings we got back from the springs, I sat out on the lawn chair to dry off before getting redressed for when the sun fell below the horizon—this was after the camp host told us that I had to tear down my bathroom tent because only self-contained vehicles were allowed on that side of the LTVA. I had told Fred that with no more bathroom tent, I noticed that when I tried to hide behind the tall weeds and do my best to be modest on the other side of my car, our neighbor about a football field away would send up his drone and have it hover nearby—another one getting a free show. So, on this early evening, I changed on the driver's side of the car and hid behind my open back driver-side door, with Reflectix covering the window and whatever privacy the overgrown shrub between Fred and me could provide.

While walking back to the lawn chair around the fire, Fred was grinning. I finally said something about the free show he got, and then he blushed, fidgeted, kicked the rocks around his chair, and shrugged. I called him a "cheeky monkey" and got another laugh out of him. I didn't mind giving him those free shows; had he asked for more, he probably would have been a very lucky boy.

One evening, we had returned from a movie in El Centro—I forget which—but it was raining on and off. We pulled into our spot, and the rain was still falling. I had asked if I could sit in the truck until it stopped raining, as I was still living in the back of my car and would have to open the back hatch to crawl in, and didn't want to do so with wet clothes. He agreed, and we sat in the truck listening to the radio and checking the radar on our various weather apps. Let's say, from my point of view, the electricity in that truck cab was quite obvious and palpable, but as usual, I felt awkward. I'm sure he was sitting behind the steering wheel, feeling the same thing, but didn't know what my deal was. It wasn't too hard to figure out that I became an absolutely enraptured, doe-eyed, permagrin, gobsmacked, female-in-love whenever he was nearby, and even if I did my best to hide it, the energetic vibrations oozing out of my pores betrayed me. But I wasn't making any moves, and I wasn't asking any questions (I was waiting for him to continue with his conversation prompts about his "very good friend," but he would always drop the subject as quickly as he brought it up.) Again, two grown-ass adults who couldn't communicate. I later found out why, but at the time, there was a definite electricity between us, with no resolution in sight.

I know this may sound trivial to some, but when the camp host told me I had to take down my bathroom tent, I had to drive a mile to the public bathrooms near the hot springs any time I needed to "take care of business." Fred was kind enough to suggest and allow me to use his truck to get up there, rather than having me tear down my car setup to drive. Again, I know this may seem like a small thing, but seeing that Fred trusted me to drive his truck—his only long-haul transportation—really stood out to me.

When I camped with him, he would occasionally lapse into long periods of daydreaming. He'd be staring at me, but he was definitely somewhere else. He'd be rather embarrassed when he snapped out of it, and when I asked him what he was thinking about, he'd grow quiet, shrug, shake his head, and tell me he didn't know. But those daydreams would always be when he was staring at me, and would happen either at camp, in a restaurant, or out at the hot springs, etc.

While in the Holtville area, he continued to willingly act as my personal tour guide. He showed me the layout of El Centro, took me down to Calexico, drove along the border for a bit, then we would drive through the fields south of Hwy 8, the canals, and more fields north of the highway.

From the road, we would take guesses at what the crops were and watch the harvesting equipment at work. He would point out the various irrigation systems and explain how they functioned. I asked more questions to get him to continue talking. Although I thoroughly enjoyed any subject he/we chose to talk about, in reality, he probably could have talked to me about an ice cube, and I would have been fascinated.

It's not that I was hanging on his every word, or that I don't know quite a bit about a lot of things, but it ensured that he and I were still wrapped up in one of our conversation bubbles. As for the new information, I very much appreciated the explanation and the opportunity to learn.

He took me to Old Plank Road—the original highway between San Diego and Yuma. We spent an afternoon at the Official Center of the World in Felicity, CA—a town the land's owner named after his wife—and the attraction is quite impressive. He took me to Salvation Mountain and Slab City and gave me a tour of the area. We stopped by East Jesus—the art installation in Slab City. One of the pictures used in the Facebook photo montage his nephew made to honor him is one I took of him in the cab of his truck, with the Slab City outbuilding in the background. It was the same location as the picture he took of me standing next to it. *(videos)*

I did tell him once that I was horribly allergic to cats, and mentioned that if anyone wanted to get rid of me, they just needed to throw a cat at me and I'd be gone. So, with those mixed signals I've been mentioning, I forget which intersection we were at, but I asked him where we were going, and with a deadpan delivery, he said, "A cat farm."

I didn't respond but instead sat there in silence, feeling like that nuisance little sister of the annoying kid down the block, again. After a few miles, he started another conversation, and everything returned to normal. However, these little pings would also stand out, suggesting he might be getting tired of my company. However, there were many other times when I could see he liked having me around.

One morning at the hot springs, he was sitting in the hotter tub along with another guy, and I asked if I could get in—there was room for four people if everyone sat together, and three could definitely sit in the tub. Two could spread out easily.

I asked and he, with a challenging look on his face, told me "no." The guy in the tub with him interjected, inviting me to sit in the tub next to him, so I did. That hottest tub is the one I preferred, plus you get to sit rather than stand in the medium-temp one. The coolest one, you could sit in, but the temperature wasn't for me.

So, I got in, talked with the other guy for a minute or two, and then he left. I moved to where the other guy had originally been sitting, and Fred remained where he was. He was looking off to his left, and I wanted to get his attention to say something, so using my hand, I tapped the top of his hand that was hanging over the water because his arm/elbow was propped on the side. He spun his head around and shot me a look of surprise/shock/alarm/shallow offensiveness. Instead of saying what I was planning to say, I defensively told him to chill out and that I wasn't giving him cooties. I never did say what I wanted to say at that moment because he looked at me with such shock. After my comment, he was quiet and looked back to the left and eventually got out of the tub, leaving me there. Again, another example of feeling like the annoying little sister of the kid down the street, who no one wanted to play with.

I never did get an answer to what that was all about, nor did I ask. I chalked it up to one more mixed signal. Because within an hour of that, we were back to talking about everything and anything. (On one of his connections with Kimberly, after his death, he told me why he gave me the look he did: He felt an intense shock of electricity when I tapped his hand. He was surprised, not upset.)

I will say, though, he had several women flocking around him while he sat in the cooler pool. I was usually in the hottest one that his heart couldn't handle for as long as I could. There was one female in particular, with green hair (on purpose), who made sure she was down at the springs every morning we were there, at damn near the same time. She'd see him, say "hi" as she was walking in, and then sit in that cooler pool with him, chatting his ear off. He would carry on any conversation that came up with anyone in the pool, and I'm sure he also figured out he had an admirer. Dare I say he knew he had many admirers?

When he had had his fill of hot water or ongoing conversation, or both, he would look at me, and I would *know* to look at him. He'd nod his head, I nodded back, and then we would meet at the fence where our towels were hanging, talk as we were getting dried off, and then leave together. (She may have had a chance to talk with him in the pool, but I was going back to the campsite with him. Again, I can be a conniving bitch with knives out.)

I will note, when we weren't in proximity, we would always have a connection that would cause us to look at the other when something was needed; anything from the time to leave to thinking the other person might need something, and this extended to knowing what the other one was most likely thinking and at times, we'd be able to finish each other's sentences/ trains of thoughts. The couple of times he showed up or was near me, I knew he was close before I saw him. I felt him even if we were fifty yards away from each other and weren't yet in each other's sights.

Beyond what I have noted here (what I can remember from two years ago), we regularly visited restaurants, theaters, candy stores, flea markets, fruit stands, and shopping outlets. We drove along the canal and field roads, and we watched the helicopters fly over us—back and forth along Hwy 8. Both of us enjoyed "catching some rays," sometimes for entire days, then we'd go into town in the evening to do something. It was truly living/camping with someone who was quickly becoming one of my best friends— especially since we learned so much about each other, got along so well, and looked forward to hanging out every day. *(videos)*

So, needless to say, when I had to leave Old Fogey Hot Springs on February 6th to take possession of my RV in Quartzsite, Fred was forlornly sitting on the steps of his toy hauler, watching the great packing adventure of me getting everything back into my car in some semblance of order. Definitely entertaining, I'm sure—especially the part about curling up that 4 x 4 x 7 bathroom tent into an eighteen-inch circle that I could put back into the zippered bag it came in for so-called "easy transport."

I got the tent into the carrying bag and loaded it with everything else back into my Murano. As I was doing this, we were talking, and I mentioned to him that I also like watching people, and confessed that I had been watching him over the weeks we had just spent together, as well as the four weeks prior in Quartzsite. Then I complimented him again on how much I appreciated him sharing his time with me, as well as his other traits, and wrapped it up by telling him I thought he was a very handsome man.

He blushed and resituated himself on his trailer steps, then quietly but assertively told me that he had been told that before. I told him that whoever had told him that in the past wasn't lying.

At this time, I also pointed out to him that I had seen a good seven different types of smiles from him, and then named them off:

- ○ His really happy, ear-to-ear grin (usually when he saw me).

- His give-it-a-whirl, opportunistic smile (suggesting crazy ideas—even in jest).
- His in-the-moment, being-present smile (around the campfires and chatting).
- His I'm-being-sneaky smile (sneaking into the Cocopah Race Track).
- His cheeky-monkey, I-got-caught smile, usually accompanied by blushing and fidgeting (him getting a "free show" from me).
- His relaxed, chilled-out smile (sitting in the hot springs/after a good meal/lying out in the sun).
- His amused-by-a-situation smile (when an amusing situation is happening but doesn't directly affect him).

I did not mention his come-hither smile (which is a whole thing in itself—dangerous, in fact, and hard to feign no interest in—good grief!), or any of his other smile variations. But those seven (along with the eighth one I didn't mention to him) stood out to me most often. He was surprised by all of that info, and once again, he fidgeted while sitting on the steps of his toy hauler, and I smiled at his nervousness.

I put a couple more things into the car and then walked over to him. He stood up, and I stood in front of him. I asked him if he wanted either a handshake or a hug. He looked down briefly, shuffled his feet, and then quietly said that a hug wouldn't hurt. I may have held on a little longer than I should have and longer than he did, but you know, why not? I had no problem with it.

Once the last "see you later down the road" was said, I got in the car and drove away. As I did, I looked in my side mirror (I couldn't see out the back window) and saw him standing there, watching as half of his little neighborhood drove away, leaving him alone. And that still kills me, but I had to get back up to Quartzsite.

Chapter 11

If he was standing there looking sad when I left, I was equally torn apart on my drive out of the Old Fogey Hot Springs LTVA to go back to Quartzsite for my RV. To this day, I still feel like an absolute shitty person for leaving him there.

But, I will point out that between mixed messages, omissions of a certain someone he could never bring himself to explaining, the fact that the camphost told me to get out of that area if I wasn't "self-contained," and sometimes feeling that he thought of me as the annoying little sister of the neighborhood kid down the street, I didn't want to overstay my welcome. After all, he was a sixty-one-year-old bachelor with this googly-eyed female (although I did my best to hide it, it didn't work, I'm sure) in his midst. As I said, I didn't want him to get completely tired of me, and I had to pick up my new money pit… I mean RV.

I got back up to Quartzsite, picked up my new-to-me RV, and then began two months of the loneliest time any human being has ever experienced. Maybe not *any* human being, but good grief, I was depressed. Sure, I had work and countless trips to the repair shop scheduled, but I missed him. Badly.

On February 9, 2024, I wrote and posted the "Travel Review" I had promised him on Facebook. I didn't tag him, but it was quite obvious who I was talking about, and I'm sure this stunt cemented his hunch that he was dealing with a loony.

5-STAR REVIEW Facebook entry:

The only time I leave a review is if something really stood out to me, good or bad. This review is because of something good and meaningful. I also have incredibly high standards and can be described as "very picky" and "hard to impress." (Really hard to impress.)

I had the pleasure of spending a month with the proprietor of "WFN"–a small tour company that isn't technically a business or a tour company of any sort, but I'll refer to it as such for this review.

I was looking for a change of scenery, and the proprietor agreed to let me camp near him. I told him that he was not responsible for me, my expenses, or my entertainment–I only wanted to camp next to someone I knew, and at that point, I had only known him for one month.

Upon arriving at his location, he helped me set up and then took me out for a drive to see the "lay of the land"–get acquainted with where I'd be staying for the next handful of weeks. We actually stayed in two different locations, and he shared his knowledge of both areas with me, as well as sightseeing opportunities. I did and saw more things, as well as visited more places, during the month of January 2024 than I have done in the last six months, if not longer:
  ◦ We went to the Winter National races
  ◦ We took a day trip to Mexico
  ◦ We visited a casino
  ◦ We went out for a lot of meals
  ◦ We spent a week soaking in hot springs
  ◦ We played music bingo at a local saloon three weeks in a row (while we were near

```
    that establishment)
  ◦ We visited various towns/cities and land-
    marks
  ◦ We went to a huge flea market and an or-
    chard
  ◦ We saw a couple of movies
  ◦ We continuously waited for SpaceX launch-
    es that were always called off
  ◦ Nearly every night, we had a campfire; as
    a matter of fact, the only times we didn't
    have a fire were when we weren't at the
    campsite or when the weather wasn't coop-
    erative
To top it off, this proprietor was a gracious
and thoughtful host whom I got to know over the
course of thirty days, and I gladly give him
five out of five stars on both Yelp and TripAd-
visor.

    If you have the opportunity to stay next to
the proprietor of "WFN," please take it. He's
a little shy at first, but he's really a great
conversationalist and knowledgeable in several
areas. If he's unfamiliar with it, I guarantee
he'll look it up on his phone and learn about
it. He has a great sense of humor, too, but the
highlight will be his company.

    I look forward to my next stay with the WFN
proprietor, whenever that may be.
```

I did text him every so often. Sometimes I got a response quickly, other times it was delayed, and sometimes I got no response. I remembered he had told me that unless there was a question or pressing matter, he probably wouldn't reply because he wasn't interested in idle chit-chat texting.

My birthday weekend showed up—the tentative plan was to go to Palm Springs for the Aerial Tramway. He didn't call, I didn't call. I was bored, lonely, and sad. Although I never got confirmation from the Facebook post he made on February 16th about finally getting around to making a fire, I could tell from the way he typed the caption that he was, too.

Unfortunately, my RV needed new brakes and brake lines. I wasn't about to take that thing anywhere, out on the open road. So, there I sat, grounded, waiting for an opening at the only place in Quartzsite I'd heard of that had some decent reviews. This place had just put six new tires on it before I picked it up (but after I bought it). Since it's the only place in town that doesn't scam and does a good job, and February/March is also when people start heading out to go back to wherever they spend their summers, I was held captive in Quartzsite until I could get in for an appointment, which happened toward the end of March. I will note here, too, that I was keeping Fred informed about all of this and posting on Facebook. So, he did know why I was unable to come back.

Sunday, Feb 18, 2024 • 6:03 PM

It's been nearly 14 days at Dome Rock - I need to move this week. I'm thinking Tyson Wash. I need to go scout a place, though.

Also, I have to say, even though I appreciate solitude, I've been lonely the last two weeks after going cold-turkey from your company. Again, not blowing sunshine up anything... but I sure do miss hanging out with you. Staring at a bonfire in silence, with someone, is a lot more fun when done with someone else.

Yes, I know you're a loner, and neither of us is looking for a lifetime commitment, but I thought we were good at being loners together. :-)

I was so lonely. And bored. And sad. I was utterly miserable. I'm miserable, and my tear ducts are beginning to leak as I type this. Plus, this was the first year that I began to equate the month of March with depression in Quartzsite. The next year, Fred died in March while I was in Quartzsite. Needless to say, I need to be anywhere in the world other than Quartzsite in March.

Through February and March, I texted him. I had invited him to stay at my campsite if he was heading back through Quartzsite on his way home for the summer. He assured me he wouldn't be going through Quartzsite and would be in Montana halfway through March. I wondered why anyone would go to Montana in March, when that part of the country still gets blizzards well into June. But I accepted his statements and didn't question him.

Monday, Mar 4, 2024 • 6:33 PM

I'm going to Mexico to get my crown fixed in early April. My mom wants me to ask if you'd go with me since I'm a solo female. I told her not to hold her breath but promised her I'd still ask. Thoughts? I believe it's the first Monday and Tuesday, if it's the first Tuesday and Wednesday- can't remember. Calendar is in the rv. Either 4/1 & 2, or 4/2 & 3.

Hope to be in Utah by then. Plans are to be in Bozeman MT by the first week in April.

That's what I thought. Thanks for getting back to me.

Tuesday, Mar 5, 2024 • 3:00 PM

Safe travels. ☺

That was last night's message before I shut my phone off. I forgot to hit send.

I captured the SpaceX Launch on March 15, 2024, and carried on like a howler monkey outside watching it shoot across the sky. A couple of days later, Fred texted to ask if he could use the video in his #WFN videos on Facebook. He said he'd give me a mention for credit. I told him "sure," but he sounded very businesslike, not the best friend I had been hanging out with for a handful of weeks. Also, divulging that he was in the hot springs while it streaked across the sky told me he was still in the area, rather than halfway to Montana, as he suggested he would be. *(video)*

Friday, Mar 22, 2024 • 11:36 AM

Good morning. Like your video on the spaceX launch. I seen it but I was at the hot spring, so no pictured. Wondering if I can steal your video? I will certainly give you credit. Hope all is going well in Q. Going to start my drive north soon.

You can use it, but I apologize for my vocal carrying on. You just don't see that kind of stuff in MN. ;-)

Will you be stopping for an overnight in Q? I have room (not many people left out here) and wood for a fire.

It's looking like I'm going to be in Cody, WY for the summer to get off the desert floor. I like heat but not that much heat... at least not for that long.

If you'll be doing an overnight in Q, I can send you my location (a Google map pin.) I'm in Tyson Wash, and will be this weekend through next Thu   then it starts getting dicey.

I really didn't know what to think. Had I been reading the situation wrong the entire time? Did I manage to make an absolute ass out of myself by hanging on his every word and gazing at him? Was it that he couldn't get rid of me fast enough?

Had I known that I could have left one vehicle in the desert and disappeared for a while, I would have done that. But again, I really didn't know where I stood with him. Plus, leaving the "not-yet-road-worthy" RV in

Quartzsite to go back down to Holtville in my car, I would have still had to contend with the camphost complaining about me not being self-contained, and I would have had to drive a mile up to the bathroom every time I needed to use the restroom—so many unknowns, hassles, and again, the unsureness.

I will say, though, if he had responded to any of my texts or called me and said, "Please come back," I would have torn down Hwy 95 at a moment's notice towards Yuma and west on Hwy 8 to Holtville. I would have gladly moved back into the trunk of my car for as long as he was still in the area, and I would have stuck my rig in storage or in the back lot of the mechanic's shop for safekeeping.

There's not much to say about these two months except that I was lonely, bored, and sad, and was dishing out copious amounts of money to repair shops to get my RV safe for the road so I could get off the desert floor for the impending summer.

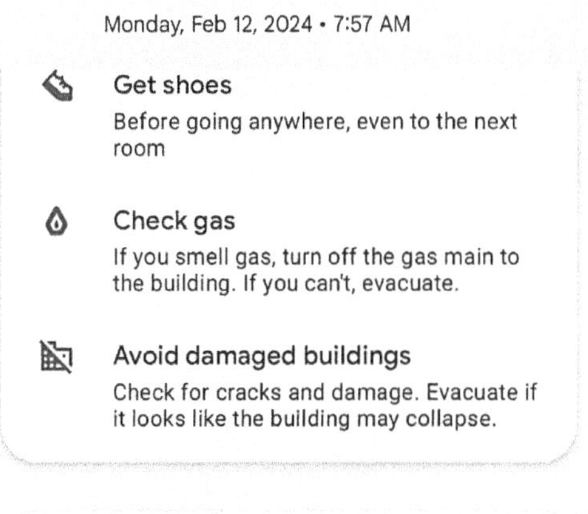

Monday, Feb 12, 2024 • 9:47 AM

Yep, woke me up.

Congrats on checking off 'experience an earthquake' on your bucket list. :-)

One thing that struck me as funny was that on February 12, 2024, Fred experienced his first earthquake. When I texted him (shown above), I congratulated him on crossing something off his bucket list. He was quick to say he didn't have such a thing, but after that experience, he began mentioning that he was "crossing things off his bucket list" a few more times: The SpaceX Launch, his trip to Rachel, NV, and one other thing that I can't remember right now.

I will add that during that March, I picked up a summer work-camping job in Cody, WY, to supplement my bank account, which was being drained by RV repairs and gas. I've got an eighty-gallon tank. I won't discuss the anxiety I get whenever I stop at a gas station.

Chapter 12

My first adventure in the RV showed up on Sunday, March 31, 2024. I had a dental appointment in Los Algodones for a root canal (oh, joy) the following morning. I wanted to get into town the night before because, as a non-morning person, I wasn't interested in driving two hours to an appointment scheduled for 9:00 a.m.

To say I was nervous was an understatement. I had new tires, new brakes, new brake lines, and a lot of other new stuff, and now I was going to take it out on the open road for a longer ride than just limping it into Quartzsite to get it fixed. Out on the road, other people want to go fast, and I hadn't pushed this thing past forty miles per hour because of bad brakes. Today was the day to see if I could drive this thing at highway speeds, be able to stop, and effectively not take myself out in a fiery crash. I really was nervous, but I needed to take this thing out on its maiden voyage with me at the wheel. Gulp! Thirty feet of fun, screaming down the road with a freaked-out driver. Sure, uh… I can handle it. Right?

Before starting the engine, I went live on Facebook, and Fred was the first to hop on. I recorded the video from where I was parked at the Tyson Wash LTVA, just south of Quartzsite, to the intersection of Hwy 95. Then, I turned off the video and made my way down to the Yuma Proving Grounds to check out the outdoor museum. I wandered from exhibit to exhibit, and even took the time to stop and photograph close-ups of the fat caterpillars clinging to the bending blades of grass on the grounds. After futzing around out there for an hour or so, taking my sweet-ass time since I had nothing better to do that day, I figured I would take the backroads to Winterhaven, CA, and then continue onto the Pilot Knob LTVA, where I would spend the night—the same place I had first started camping with Fred. *(video)*

Taking the back roads, I looked for the entrance to Imperial Dam—another camping spot that many snowbirds rave about. Instead, I experienced "baptism by fire" regarding the RV's responsiveness and handling while swerving around deep potholes on a poorly maintained road. At one point, I slowed to fifteen miles per hour to navigate this course of hazards I was desperately trying to avoid, because I didn't need more repair bills for suspension, alignment, or anything being jarred loose. I never did find the entrance to Imperial Dam, either.

I got to Winterhaven, got onto Hwy 8, and went through the California checkpoint without my vehicle being searched (I worry about these things), then pulled into the Pilot Knob LTVA around 12:30 p.m.

I had been texting with Fred about where to park, etc., the night before, and he suggested that if I wanted to skip the drive in the morning, I could just stay at the border for $40/night. Since I had already donated my lungs and one of my kidneys to the repairs and to fill the tank of the "Beast" I now called home, I was feeling rather frugal, so I pulled into Pilot Knob because I had already paid for that seasonal pass.

When I drove in, I thought about parking where Fred and I had stayed a few months earlier, in January, but I didn't want to depress myself further. So, I veered to the left and parked elsewhere.

I turned off the engine, started setting things up, put out my solar panels, then went back inside and glanced out the window toward the spot where we had been during January.

I couldn't believe my eyes! There was another Jayco Octane toy hauler, with a cranberry-colored Ford F-150 and a motorcycle parked in nearly the same spot we had camped.

Now, according to Fred's texts, he was supposed to be in Montana by the middle of March, or at least, heading that direction. So, I grabbed my phone, zoomed in, took a picture of this person's setup, and then texted Fred:

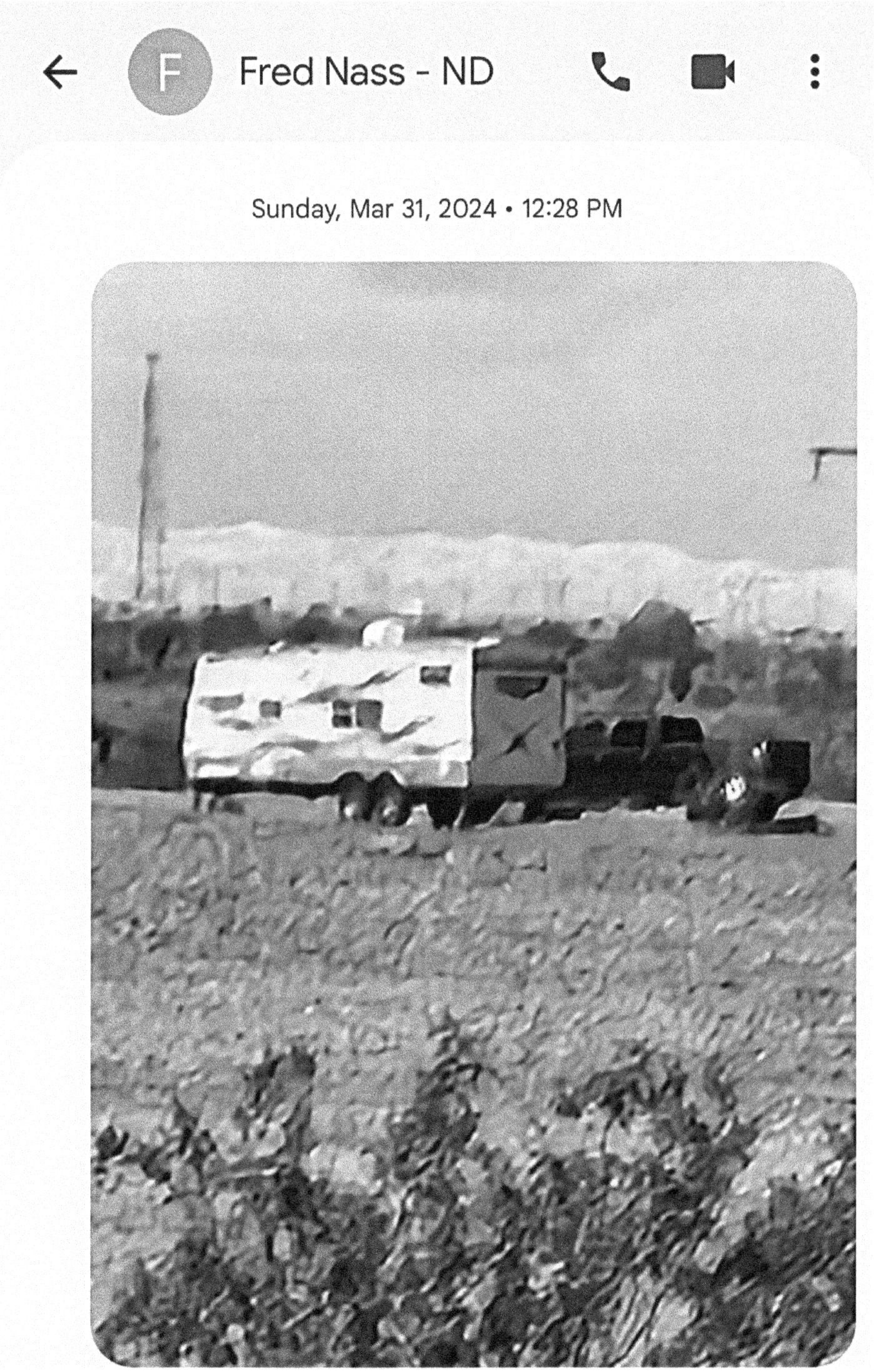

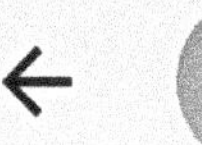

Fred Nass – ND

Sunday, Mar 31, 2024 • 12:28 PM

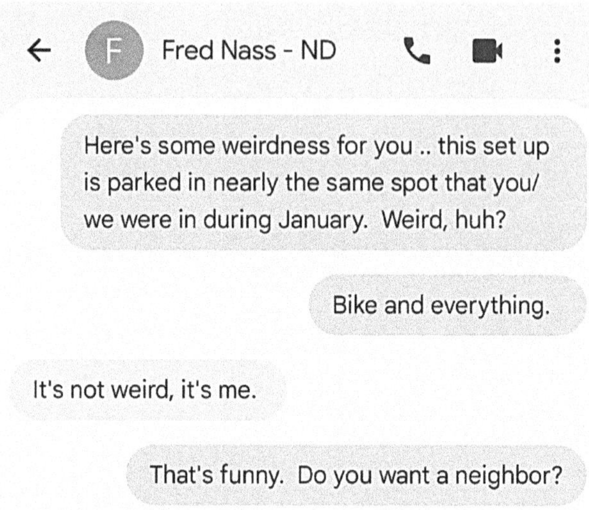

After he texted me back immediately, I asked if he wanted company. I didn't give the message a chance to be delivered before I called him and suggested we camp together again. He said sure, and my heart leapt out of my chest!

No one, to date, has ever seen me move as fast as I moved to get ready to move the RV. I was absolutely giddy to see him again! It was truly comical—my mom called me "molasses" throughout childhood because I got where I needed to be on my own schedule; things got done when they got done, and not a moment sooner with me.

Had my solar panels not cost me a pretty penny, I would have haphazardly thrown them back into the rig. Instead, I quickly folded up the panels and carefully put them back where I stored them. Everything else inside was thrown back onto the bed. I checked that the cupboards were shut, started the RV, and moved over to him.

I rolled up and jumped out. He had watched this lumbering older-model motorhome drive up to him and saw me jump out with my ear-to-ear permagrin on. Bright-eyed and bushy-tailed to find him there when I thought he'd be in Montana.

I found him sitting in one of his low-slung lawn chairs at the back of his trailer in the shade. I will note here that when I took the picture, there were no lawn chairs at the back of his trailer. When I got over there in two and a half minutes (or less), there were three chairs back there, and he was sitting in one, looking a little worn out.*

He didn't really have a reason why he hadn't yet left, and I didn't push it; I really didn't care—I was simply over the moon to see him again!

Per our track record, we sat together from 12:30 p.m. to about 3:30 p.m., talking nonstop, as if nearly sixty days hadn't passed since we last saw each other in person on February 6th, when I drove back to Quartzsite for the RV.

Around 3:30 p.m., he said he planned to go into Yuma to get some propane, and I asked if he would like company. He sort of shrugged, nodded, and quietly said, "Yes."

As far as I was concerned, that was good enough for me as an emphatic "yes," and I told him I'd get myself together—basically pulling in my solar panels, and getting my purse.

I came back out of the RV to find him changing out of his Sturgis HD shirt into a clean Polo. He spritzed himself with cologne and used the side mirror of his truck to style his hair. I didn't mention this, but I did take note.

I got in his truck like it was an everyday occurrence, and he put his empty tanks in the back, and we set off east down the highway to the propane station he used in Yuma.**

---

*I didn't realize this until a few months ago, when I took another look at the picture I sent him via text. In the time it took me to darn near throw everything back into the RV and get it moved over, he had set up an area for our next conversation.

**I'll note here, too, that had I followed his suggestions for staying down on the border, I would never have known he was just over the hill. Also, my intention that day was to find the Imperial Dam and possibly stay out there that night, which would have cheated me out of seeing him again. Even if I had wandered around out there and then driven on to Pilot Knob, that would have chewed up the entire day, causing me to lose time with Fred. So, with my decision-making skills urging me to go to Pilot Knob, and being so wrapped up in the obstacle course I was driving through, north of Winterhaven, I completely missed the sign for Imperial Dam, and showed up earlier to Pilot Knob than I had intended, which gave me darn near a full day with Fred. What a fantastic surprise! Was the universe pushing us together?

On the way into town, we talked about future events—what we could see next season if we were both back down in the area (I was already hoping and praying and crossing my fingers that I would see him the following autumn/winter). We got to the station, and he filled the tanks while I thought I'd be useful by cleaning up a few pieces of trash from his front seat.

After getting the propane, he asked if I wanted to get some food somewhere, and I told him I was famished and could skip fast food, to which he nodded in agreement. Then I suggested the Texas Roadhouse, and he agreed—especially since he hadn't been there yet that season.

We pulled in and saw that the parking lot was full. He was going to back out of the idea, and I suggested we give it a try, just for fun. Apparently, everyone in Yuma goes to the Texas Roadhouse for Easter, but true to his track record, a spot was open right up front (he lived a charmed life of getting prime parking spots up front while I usually had to hoof it in from the north forty).

He was still hesitant when we walked into the full lobby, but I checked the wait time, which was only about twenty minutes, and he agreed to be patient. The seating area was crowded, so we had to sit next to each other on the only available bench. I placed my purse between us, though it got squooshed.

He had reminded me of a time when this restaurant offered in-the-shell peanuts to people waiting to be seated and while at the table. After a moment, I asked him to watch my purse and moseyed up to the hostess stand to ask if they still had the in-the-shell peanuts available. She handed me two bags, and when I returned to where he was sitting, I saw this handsome man tucked against the wall, his left hand on my purse to keep it beside him, watching for me to come back. I smiled when I approached and handed him a bag of peanuts. He was surprised to see them, and I told him, "I had connections and could get things done." We sat there for the next fifteen minutes, eating nuts and throwing the shells on the floor.

Eventually, our table was ready. I followed the hostess first, and Fred was right behind me. The hostess, who was seating us, abruptly stopped to get something before continuing, so I stopped too, to avoid running into her. Fred was right behind me, and to avoid running into the back of me, he reached out and touched my lower back.

Holy monkeys! A surge of electricity blew right through me. A shock or a zap doesn't begin to scratch the surface of what I felt.* I liken it to those movie effects where a blazing burst of energy and light shoots out of every pore and orifice of a person (think of that final scene in *The Fifth Element*). I've never been struck by lightning, thankfully, but I would imagine it would be similar. I can still feel that spot on my lower back, and with everything that has transpired over the past couple of years, I've been thinking about getting a tattoo there. But of course, I need to come up with the perfect design since there are no "backsies" with tattoos.

We had a lovely dinner. That was also one of the restaurants where the waiter asked how long we had been married. He blushed, and again, I clarified. When the waiter delivered the bill, he showed up with another four bags of peanuts and told us he couldn't believe we weren't married, and thanked us for coming in. He got a good tip.

What was planned to be an overnight and then back to Quartzsite, believing Fred was in Montana at that point, I extended my stay with him to a week and wound up leaving on April 6th. Writing that out, I'm realizing that I met him on December 6th, he told me I could camp with him in Yuma on January 6th (but left Quartzsite on the 7th), I left to go back up to Quartzsite to take possession of my RV on February 6th, and I left him again on April 6th to start my trek northward.

Anyway, April 1st came and went with the "consultation" appointment, and I returned to Mexico on April 2nd for that root canal and a temporary crown. He asked when I was planning to leave, and I told him I had changed my mind and was going to hang out with him for the week rather than sitting in Quartzsite, lonely again. That worked for him. We continued our conversations, went out to eat a couple of times, and spent a day lying in the sun and listening to music. He finally saw the SpaceX launch from Vandenberg AFB, after all the times we sat outside a couple of months earlier waiting for one. Another beautiful week in the Arizona sun and warmth with a really cool person.

---

*I'll add that I tease him about those moments when he touched my back and I touched his hand, and we both felt that mind-blowing zing (and that doesn't even scratch the surface of explaining the feeling we both received); had we been physically intimate, we would have had enough energy between us to move tectonic plates. OMG! The energy was and still is indescribable!

When it was time for me to get on the road, I remember him standing by the bed of his truck watching me get everything together, and that unfortunately familiar, sad look was on his face. A couple of days prior, I had decided to kiss him on his right cheek when I hugged him goodbye for the second time.

Again, I asked him if he wanted a handshake or a hug, and he chose a hug, but I chickened out on the cheek kiss. I wish I had followed through on my plan, but, again, because I hadn't figured out his full opinion of me, I didn't spring any surprises on him. I didn't want to offend him or upset him, so I just hugged him and left it at that, although it was fairly obvious that both of us were crushing on each other. It was a strange partnership, and although I hadn't understood why at that time, I understand now what the overarching problem was (more on that further into the book).

I would have happily stayed a few more days, but I had to get up to Wyoming by April 21st for that summer work-camping job I had arranged to earn more money for the never-ending repairs I had taken on with my new-to-me, money-pit motorhome. I also didn't know how well it would travel, so I wanted to give myself as much time as possible. (I made the trip in four days—I should have stayed longer with him.)

Chapter 13

Much like February and March, when I was lonely, sad, and depressed, my 2024 summer was equally so. Sure, I was surrounded by people and went to a few rodeos, but I really wanted to be with Fred in North Dakota.

I had seriously considered pulling out of Cody and driving to Rhame or Cando, but he wasn't expecting me, and I didn't want to barge in, especially if he was spending time with his "very good friend." I was still not entirely sure what I meant to him: convenient friend or possibly something more? Plus, I had given this business my word that I would help them that season, and with that damn integrity I live by, I stayed true to my word and commitment by remaining in Cody.

During the time apart from April to November 2024, we texted every so often. In April, he filled me in on the term "speed goats," which still makes me break into a fit of giggles to this day. I have no idea why, exactly. It just does.

APR 19, 2024 AT 7:33 AM

Since posting 'Wyoming speed goats' - which still has me laughing, I've had multiple people message me about them googling it and laughing, too. I think that word combination is funny, and how much do you want to bet when I have to be quiet somewhere/I have to be 'professional', that word combo is going to pop into me head out of nowhere and throw me into a fit of giggles? 😣

MAY 16, 2024 AT 4:32 PM

I watched your video. Good to see you got home safely and to your doctor's appt. I was going to comment 'nice buttes' in your post, but I figured your friends wouldn't get my twisted and often inappropriate type of humor. 😉

Obviously, you know I'm odd, and I told you plenty of times how much I enjoy the western side of the Dakotas, so it would make sense to you. 😊

MAY 17, 2024 AT 11:35 PM

Hey, if you're looking for a new truck name, (don't be offended if this sounds too forward, too) but 'Silver Fox' just popped into my thoughts. Perhaps corny/clever/both, but it's apropos. Ciao.

In June, I arranged with the owners of the Cando Bar & Grill to buy him dinner. He was up in Cando, ND (his hometown) for the last part of June and through the Fourth of July holiday, and I wanted to do something special for his birthday. I called the bar and spoke with one of the owners, who said there was no official way to purchase a Gift Certificate for Fred other than in person. I reiterated that I was nowhere near Cando and wouldn't be anytime soon, but I really wanted to buy Fred dinner. I then suggested PayPal or Venmo, and he handed me off to his wife, who had a Venmo account. I made the purchase, thanked her and her husband emphatically, and they then informed me that Fred would be in that night with his friend. So, I didn't tell him what was waiting for him and kept it a surprise, letting the bar owners tell him who the gift was from.

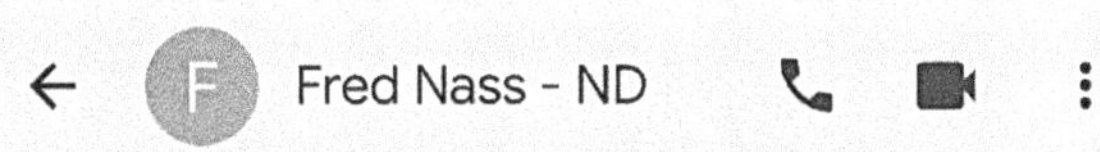

Thanks for the birthday tab. I had the chicken tonight and was very good. Thanks again

You're welcome. I'm not saying 'HB' though until tomorrow. ;-)

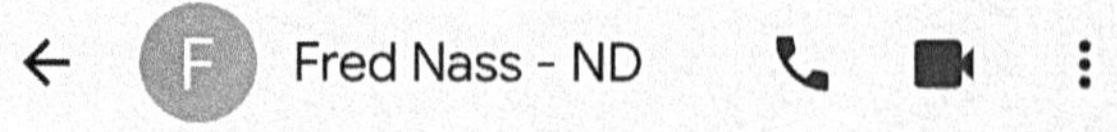

Fred Nass - ND

Monday, Jun 24, 2024 • 10:02 PM

Happiest of birthdays to you! I truly wish you a fabulous day. :-)

If I see you this winter and you're interested, I'll take you out for another dinner to round out tonight's gift certificate to an even $62. I suppose if it's winter, and you'll be 62 1/2, I'll have to pony up another 50 cents to make it correct. I'll start saving now in case it's a go...

*I do know you're getting this text in the Central time zone, so it's officially your birthday. Over here in Mountain time, I'm going to sleep. ;-)

**Yesterday's snafu was because I thought it was Monday after I had brought up the Cando Bar's web listing as a reminder to myself to buy the gift certificate on Monday because I wouldn't have the time on Tuesday. In that short amount of time, I got my days mixed up. Oops, and quite embarrassing.

July came and went, and I carried on to all of my summer work colleagues about this really great guy in North Dakota, and I could tell they had had their fill of my incessant chatter about this one person. I showed everyone his pictures on Facebook and basically conducted myself as a lovesick teenager for nearly six months. I couldn't help myself. Some of them tried to goad me into driving out and surprising him, but I didn't think that would be a good idea, especially since I didn't know where I stood in this entire relationship—if it was even considered a *relationship.*

Plus, I was still unsure about my RV's potential for future breakdowns, the cost of gas, and the time required to travel to and from (or I might have just stayed out there, since I wasn't enjoying this job in Cody very much), but I didn't do it.

I also knew that he would be attending Sturgis—an annual event for him—and that his special friend would most likely be there. Again, I had no idea what that was all about. But on his Facebook page, when people were posting "Happy Birthday" wishes to him, I sent one and received a thumbs up—as did most everyone else. But when he got a birthday wish from L.M., he replied to her post asking if he would see her at Sturgis, then followed up with a double-heart emoji.

Yeah, that didn't sit well with me, but I instantly chalked it up to my suspicions being correct: he was a taken man, and I was simply a friend who bought him dinner. Again, so be it.

My brain started mocking my heart, and my heart kept telling my brain to stick it up its ass. I had gotten used to this internal war going on since December 6, 2023.

July came and went—I saw his posted pictures and videos of friends shooting off fireworks, and his campfires.

After he announced he was going back home to get ready for the Bike Rally, I folded inward (still with my internal conflict) and steadied myself with the thought that he would be spending time with L.M. doing… whatever… in Sturgis. Yes, I was jealous. But again, it wasn't any of my business.

I liked his various posts from the event and kept myself busy counting down until I was done with the job that had managed to suck the fun out of that summer.*

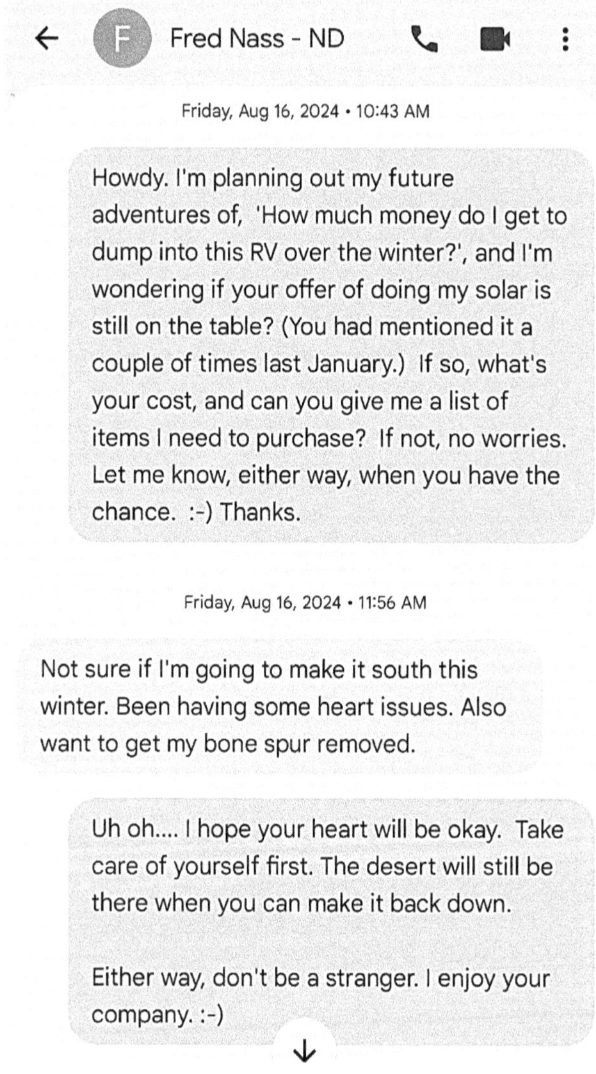

---

*I've been self-employed for thirty-six years, as of the time I'm writing this, and am used to writing my own schedule. So, having to clock in on someone else's schedule and then *fall into line,* or, as they put it, constantly *stay in your own lane,* made me absolutely miserable. And having the guy I like five hours away, and most likely cavorting with this one person he could never bring himself to explain to me, also made me very depressed.

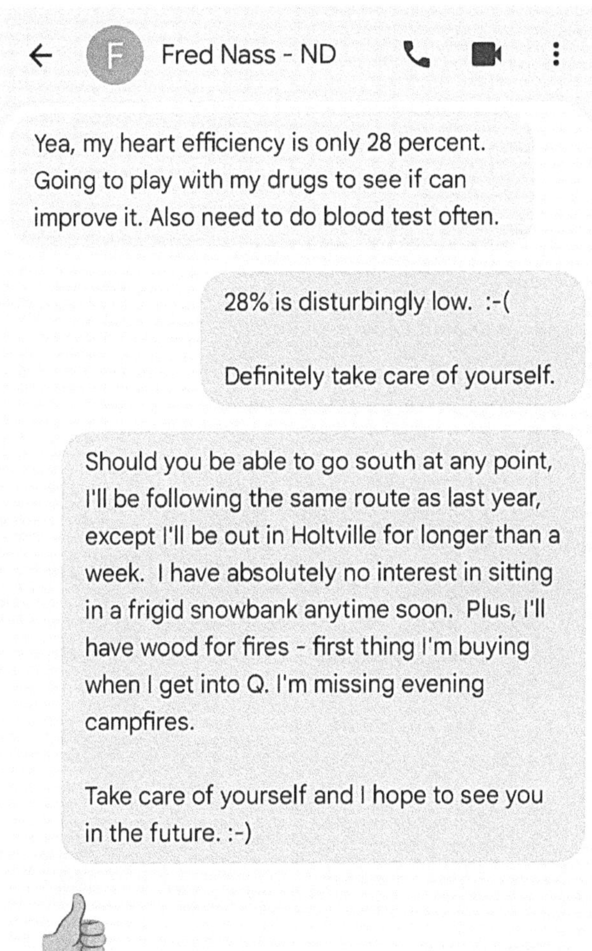

I gave it until after Labor Day to reach out to him again, and asked him about his plans for the upcoming winter season, and that's when he told me about his continuing and newer health issues, then said he wasn't coming back down that year. I was crushed, and true to the writer's form, I got onto Facebook and bared my soul with vague-booking, knowing full well he would read it.

September 12, 2024, Facebook entry:

In extreme anticipation of getting the heck outta here and back down to the desert, and the combination of listening to Robert Plant's Big Log on my shuffle, I'm brought back to quality time last winter–someone said he liked this song while we were listening to tunes either sun tanning/around the nearly-nightly campfire.

Oh... You know, when you find something/someone good, and it's a freakin' blast of fresh air, and it's awesome, but life enjoys kicking you around for its simple amusement? Welcome to my world.

Yes, I'm attracted to positive energy, someone/something with a chill personality–and really, aren't we all? I lead such a hectic life/ calendar that when you find a friend to kick back with and shoot the $hit, or stare into the abyss just for S&Gs, it's freakin' crack. I've never had crack or most other substances, but I would imagine this is what it's like–withdrawal from crack.

Well, that gift of a person (I will use that description because he was truly a gift for my soul–again, not blowing sunshine up anyone's butt, here, but those six weeks were so needed, so appreciated, so calming) will not be down in the desert this winter due to some personal issues that need to be taken care of this year.

I know so many people. So many, many people. But it's that rare person who crosses my path of insanity and is allowed into my life (and rarely do people get to be "in" my life beyond a work or acquaintance status) who is a breath of fresh air.

No one is perfect, but he was the perfect person to be a part of my life this past winter– what I needed to introduce me to the nomadic life and the upheaval of life as I knew it. Kindness, real, genuine, fun, chilled out, relaxed, helpful, entertaining, and funny, and more—a helluva person.

I'd be weirdly lucky to find another person I could kick back and chill out with this winter. But since I'm as picky as he!!, I'm not holding my breath.

I know he read it because we kept Facebook stalking each other. He didn't say anything to this post, and in a way, I'm glad he didn't. Although it might have been embarrassing that I didn't know his full story, I needed to write it and get it to him somehow. Get it out into the universe.

I left Cody at the beginning of October and headed down to Denver for a week to hang out with my kids, then continued down into New Mexico, where I had my next expensive breakdown with a fuel pump just north of Alamogordo. I got out of there after an unexpected twelve-day deviation from my route and schedule, and pulled into Quartzsite on October 30, 2024.

I found a spot, got myself set up for the season, and put myself in the headspace of knowing I wouldn't see Fred that winter. He was, as far as I knew, staying up in North Dakota for doctor appointments and such. I had no idea if I would ever see him again.

However, while stalking Fred with my now-daily, habitual multiple-times-a-day checking of his page, I found his three posts on November 7th. The driving one piqued my curiosity, which led me to start gauging how often he was or was not on Facebook; he was damn near always on, so if his profile timer went over three hours and that timestamp fell off, I knew he was traveling. Not that I had become really good at stalking him, or anything…

Toward the evening, he posted a new selfie, which, although one might glance at it and think he was being grumpy, I could see he was hiding a smile. And the last picture—the shot of the empty beer mug reviewing Speed Goat Ale from Green River, WY—I knew that message was for me, and that confirmed he was heading down to Quartzsite, AZ, for the season. My heart soared, and I walked on clouds with impatient excitement as I waited for his arrival.

I didn't know how long he was going to take, though. His normal travel schedule had him at various stops for a few weeks—usually waiting until his tanks were full to move again. He usually drove right through Utah on I-15 and would stop in Overton, NV, for a few weeks before continuing down to Quartzsite, with a stop at Walmart in Parker for supplies and food.

I continued to track him with excited anticipation, and when I saw his post from Las Vegas on November 15th, sitting in traffic on an overpass, I began timing when he was on Facebook that day. Over a three-hour absence, he was driving, and if he was coming out of Las Vegas, he was driving south; Quartzsite is shy of four hours away. Cue the giddy butterflies in my stomach!

A couple of hours later, he posted a familiar barren picture of an empty highway—I'm going to guess it was taken just north of Quartzsite on Hwy 95 —and then he posted a video of his spot at La Posa South at sunset.

Friday, Nov 15, 2024 • 6:32 PM

Hey. Just saw your fb post. Which ltva are you in? Glad you got here okay with the wind. :-)

South. Not far from where I was Last year. I like it because of good road and not far off the blacktop. Much easier with the motel.

Motorcycle

I'll be out there tomorrow night for a drumming circle. There's a music camp out there, somewhere. Have to find it.

I have to dump garbage and get water tomorrow. If you're interested, I can stop out and say hi, too.

HOLY SHIT!!! I get to see him again. To say that I was ecstatic that night didn't even cover a fraction of what I was feeling knowing that this guy, who has been living rent-free in my head every second of every day since December 6, 2023, was safely off the road and in his spot next to his favorite cacti for the night.

My world was complete.

Chapter 14

The desert mornings are cool, so I got dressed in a short-sleeved shirt and a brand-new pair of black fleece sweatpants. All nice and fuzzy-wuzzy warm. I had some breakfast, washed the dishes, and got the garbage together for dumping, and then around 10:00 a.m., drove across the highway over to La Posa South, dumped my garbage, and then set off further down the road to find the campsite he'd referred to by throwing his arm out in a general direction the year before. I figured I would find it since most people hadn't yet come in for the season. How hard would it be to find his spot, somewhere "over there?"

I drove out another mile or two into the desert on a very bumpy, not-very-often-used road with no new silver-colored truck (he had purchased a new truck in May of 2024, when he got back from Arizona for the summer), Jayco toy hauler, or motorcycle in sight. So I turned around and got on the phone.

He picked up right away, and I told him I was coming over for a visit, or at least to say "hi," but I was in the middle of nowhere and couldn't find his campsite. He told me he was going to run up to the Ranger's Station and get his pass, and I could meet him up there.

I started making my way back up to the Ranger's Station, and as I was driving back into the "civilization" of other RVs (I was way out there), I glanced out my driver's window and saw him at a perpendicular angle driving in the same direction as me, in his new silver truck. Had we kept going at the same speed, we would have run into each other.

He was making good time until he saw me on the right side of his truck, and he slowed down. To not make it look like I was too eager to see him (back to playing it cool)… I pretended not to notice him and kept looking straight out the windshield. As soon as I passed that intersection, he showed up behind me and followed me up to the front of the LTVA. I kept playing it cool and resisted the urge to roll down my window and wave madly at him as I drove the last mile up to the front at fifteen miles per hour—a slow drive filled with massive anticipation and pure excitement.

I parked and got out, and then he rolled up to a stop in front of me and got out himself.

He wore baggy jeans, a red shirt, a ball cap, and had a great big ear-to-ear grin. A warm, great big, friendly smile. (How I wish I had a GoPro strapped to my head for times like these.) And even typing this now, I can see him, his smile, and the positive, happy energy that just radiated from him. I'm also tearing up again.

Now it was my turn to beeline to him, which I did, and although I didn't hug him (I wanted to, though), we stood along the side of his truck, easily falling back into conversation. As cliché as it sounds, we always picked up right where we left off, the world quieted, the bubble showed up, and we were connected. So connected that he abruptly remembered where he was and why he was there after a few minutes of mutual permagrin.

He walked over to the Ranger's Station to buy his pass, and I hung back waiting for him to finish that transaction. When he came back to the truck, I asked him if he'd mind a morning visitor, and he said that would be nice.

I followed him back to his spot, finally learning what "over there" meant regarding his campsite location. He set up some chairs for us to sit in the shade of his trailer, and the conversation began.

Of the things I told him, he gave himself and his stalking maneuvers away by practically finishing my sentences and/or telling me he had seen it on Facebook. I, on the other hand, pretended to be surprised at hearing "new" things about his life over the past summer. Again, I wanted to play it cool. Didn't want to appear desperate. I'm sure he knew otherwise.

He shared his medical issues with me, showed me various X-rays of his foot on his phone, told me what he did that summer (his abridged version), and asked me about rodeos and whitewater rafting. He thanked me again for his birthday dinner, and I told him it was my pleasure. I began to get cold in the shade of his trailer while we were talking, so he moved a chair for me to a sunnier spot in his campsite, and we continued our conversation about everything and anything under the sun. For all the grief he would give me for all of my talking, he sure did a good job keeping pace with me. I didn't take my eyes off of him, and he didn't break my gaze, either. He told me of his trip to Area 51 and the Little Ale'Inn in Rachel, NV. He told me of some of the places he visited in Overton on his way down and that he had won $40 in scratch-offs at one of the bars up there. We talked, and talked, and talked, and the world continued spinning, and people drove by and carried on with their own errands and business, and Fred and I sat in our permagrin bubble of happiness.

An hour into it, though, I shifted in my lawn chair and remembered what I had dressed myself in that morning. It was approaching noon, and I was sitting in direct sunlight in a pair of brand-new fuzzy-wuzzy, fleece-lined black sweatpants. I moved back into the shade and kept smiling, but what I really wanted/needed to do was change into a pair of shorts, but I didn't bring any with me. By the time I had moved back into the shade, though, the noon sun was beating down and warming up the air, and when I moved, I noticed my back was drenched in sweat, and I was broiling, and I hate wearing wet clothes. But I didn't want to break that connection—it had been a whole seven months of not laying my eyes on him in person, and sitting in a permagrin bubble of conversation. As far as I was concerned, I was going to sit there with a smile on my face and deal with my bad wardrobe choice from that morning, whether I liked it or not. The most important thing was that I was sitting next to Fred again, and with that, I could deal with anything.

I baked from 10:30 a.m. to roughly 3:00 p.m. Oh, gawd! Just writing this, and I can still feel the discomfort of literally baking in those black sweatpants. Yuck!

We were both getting hungry, and he had gotten up and walked to the back of his truck to get something from the bed. As he was coming back, he defeatedly said, "Well, I can see I'm not going to get anything done today." I smiled, and so did he. He then leaned over to pick something off his trailer step, looked at me over his left shoulder, and asked if I'd be interested in meeting him up at Beer Belly's in an hour to get something to eat. I wholeheartedly agreed, then got up and sloshed my way back to my car.

I waved goodbye and drove at a respectable speed out of his sight, and then, when I knew he could no longer see me, I stepped on the accelerator and broke the speed limit, getting out of La Posa South and back over to my RV in Tyson Wash across the highway.

Do you remember the part on March 31st when I saw him out at Pilot Knob, and it took me less than three minutes to throw all my crap back into the RV and move over next to him? Well, this situation was at the same breakneck speed but now in swampy sweatpants. Oh, gawd, it was disgusting. I needed a shower!

On my way to my RV, I had briefly thought I could just freshen up with some new clothes and be good as new, but when I got into the RV and looked in the mirror, I immediately switched on the water heater and started the impatient countdown to hot water.

I now had less than forty minutes to shower (my showers are usually twenty minutes), get dressed, put my hair up, do my makeup, and find my earrings. I had less than an hour to transform myself from morning-troglodyte-broiling-in-sweatpants to something fit for public and attractive to Fred, and then drive into town and meet him without being too late.

Well, I did it. The universe managed to span out those forty minutes into a hot shower, drying off, getting a nice outfit together and on my body, doing something with my hair, putting on make-up, and successfully finding my jewelry to accessorize with. Got my shoes on and ran out the door and did my best not to break traffic laws getting into town, finding a parking space on a Saturday afternoon in the Tyson Wells area of Quartzsite, and getting my arse over to Beer Belly's, where I found him sitting with a beer and watching the band. He said he'd been there for about five minutes when I rolled in.

I had a cheeseburger and a couple of hard lemonades, and he had a couple of beers, but I don't remember him eating anything. He probably ate in his trailer while I was losing my mind on the other side of the highway, waiting for my water to heat up for a much-needed shower.

We talked a bit more and listened to the band. He asked me what I was doing that night, and I told him I was planning to attend a drum circle. He told me he was going to go out drinking.

Oh.

Well, in case he would change his mind, I showed him the post and gave him the coordinates, and after an hour or so, we went our separate ways.

Since I had woken up early that day, not even sure I had really slept the night before, knowing he was on the other side of the highway, I tried to lie down for a little nap before heading over to the Drum Circle. The event started at 6:30 or 7:00 p.m., and I didn't leave my site until 7:15 p.m.—being fashionably late.

When I got there and pulled my lawn chair and drum out of the car to find a spot, I noticed someone who looked a lot like Fred, about fifteen feet away to my left. With my old prescription glasses, I strained my eyes through the dark and then crept closer to make sure it was him—because as far as I knew, he was going to the bar that evening.

Yep, it was him (permagrin time!!!!), and I nonchalantly asked if he was okay with me sitting next to him. He nodded and gestured to his right, and I planted both the chair and the drum down and plopped myself into the lawn chair. We sat there, quietly. After a bit, the organizer told everyone we were going to have a howling-at-the-moon contest, and people started stepping up to wait for their turn. I had said quietly, but loud enough for him to hear me, "I prefer to howl in private," which elicited a short chuckle from him that was dripping with suggestive tones, and then he shifted his body in his lawn chair again. With his suggestive chuckle and his tell of shifting in his chair, he gave his quiet thoughts away.

After the howling contest and the fifty-fifty firewood split drawing, he bade me a goodnight and left for much-needed sleep.

I eventually left myself for some much-needed, hopeful sleep, too, if I could muster it while skittering across the edges of the universe, filled with absolute excitement.[*]

---

[*]I'll add here the reason why we weren't camping next to each other this time around: He liked the asphalt driveway in La Posa South for riding his motorcycle on, and I appreciated the four and five-bar 5G in Tyson Wash. I could only get one or two bars of 4G in his campsite, and that wasn't going to support my workload. I also hadn't bought into Starlink yet. Again, any extra money I had went into the RV rather than on an overpriced monthly subscription. The hotspot on my phone worked just fine in most locations across the US. So, "practicality" on both of our parts.

Chapter 15

November 16, 2024:

The next day, I laid low and didn't reach out to him. He still needed to get set up and organized, and I figured there'd be at least one hundred thirty-six more days of the season to "bother" him.

November 17, 2024:

Late afternoon, I texted him an invitation to come over for a campfire on Monday, the eighteenth. An hour later, the universe decided that I needed to go shopping for coffee! Right now! I was busy working, but that voice said I really needed to go shopping for coffee right then. What a weird urge, but whatever.

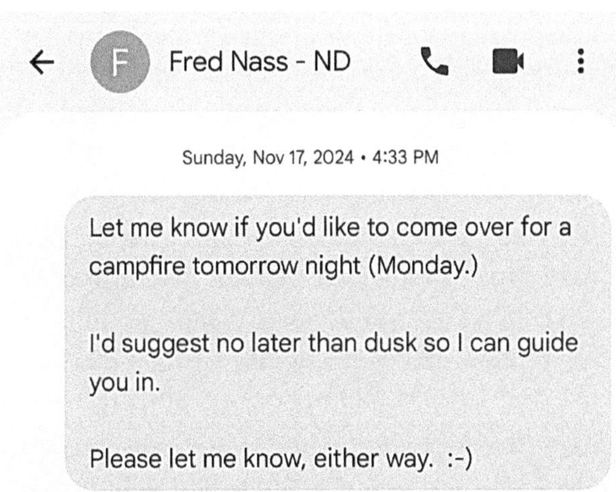

So, I put on my shoes, grabbed the keys, locked up the RV, and drove out of the campsite. I first checked one of the local grocery stores, and I didn't find whole beans or coarsely ground beans (I bought a French Press in August of 2024, and still haven't used it—it's still in the box as I write this).

Not finding anything there, I went over to Dollar General—fairly sure they wouldn't have what I was looking for, either, but apparently this voice really thought I should look at the coffee options at the new Dollar General in town. Again, whatever.

Five minutes later, I was in the coffee/soup/cereal aisle, having a lovely conversation with myself. The voice in my head was adamant that I stay there and look at *ALL* of the containers of beans, and taste intensities, finely ground coffee, freeze-dried coffee, and coffee pods; essentially everything I was *not* looking for. After ten minutes of looking at everything I didn't need across four different shelves, I stood up and looked to my right. There was Fred, about ten feet away, looking at the soups and listening to my conversation with the coffee containers. (Yes, I talk out loud sometimes—a lot of the time, actually.)

The outside windows were behind him, so I wasn't sure, initially, that it was him looking so intently at the cans of soup. But through my old prescription glasses, squinting to see him better in the brighter light behind him, I confirmed my suspicion, walked over to his cart, and said, "Hi." He told me he didn't want to interrupt my conversation with the coffee cans. With a smile, I asked him how much he had heard, and he shrugged with that smile of amusement.

I can't remember all we talked about in that short conversation, but when I walked away to finish my shopping, I remembered I had sent him that text an hour earlier. I snapped my fingers, exclaimed "Oh!" and turned around. In six paces, I was back to talk to him, but this time, instead of being a cart's length away, I was standing right in front of him.

When I walked back to him, someone else entered the aisle and needed to get past me, so I moved closer to him. In response to my invading his personal space, he backed up, but the cereal shelves didn't budge, and now he was practically pinned between Captain Crunch and me. Every muscle in his body tensed, and I could feel his energy shift from relaxed to *OMG! She's standing right in front of me! Now what???*

He said he was a little over six-foot-five, and with my shoes on (and if I stand up tall), I'm close to five-foot-eleven (on a good day). There was probably less than four inches between our stomachs—I was definitely invading his personal space—and his eyes widened in surprise. Sure, I had hugged him a couple of times the season prior, but now I was practically shoved up against him, looking into his eyes—and they were wide open—with a damn near expression akin to seeing a UFO or Santa Claus fly by.

I saw two wide open, unblinking, bewildered eyes, bushy white eyebrows, and some drier skin around his brow. Fred's stocking cap was pulled down with some of his white hair peeking out from underneath. I smiled at him and asked if he had read my earlier text. He sputtered and finally said that his phone had been on the charger and that he hadn't looked at it recently. So, I repeated the invitation I had sent him, and asked him point-blank if he'd like to stop over the following evening for a campfire. Again, without blinking and still frozen in nervous fear, he nodded and eventually eked out a "Yeah, sure."

I continued to smile and told him I was pleased he'd be joining me, then I backed up, said "Ciao," and walked out of the aisle. I didn't look back, but I could feel his eyes tracking me.

I went to Dollar General to find coffee and ended up with a campfire date instead.

November 18, 2024:

Monday, Nov 18, 2024 • 12:44 PM

I'm hoping this wind dies down. It's supposed to, according to the wind app.

Me to. I have a cooler with a 12 pak in it and it blew over.

It's not that bad over here. It's the occasional gust.

The wind app claims it'll settle down, though.

Monday, Nov 18, 2024 • 3:16 PM

Although the wind app is reading those speeds at the Blythe airport, I haven't felt any gusts recently. Wind usually dies down in the evening... usually.

If you're coming out here, please BYOE - bring your own everything. Chair included. :-)

4pm or 4.30pm at the Rangers station? Bring your own chair, too.

I'm at beer Belly's. Can we making it 4:45? I'm on the bike and need to go get my pickup

Sure

He was originally scheduled to arrive at 4:30 p.m., but arrived around 4:45 p.m. I told him I'd meet him at the Tyson Wash Ranger Station and lead him to my campsite. I was in my car, looking at my phone, when he arrived. He had just pulled up, and I looked out my window to see his smiling face, looking at me from across the front seat and out the passenger window of his truck. I waved and pulled forward to lead him to my campsite.

Once at the campsite, we turned our chairs toward the sunset and watched it happen, then flipped them around to tend the campfire, which was having a heck of a time lighting up since it was so windy.

During that evening's campfire conversation, I asked him if he remembered telling me how he hated people the first night I was at Pilot Knob, and asked if he remembered my response of laughing, and he did. Then I told him why I laughed—that was the very same sentence I'd been saying all of my life. So, I understood what he meant when he said it.

We were sitting side-by-side, and somewhere during our conversation, he turned his body toward me and once again pointed out how his heart can't handle any activity that would cause his body to bump and slam around. I nodded and said I remembered him saying that a few times the previous season, but didn't delve further into it. As usual, he dropped the subject with a somewhat confused look, wondering if I understood him. (I will add, I still didn't know where I stood with him, what his relationship status was; I knew nothing except that I really enjoyed hanging out with him, and I was madly in love with him.)

He asked me if I would do another off-roading adventure—he had seen my video from Wyoming, doing off-roading in the Absaroka Mountain Range. I vigorously nodded my head and told him I hoped to again soon, and that I really thought I should have my own RZR. I mused about how much trouble I could get into, and he wholeheartedly agreed that I would probably get into a bit of trouble.

He initiated a discussion of the season's plans. He pulled out his phone to look up dates for area events we could attend together, including the upcoming Fall Festival that Saturday. From his phone, he told me the band, that admission was free, and that vendors would be at the town's park, so we made plans to attend together.

We also talked about potential dates to see various bands, check out different restaurants in the area, and attend boat races, sand drags, and tractor pulls—all the usual things we liked to do. I filled him in on the fact that I had promised a friend I would help them at their booth during the Big Tent RV Show in January, but that I would join him down in Yuma afterward. He added we'd follow the same route and get out to Old Fogey Hot Springs again for February after Pilot Knob.

He continued to stoke the fire, keeping it going despite the very windy night. Usually, the wind dies down at night, but that evening, it seemed only to get stronger and colder.

We talked about other things, and then he told me he was going to hang around with the group that had kicked me out the previous year, too, while he was in Quartzsite for the next six weeks. He said it was for amusement, to see them fall on their faces because of their immaturity. Again, since I had no say in his schedule, I added the hope of hanging out a lot while we were both in Quartzsite—especially since we had just spent the past hour talking about and looking up various local events. He even said he'd be open to going to Phoenix with me to visit some of my friends for dinner in early December.

I told him that, as much as I would love to move over next to him, I needed the internet service where I was camped, but that on some mornings I could get my butt over to his campsite to watch the sunrises. I told him I missed watching the sun come up over the mountain ranges and spending time with him. And after that confession, I saw his energy shift; his face sort of contorted, he looked at the ground, and he shifted in his chair.

After a short lull in conversation, and as the wind grew colder, he nodded in agreement with my sunrise confession and then said he was going to call it a night after being there for not quite two hours. He thanked me for the invitation, got up, picked up his chair, placed it into the back of his truck, got in, said goodbye, and drove away.

Between the creeping darkness, the cold wind, the quiet nod, and the abrupt departure, the vibe was off. I watched his taillights drive away through one of the washes, head out of the main driveway, cross Hwy 95, and disappear down the La Posa South driveway toward his campsite.

A switch flipped. Something changed within a moment, and I couldn't put my finger on it, but the world was growing darker and colder as I stood there watching him drive away; his taillights disappeared down the La Posa South driveway.

Ever the good hostess, though, I sent him this text and never received a response.

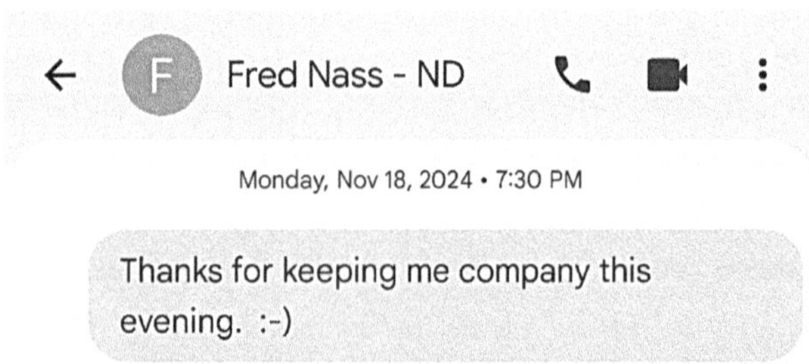

> Btw, I actually can cook (tell no one), and one of these days, I'll make my cheese fondue for you. There's garlic in it, and I serve it with steak (out here, on the grill), assorted veggies, tomatoes, and slices of baguettes.
>
> It's kickin' delicious. Unless you don't like cheese... 😉
>
> Dag nabbit, now I'm hungry for that.

November 20, 2024:

I had another fun-filled root canal scheduled in Los Algodones a couple of days later. On the way back, I stopped at the Quechan Casino right next to Pilot Knob to inquire about their New Year's Eve festivities. Based on our conversation at the campfire two days prior, I thought I would stop by and get a membership card so I could buy two tickets for NYE for us to attend—figuring we could be down there after Christmas, given the previous evening's arrangements. I was going to buy two tickets at $45 each and surprise him with them, but then I thought, maybe I should hold off to see if he wants to go.

Further into the week, all I got was sporadic, cryptic, vague texting. I figured he was establishing some kind of boundary for some purpose (???). I wasn't going to commandeer his calendar—I hadn't the season before, why would I now? We hung out together, had a weird, attraction-filled vibe, and stalked each other on Facebook. Other than that, we got along great and enjoyed hanging out. Same sense of humor and snarkiness; we could roll.

November 22, 2024:

Text for chicken wings—no. Apparently, he now goes to bed by 9:00 p.m. (Sure, whatever.)

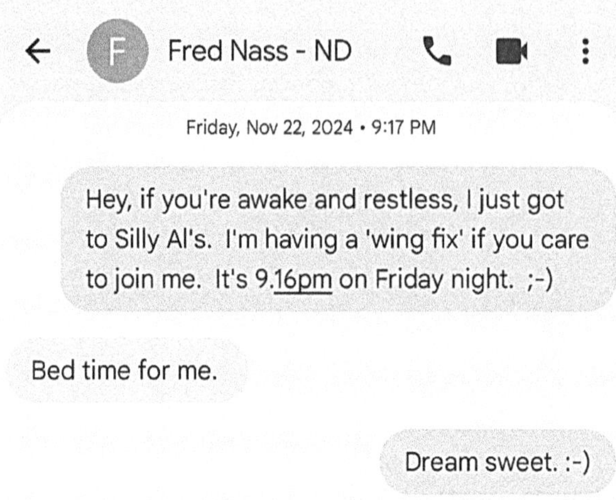

November 23, 2024:

Quartzsite Fall Festival: He was vague in his texts. I took a shower that morning, got dressed in clean clothes, and did my makeup and hair—a feat for someone in a desert who takes maybe two or three showers per month, four if I'm feeling really fancy. Drove to the park and texted him. Vague texts again. What in the hell? It was his idea not six days prior to attend the Fall Festival together, and now he's hiding from me?

Saturday, Nov 23, 2024 • 5:47 PM

> Are you doing anything fun tonight? It looks like the drum circle at ███████████ isn't happening tonight.

That night, there was no answer on either phone or text. Radio silence.

November 24, 2024:

I needed to get into town to pick up some dinner before the stores closed at 6:00 p.m. I rolled up to the intersection of the Tyson Wash driveway and Hwy 95, waited for a few cars to pass, then saw a motorcycle approaching, and my mind told me it was Fred on his bike. Sure enough, it was him, and I waved through the car window. He looked at me and then did that whistling-while-looking-away-to-pretend-you-didn't-notice-someone schtick. He turned into La Posa South, ignoring me completely, and that was that.

What the actual fuck was that all about?

I knew that over the past week, conversation was at a minimum, but both of us were busy—or at least that's what I had told myself. I knew a few days prior that he had attended a movie night with the group that kicked me out, and I hadn't said anything; again, not my business. But to outright ignore me so blatantly? I know he saw me. Did those bitchy women get to him? Did they convince him that I was a horrible person? Did he only want to hang out with the "cool" people and leave the boring loser across the highway alone? The very person he initiated potential plans with six days prior, he was now going to completely ignore?

Typing this is causing tears to well up in my eyes again. Now I know what happened, but at the time, that event sent me into a tailspin, wondering what in the hell had just happened and why? Did I say something wrong that Monday night prior? I ran our conversations over and over, turned them inside out, and hung them upside down to glean any miscommunication/insult/misconstrued comment I might have needed to apologize for, but nothing came to mind. Everything was fine until I mentioned going to his campsite every so often to watch the sunrise with him; that I would make the effort to get up at the ass-crack of dawn to drive a few miles over to hang out with him. Was that an offensive thing to say? That I wanted to hang out with him and missed our tradition of watching the sunrise?

Again, what the actual fuck?

After a day of wondering what in the hell was going on and talking off the ears of both my mom and my daughter, overanalyzing whatever just happened that I wasn't privy to, but was the other half of the equation, I decided to write him a letter and bare my soul. If he was going to shut me out for no obvious reason and not have the spine to tell me, I was going to bare my truths and shut him down completely. If he wants to implode our friendship, I can put the final stick of dynamite on the pile of crap, blow it to smithereens, and walk away mostly unscathed. I've done it before, and I'll do it again. No hair off my ass shutting this party down. Sure, I was hurting, but I don't take kindly to people treating me this way.

I had put up with his avoidance of all things "L.M." I had put up with his sometimes radio silence, figuring he was busy with the life that he had had for sixty-plus years before meeting me. I tolerated his mixed messages and the vibes he sometimes gave off that made me feel like the little sister of the nuisance neighbor kid down the street, whom no one wanted to play with. Again, giving him the benefit of the doubt and remembering that he was now a sixty-two-year-old bachelor who didn't need or want a woman around all the time, and quite frankly, I was rather busy myself and had been divorced for nearly twenty years. I had no problem being by myself, either, but when someone disrespects me to my face, I'm out.

I had slept on it and decided to send him this text. I was officially putting the ball in his court, and based on his answer, he and I were either going to have an open conversation about what in the world this was all about, or I was going to excommunicate him, and he'd never see me again.

Monday, Nov 25, 2024 • 10:54 AM

11-25-24

I'd like to talk with you, in person, but I'm guessing that's not going to happen from the cold-shoulder you've been giving me over the last week. So, here's my two cents:

Yes, I will admit that I found you 'interesting' on 12/6/23 when you got out of your truck, walked right up to me, and said, "Hi, I'm Fred and I have a motorcycle." I will add, between my initial attraction to you and being tongue-tied/confused, I wandered away but my interest was still piqued. The day after becoming FB Friends, I gained some clarity including learning about L.M. My thought on it was (and still is) so be it, 'another guy off my radar', BUT I appreciated you as a person and eventually counted you as one of my very few friends. I have a shit ton of acquaintances but very few friends. Over the month of December '23, I had only detected indications of a level-headed, kind person - someone I'd want to be friends with.

Last January when leaving Quartzsite, I asked if I could stay near you for safety, first and foremost. I knew you had something going on with L.M. , and although you didn't elaborate on it, your suggestion of talking about her in early January confirmed that you were off the market. Your FB page might say you're single, but you're not. Interestingly, though, you've brought up the idea of talking about her three times now, but never go further. (One of my many observations.)...

So, yes. I have one helluva crush on you. It's all Fred every fucking minute of every fucking day in my head which is absolutely fucking annoying. HOWEVER, I maintain my distance out of respect to you, as a friend, that you have something going on with L.M. . Trust me, if I didn't have respect for myself, or you, or whatever relationships you have, or if I hadn't detected anything last winter, I would have been all over you within a week of getting out to Pilot Knob. And yes, I've picked up on the 3 or 4 times you've given me the 'come hither' smile which I would like to act on but I don't because you have something going on with L.M. . The friggin' high levels of standards and integrity I hold myself to...

So, why in the world do I continue to (try to) spend time with you? Because I also really like you as a person. Besides all of my attraction for you, you're a decent person, intelligent, conversational, funny, and you bring a calming aspect to my life. I really, really like chilling out with you. Talking or not talking - I don't care. I like spending time in your presence. You chill me out which inevitably causes me to be happy. I also like doing things with you and going places with you - we seem to have things in common.

From the way you always light up & smile when you see me, I thought you enjoyed hanging out with me, too. We don't seem to have any problems picking up in conversation where we left off, either. Those two things would be a good basis for a friendship. I do miss our morning soaking in the sun times, and I enjoy our campfires, and the other things we have done in the past. I might not be able to have you as a partner, but the friendship thing worked for me, too. This past week of getting the cold-shoulder has hurt, though. I don't know what happened at Monday evening's fire? I minded my manners, couldn't do much about the wind, and then you set about ignoring/avoiding me for the rest of the week. So be it, I suppose.

A side note: The ███████████ crowd - I know I had touched on this subject last January but I'll give you the full story now: I know I had told you about ████, ████ and ████ being hellbent on getting me laid last season (████ was busy screwing ████ and wasn't always part of the side conversation.) I laughed at every guy they could name off... even ████ suggested that she got ██ down there so I could screw him (I don't think so.) But when they said your name, I gave them a firm 'no' pointing out that I didn't think it was a good idea to take a guy for a ride simply for the sole benefit of their amusement; that I had more respect for myself and the potential guys than giving into their tauntings simply for their entertainment.

  Fred Nass - ND  

From there, the rhetoric got more disrespectful/mean towards me and the few names of guys, who kept being brought up, but eventually dwindled down to only your name and you being disrespected. After a few rounds of this, I shut it down and that's when ████ spouted that if I'm not going to take you, she'd do it herself. I didn't answer her. A couple of days later, she asked you to walk with her on NYE but couldn't say anything. (It's because she didn't know what to say - she hadn't put much thought into it because she was fulfilling her taunt - that was made in front of ████ & ████ - to have a go with you to screw with me.) I never outright said anything to any of them about my feelings toward you, but I'm going to guess that when I told them to shut their BS down when your name came up, that was probably a good signal for them to go after that angle. Essentially, you were a pawn for their entertainment, and since I didn't take them up on it - plus, I'm not a raging drunk - this only added to their distaste for me. Strangely, I grew out of the age of 7th-grade antics which they ˙ive in.

The facts of the matter are:

Yes, I'm incredibly attracted to all of you and what you bring to the table as a person.Yes, I know about  and because of my integrity and standards, know that you're a taken man, and don't act on any of my impulses.I was hoping we could be friends since we seem to get along well.Based on what I know about you, I was not looking for anything besides friendship from you.

Thank you for the time you shared with me.

~ Kiersten

←   F   Fred Nass - ND 📞 🎥 ⋮

Tuesday, Nov 26, 2024 • 11:59 AM

So guess I should address you lengthy text. First some of the things you assume are correct, but some are way off base. As for last year I don't care what people do or think as long as it don't effect me.
I'll update you on stuff. First I felt like shit last winter. Didn't know why tell me April doctors appointment. My heart is at 24-26% effective. A normal person is 40+. That why I was feeling the way I do. Doctor, I will just have to deal with it. Damage to my heart is all ready done. I traded by pickup off and s few months later not happy with the deal. But had to do something. August my brother contacted me and wants to sell our 4 generation farm. His part anyway. I can't afford to buy him out.

 Fred Nass - ND  

Went back to doctor in October, no improvement. The word possible heart transplant comes up. Then two day before leaving, my water heater starts leaking. Oh great, something to look forward to when I get back. As you can see my summer wasn't the best. Oh yea, I also died. If it wasn't for my pacemaker I would have been in a pine box. So, how was your fuckin summer?
I come here to unwind, relax and regroup.

 Fred Nass - ND  

Tuesday, Nov 26, 2024 • 5:26 PM

I'm relieved that you are not residing in a pine box. I was worried about you with your text about your heart and such. I'm sorry that your heart is damaged & that you have health problems - I really am. Whether or not you like me, I care for you since you are in my orbit.

Of the things that are way off base, I apologize for any incorrections, but the only story/side/perception I know is from my own experience.

The length of the text was due to me opening the floodgates of my emotions, which I rarely do, and that was the condensed version.

Obviously, you can do whatever you want, whenever you want, with whomever you want. What hurt me was the perceived cold-shoulder of seeing your videos of the ██████████ when texts of doing something with me either went unanswered or have very short/vague answers (you told me about your reasons for doing this last season.) The last 'sting' was when you saw me at an intersection and didn't bother to wave. And I know you saw me/my car.

Over the last week, I felt as if you were shoving me out of your life (what little space i take up, if any at all), and I didn't understand why. In reality, I don't need to know 'why' since it's your life, but I was thinking/still do think you're a decent individual who would give an explanation besides my perception of being ghosted.

Now that I've bared my soul/heart, I will admit my spirits soared when I realized you were coming back down for the winter. I didn't think I'd see you again. I would imagine my excitement wasn't hidden very well when I commandeered your first day down here. Not that I was planning on overtaking your calendar by any means, but the heart palpitations started up again when I was feeling ghosted and left out. Again, not your fault with the mean girl bunch, but I felt sad & alone, and couldn't figure out why I was being shunned.

My goal is not to cause you stress, and I only want the best for you. You're an awesome individual.

> The last text wasn't allowing me more room to type. But if you ever want to hang out, please ask. I promise I won't bring up stuff, and I'll stay on my side of the fire, as I usually do. I'd rather not give up a friendship with you, but can certainly understand if you'd rather not.

My mom said I should go over there and confront him. I said I didn't want to cause him more stress, especially because of his heart. I was also unsure of the reaction I would get from him. It was an open-ended email, but I wasn't willing to risk it all and get a confirmed-to-my-face ending, such as "fuck off." I was holding out hope that I would hear more. I put the ball in his court, and rather than excommunicating him as I planned, I backed off.

That was the last time I ever heard from him.

Chapter 16

After a good few days of still wondering what I had done so wrong, and being unbearably mopey that I had lost someone who I considered, for the most part, to be a best friend; gawd knows he knew everything about me, plus some. I made a decision. And it was heartbreaking, *but* I don't let anyone treat me this poorly. Ever.

I logged onto Facebook and sat there looking at his profile picture, with the *Block* option displayed on the screen. Typing this—even now, I'm starting to cry again—realizing that I was even tempted to do such a thing.

I sat there, staring at that screen, running through the pros and cons of leaving it as is. No one was allowed to treat me that way. Sure, I knew arguments and petty disagreements occur in every type of relationship. Still, as long as there is open communication and a mutual willingness to work things out, I wouldn't resort to the *Block* option on Facebook. But this being ghosted thing? Fuck that. I don't have the time nor the patience for that bullshit.

I can't tell you how long I sat at my desk, staring at that screen, refreshing it every time the computer went into standby. I couldn't do it. I could do it to anyone else in the world; I have a *Block* list so long right now that I'm sure you could wrap it around the equator at least five times in ten-point font. I have no problem blocking people and eradicating them from my life, never to think about them again.

But I could not do that to Fred.

My intuition, my guardian angels, the world, every soul to have ever passed through this universe—all were SCREAMING at me not to block him. My heart palpitations were strong, my eyes were filled with tears, and I had no fucking idea what I had done so wrong.

And I was pissed!

I was pissed that I was leaning toward giving him a pass. Why was I giving him a pass? I don't give anyone a pass. I've blocked family members, coworkers, so-called friends, colleagues, clients, random people online, and all of the men who send inappropriate pictures via social media. Again, I have no problem whatsoever with removing people from my life. But I could not bring myself to do it with Fred. What in the hell was wrong with me?

My voice of reason showed up and suggested that I ride it out.

Since I knew Fred wasn't healthy and wasn't always feeling well from the time I first met him, I let him dictate when we spent time together. I let him dictate what we were going to do and where we were going when we camped together. We did things on his terms, at the level he was able to.

The caring and consideration I showed him and his circumstances were what made the time we spent together possible. In turn, he was willing to give me his time, even on days he really didn't feel good. On those days, we would stay at camp and lie out on our lawn chairs; occasionally, he would doze off in the sun, and I was good. I was next to him, and that's all that really mattered.

On that point, I will add: Anyone who knows me knows I don't allow things to be "dictated" to me. I can compromise and negotiate—if they ask nicely. But push me? And I'm gone, never to be heard from again. Yes, that is ghosting, but usually there is a big blow-up and an obvious ending— whoever got blocked knew damn well what happened and what went down to make me leave. But with Fred, it was an absolute unknown.

My voice of reason suggested I let it ride; keep the ball in his court as I always did. Sure, he was ghosting me, but he was still stalking me on Facebook and watching my YouTube videos. Why would he do that if he hated me so much for whatever I did wrong? And why didn't he take the initiative and block me?

So I closed his page and later posted a nice selfie update video of myself. Got myself all gussied up, hit Facebook Live, and started recording. I don't remember what I said, but I figured, *Fine, if you're going to be a shit for whatever reason, and not block me... or at the very least not unfollow me, and continue to watch all of my Facebook Live videos/reels, I'm going to fuck with you, Fred.*

And that's what I did.

I made sure every damn day, I posted either a selfie or a Facebook video of myself and/or out doing something. I initially thought he might have forgotten to block me. However, he dutifully kept hopping onto my Live Facebook videos while I was still on camera. I never acknowledged him, which most likely led him to believe that his Facebook activity was untraceable.

The taunting and teasing kept my mind off being ghosted, and I secretly hoped he shifted a lot in his lawn chair every time I went live or posted a selfie. Yes, I can be petty and vengeful—I've always known that about myself—but, again, mess with me and you should expect it back tenfold. He was getting it back a thousandfold. I was pissed.

Regarding those selfies and Facebook Live videos: I believe I mentioned earlier that I did a lot of primping when hanging out with Fred. Not all the time—he got to see me when I crawled out of my car each morning, and he got to see me chilling at the campsite, by the campfire, and all the other times we weren't going to a restaurant, bar, or an event. One of the things I only started doing after I met Fred was taking selfies. I was never really good at them—I always looked pissed off in the photos. But I finally figured them out when I knew Fred was my #1 follower on both Facebook and YouTube. Also, regarding live videos on Facebook, Fred would be one of the first, if not the first, to join my live streams. Before this situation, when we were still communicating, if he joined my Live Facebook videos, I would sometimes call him out by saying "hi" midway through the stream. I don't think he ever disengaged because that would be a bad optic, but I don't think he ever engaged with a post. He was caught in a pickle because he knew I saw him, but didn't know how to respond—should he log off or ride out the video?

But since I knew he was my number-one stalker—and I was his—I would post selfies, knowing in my heart that he was seeing them. He wouldn't like or love them, but I knew he saw them.

So on Thanksgiving morning, a few days after learning that I was no longer a... *whatever I meant to him if I meant anything at all to him,* I went outside to put out my lawn chairs and outdoor rug, etc. While I was doing that, I was playing and singing along to Arlo Guthrie's "Alice's Restaurant" at the top of my lungs, as is the tradition in my family (my kids and I). While doing this, I did part of it on a Facebook Live feed, and sure enough, Fred was the first viewer to hop on and watch. I didn't acknowledge him this time around. But I knew the great stalk-athon was still on between us, even though he apparently wasn't speaking to me for whatever reason.

Around the beginning of December 2024, another guy was hunting for his fourth unsuspecting victim… I mean, a wife, and he locked his eyes on me. This guy followed me around like a lost puppy dog, and he was really "working it" to get me to fall for him. I told him "friends-only," but as usual, when it comes to my experience with men, he used selective hearing/interpretation. Even my mom wanted to see a picture of him, and when she wrote back, she urged me to be interested in him. I told him that, and I could see he thought he was closing the deal with me. The funny thing, though, was that there was no deal for him to close. The man I loved was sitting in the La Posa South LTVA, across Hwy 95, ignoring me for some reason, but still actively stalking me. I was more involved with that whole situation and the lack of action than this guy, who was trying his darndest to sweep me off my feet—albeit his tactics were mind-numbingly stupid and boring. Actually, I viewed him and his overall existence as mind-numbingly stupid and boring.

After twenty-eight days—a few days into January 2025, I told him that his *conquest of me* wasn't going to happen, and he rode off on his quad defeated. Of course, he blocked me on everything. Whatever—funny, though.

But during December, he was willing to go howl at the moon with me in Yuma and go out to the Kofa Range. He took me out to the Desert Bar—and I will admit that I did begin a Live Facebook stream while approaching Hwy 95, and sure enough, Fred was my first viewer.

I said that a friend just took me out there (because, again, you can only go out there in a UTV or a truck that can handle unmaintained roads). And I followed that line up with, "friends take friends out to the Desert Bar," knowing full well Fred would hear every one of those words while I recorded the sparkling Colorado River in the distance, out the windshield.* Immature? Sure. But I was also driving home the point that he had reneged on the plan to go out to the Desert Bar during the November 18th campfire. Lots of plans, then nothing.

December 21, 2024:

There was a Winter Solstice Drum Circle in La Posa South. I knew Fred was going to be there. He loved drum circles.

Obviously, I was going to show up with my djembe and join in. The guy who was following me around the desert was curious as to what it was all about, voicing several concerns and opinions before the day even arrived. (Yes, he was excruciatingly boring, among other things.)

Anyway, this guy and I arrived early and were sitting around the campfire before the sun went down. We were about forty minutes early.

After twenty-five minutes of sitting there, I looked up in the direction of Fred's campsite and saw him arriving. Again, I knew that he was going to be there, and I knew when he'd be there. I saw him turn down the road that led to the event, then take a left into the parking area, park his truck, get out, and take his lawn chair out of the back. I saw him walk up to the drum circle, opposite me, sitting at the fire already, and he stopped dead in his tracks. He had seen me, but I made it look like I didn't notice him. His eyes got a bit wide, and then he looked to his right and started skirting behind people. Rather than sitting up front as he usually did, he hid himself and his chair in the second row of people off to my left. If I were in the 12:00 position on a clock, he showed up at 6:00, and settled into a spot at approximately 2:45. Throughout the entire event, he stared at me by peeking out behind the people sitting in front of him.

How would I know when he'd be arriving, besides the obvious connection we still had?

---

*Fred had gone out to the Desert Bar with the "mean girls" group in November, and had driven the always-high, instruction-following sidekick to the C-Class bitch out there; someone else I had befriended told me that in December. (Upon hearing that, at that time, I couldn't understand why he would ignore me and drive one of the people he could have cared less about out to the restaurant, but whatever, I guess.)

I stared at him, too, but with my peripheral vision, doing a sweep of everyone in attendance, or by "looking through him" (the way a restaurant server can survey the dining area but *not* see you waving madly from your table to get their attention.) I used to wait tables for about eight years. I've got that skill as involuntary muscle memory now.

A couple of times, I got up to use a vault toilet and had to walk past him; he would always shrink in his chair as he watched me, peeking out from behind people. I had thought about walking up to him and, at the very least, saying "hi," but then again, I talked myself out of it because I didn't want to cause him stress, nor did I want him to tell me to "fuck off." Not that he would do that, or maybe he would. I really didn't know, and I didn't want to find out in case my hunch was proven right.

I had no idea that that night would be the last time I saw him.

December 23, 2024:

Two days after I saw him at the Winter Solstice Drum Circle, he had posted a picture of his chicken wings and beer at one of our favorite bars in Quartzsite, and mentioned that he was there enjoying his Monday night with a football game on the screen.

Uh huh… And he knows I love those chicken wings and would live at the restaurant eating them for life if I could.

That post came across at 9:00 p.m.-ish, and that's when my mental gymnastics started again:

- A month earlier, I had invited him out for wings at that establishment and told him I would pay. He texted back and said he was already in bed/getting ready for bed. (Uh huh… he's a night owl, through and through. Don't give me that 9:00 p.m. shit.)

- I was actually already in my pajamas, about to get into bed, because I was bored, sad, and lonely. Additionally, I had been utterly exhausted for the past month, which I had chalked up to boredom, sadness, and loneliness.

- If I went into town, then I would look desperate. I don't do "desperate." Sure, I didn't block him, but I still had some shred of dignity to my name.

- Plus, he probably took that picture earlier in the evening, being that he's apparently in bed every night at 9:00 p.m. these days. The trip would not have been a success on that point, but it would probably still have led to an order of carry-out chicken wings for me. I abstained that night, though.

- Or if he were still there and saw the one person he apparently never wanted to see again, that would put stress on his heart.

- And much like the day he sent back a message responding to my "lengthy text" in November, I didn't want to face him for him to tell me to "fuck off," permanently. I relegated myself to purgatory rather than being kicked out altogether. Again, I didn't want to chance it.

All of that, plus probably more with the inconvenience of getting back into clothes and driving into town in the dark, and, and, and… Not to mention, it would be my luck to pass him on the highway, going the opposite direction. So, I crawled into bed and let him sit wherever he was, all by himself.

New Year's Eve came and went. I was more than relieved I never bought the tickets for that NYE party at the Quechan Casino. I would have been out $90 plus fees, taxes, and whatever else they tacked on. I would have two useless tickets while sitting in my RV, cold, lonely, sad, depressed, bored, and still wondering WTF happened in November.

Facebook betrayed me by popping up a notification about some videos he had made at the NYE celebration across the highway with people he knew who treated me badly, and he knew I wasn't going to bother with them; he had his perfect out and the assurance that he would never see me over there. And I was still pissed. (I can hold a grudge, too.)

I'm not sure on which day he left for Yuma, but I'd guess around the fifth of January. Quartzsite felt even colder to me around that date.

Chapter 17

Fred and I kept up our mutual stalking without talking. He didn't post much, and what he did didn't sound very happy. I did my best to avoid watching his videos then, but Facebook would occasionally throw them into my feed. They were from past December events held by the "seventh-grade mentality female group." For the life of me, I couldn't figure out what I had done so wrong for him to just ghost me. One day, we were fine—business as usual—making plans for the 2024/25 season, with him instigating the conversation; the next day, I no longer existed in his world.

I was scheduled to help a friend run her booth at the Quartzsite Big Tent RV Show in mid-January. I also had a book reading event set up at a local school district a few days after the RV show. So there I sat in Quartzsite, bored, lonely, sad, pissed off, and sleeping ten to twelve hours a night, solid, with at least two or three naps per day, each lasting at least a couple of hours. Good grief, I was exhausted! I couldn't get enough sleep, even after fifteen to eighteen hours per day.

January 30, 2025:

With all of my Quartzsite obligations behind me, I arranged with my neighbor—the same guy who has worked on my rig and was the person who checked out the RV before I bought it—to watch my car while I left for at least thirty days. I needed out of Quartzsite badly.

I drove down to Yuma, stopped at Walmart, and picked up my food for the next three weeks. I was planning to park and stay without leaving for additional supplies. And I bought the ingredients for the cheese fondue I had told Fred about the night of the November 18th campfire, which he said he'd be interested in trying.

I pulled into the LTVA around 4:00 p.m.—the sun was less than an hour from setting, and I had a lot of groceries to put away. When I pulled in, I didn't have to look too hard to find Fred's trailer—it was fully loaded, locked, and parked up at the front, not too far from the camphost's site. Looking back, I should have asked the camphost where he was—if they knew, but I didn't. I figured he had parked his trailer there and went back to San Diego for a visit, like he had a couple of years prior.

However, I still found it weird that he hadn't posted since January 17th, nor had he stalked any of my live Facebook videos. Seriously, where was he? My mom even went as far as to suggest that maybe his girlfriend came down and they went on a trip somewhere. Or worse, took off to get married. I seriously didn't know what was happening, but I was definitely getting worried. I didn't have a good feeling, and whenever I thought about him, my "third eye" was just blank. No colors, no visions, no auditory, no feelings, no temperature difference, but I was extremely tired—had been since I saw him again that past November. Ten to twelve hours of sleep per night with two or three couple-hour naps throughout the day. Good grief, I was tired!

On the topic of my mom suggesting he ran off and got married, she was trying to get me prepared for the worst that one could speculate at that time, and begin the processing that my over-analytical self needed to let my battered heart down easily, or at least gradually. However, I told my mom that although I would be crushed, I'd at least be relieved in knowing that he was safe and okay. My mom again threw in another barb: "But if he's married, why should you care about him anymore?" And my response was, "Because I know he would be alright and he would be safe and happy."

First and foremost, Fred was always a friend to me—I've always only ever wanted him to be happy, safe, and good. Things I want for all my friends, and if any of them ever need anything, I'm usually the first one to twist myself into a pretzel to get them what they want. How can I fix this situation for this person? Not so much for control purposes or to be anyone's savior, but to make them happy. Their existence makes me happy, so I want to make sure they are happy.

I put away all of my groceries and spent the night at Pilot Knob, only a hundred yards from Fred's trailer, with him and his truck nowhere to be seen. The next day, I drove to Old Fogey Hot Springs just outside of Holtville, CA, and set up camp for the next three weeks. I had really hoped that I would have been able to catch up to him to make my cheese fondue with all of the trimmings and have a chance to talk with him without being surrounded by the "mean girls." I wanted unfettered access rather than a bubble of unfriendly people surrounding and protecting him from me. I wanted mature conversation, not ghosting on texts.

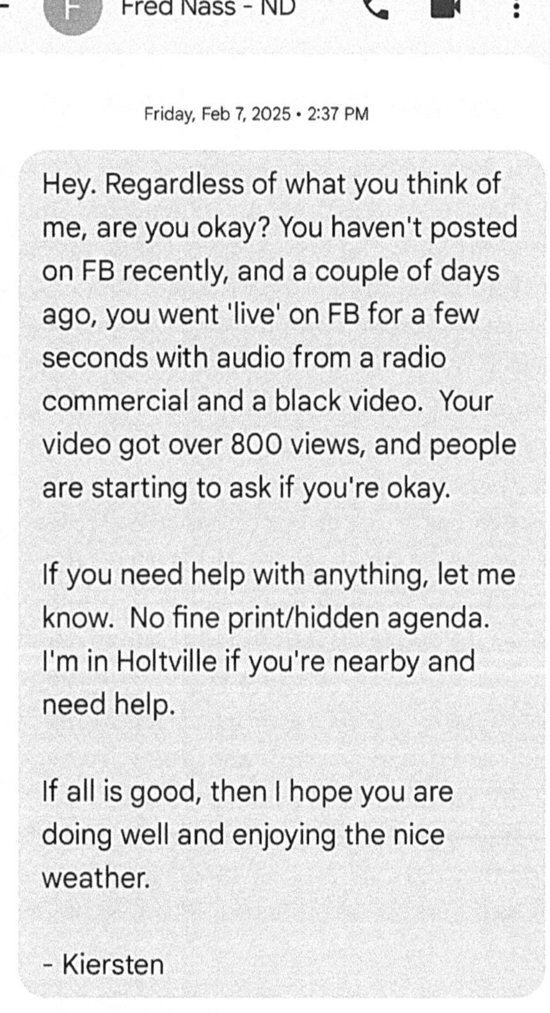

February 9, 2025:

The day after I texted him to ask where he was, he hopped on Facebook and posted about what he'd been up to, including hospital and ICU stays. At least he had been spotted; he'd resurfaced. I sent him another text.

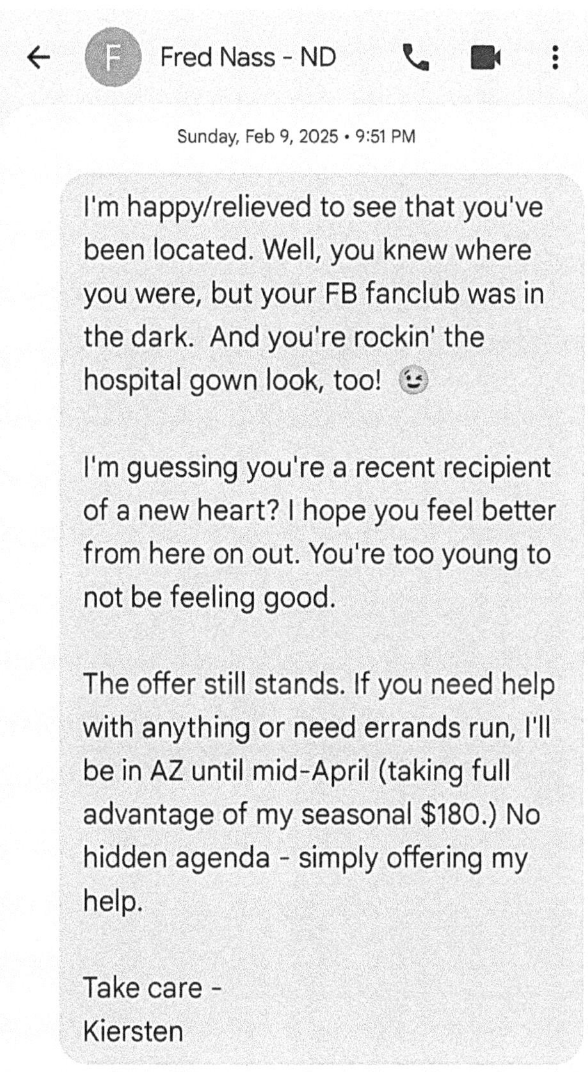

February 12, 2025:

He posted again, saying he would post at least once a week to keep everyone updated. He mentioned that his brother had been down, had put his truck and trailer into storage, and had spoken with the doctors, getting a better handle on what happened and how Fred would move forward.

However, the next week came and went—the week of February 19th, then the week of February 26th. I was getting nervous again: what was happening? I reached out to one of his cousins and asked for any updates to post on his Facebook wall, since his "fan club" was starting to get restless again regarding his whereabouts. She got back to me a day or two later, pointing out she was waiting for an answer from his brother. At that point, I knew nothing. No one knew anything.

I wanted to send him flowers and have Texas Roadhouse send a couple of bags of peanuts, but I wasn't sure if that would be appropriate, given that he had cut me off a few months ago with no warning or communication. Everything after November 2024 had me flip-flopping about appropriate protocol. I also figured that his very special friend would have been hanging out with him in Yuma to keep him company, so I didn't want to interfere. It wasn't that I had never had anyone tell me to take a hike in the past—romantic or platonic—but for someone so important, who had made such an indelible mark in my life, to disappear when I knew there was more to the story. That's what I wanted to get to the bottom of.

FEB 26, 2025 AT 4:41 PM

My trip from Yuma back to Quartzsite followed a route from Holtville up to Bombay Beach around the Salton Sea, with a couple of days in the Coachella Valley on my way to visit my sister in the Palm Springs area. I left Quartzsite on January 29, 2025, and arrived in Palm Springs on February 26, 2025, and stayed with her overnight. The next day, I told her I would drive the RV back to Quartzsite because I didn't want to pay $125/night to store it at a resort (her driveway was too short for me to park in). The plan was to return the next day and spend the weekend.

The next day, waking up in Quartzsite, I locked up the RV and got into my car to head back to Palm Springs. That was the twenty-eighth of February, and I was staying until the following Tuesday morning, March 4th.

That whole weekend, I talked my sister's ear off about this guy named Fred. I had no idea what went wrong. Should I take Hwy 86 back down through Brawley and go to Yuma on my way back to Quartzsite? To at least stand outside the window of the assisted living facility where he was building up his strength to walk again after spending the better part of a month lying in a hospital bed. Needless to say, my sister was probably more than happy I was leaving since I couldn't stop talking about him—I could turn any conversation into one all about Fred. I was so laser-focused on this topic that I didn't really talk about anything else.

March 3, 2025:

That evening, I was torn between going to Yuma and returning to Quartzsite. I finally decided on going to Yuma before going to sleep, mainly because my sister—exasperated—said, "Just go!"

March 4, 2025:

Of course, I woke up with an I'm-not-sure-that's-a-good-idea feeling, again chalking it up to not wanting to piss him off and causing stress that I dared to go near him. He was there to get better, not to see some ditz jumping around the parking lot, waving madly at him through the window.

So, before backing the car down the driveway, I promised myself that at the one-mile marker sign for the Brawley exit heading east on I-10, I would make that decision with my gut.

When I saw the sign, a resounding "NO!" went through my head, and my heart asked, "Are you sure?" and my soul/brain said, "No" again, firmly.

So, I took a deep, exasperated breath and continued on I-10 East, watching as the Brawley Exit sign passed by my passenger side windows.

Later that night, I finally heard back from his cousin: That morning, when my brain firmly said "no" to going to Yuma, he was being transported back to the ICU with a COVID diagnosis, which he contracted while at the assisted living home where he was supposed to be recovering.

I was in shock, and I knew that unless a really big miracle showed up, the end was near. I went into full business mode and started taking screenshots of all of our texts and Facebook messages. I didn't want to lose access to those if his phone was turned off or his Facebook account was taken down. After two hours of that activity, the shock hit me. The timeline of deciding not to go to Yuma coincided with the time he was probably being transported back to the hospital.

His cousin posted on Fred's Facebook page after messaging me, and the care emojis started coming in.

That week, for me, involved a lot of bribing the universe, along with the regular work I had to do, which helped take my mind off this mess.

I was waiting to hear any more updates from his cousin, who had promised she'd keep me in the loop. I heard nothing the rest of that week since she had no idea, either. Again, no one knew anything except that he was back in the hospital.

March 11, 2025:

The day started normally, except for the pressing exhaustion I had been dealing with for the past few months. Starting mid-morning, though, I began to feel a growing sense of dread that only worsened throughout the day. I had no idea why. I checked everything I could think of, including emails and bank statements. Did I miss anything? No, everything was fine. I was waiting to hear back from his cousin for any updates, but otherwise, everything was fine on my end. But the dread kept increasing throughout the day.

Journal Entries

from November 19, 2024 &
March 11, 2025 - March 31, 2026

- Fragmented thoughts, ideas, visions, and happenings.
- Sometimes I refer to him as "Fred," or I refer to him as "you" since I'm talking to him about him.
- Most days, at least one, if not more, videos pop up in my feed, ranging from Carl Jung to various tarot readers, and everything in between. Most of these videos ping at least one synchronicity between us, if not several. Not all videos pertain to our situation, though; I say this to let the reader know that I'm not just grasping at anything that comes up in my feed.
- Locations noted are places I stayed, either because I stayed longer than just passing through or because something noteworthy happened there.
- Not all dates are represented. I didn't include days where nothing happened beyond my constant 24/7/365 thoughts of him.
- Videos appeared nearly every day, but I didn't include them for copyright purposes and didn't have the time to contact each content creator for permission.

Quartzsite, AZ - Tyson Wash LTVA (BLM)

November 19, 2024:

I began sliding into a schedule of sleeping ten to twelve hours per day (overnight) and doing my best to have two or three couple-hour naps per day. It was getting ridiculous through the end of December 2024 and through all of January 2025. My ability to stay awake through February and the beginning of March improved, but the naps were still there, though I had managed to curb my overnight sleep back to eight or nine hours.

March 11, 2025:

I was filled with growing dread that day. It was cold, windy, rainy, and overall, yuck, out in the desert that week. I figured the dread was the doom and despair I usually feel when not seeing sunshine (I'm diagnosed with S.A.D.—Seasonal Affective Disorder… I *need* sunshine.) The feeling of dread kept growing throughout the day, though, and I had no idea why.

The text bubble shown below was sent to Fred because he had mistakenly posted a password on his Facebook page. Aside from him reading this message and taking that post down, he also acknowledged it with that heart emoji. He could have given it a thumbs-up, but he put a heart on it instead. And as small as that may seem to some, it was and still is huge for me.

MAR 11, 2025 AT 1:30 PM

March 12, 2025:

Woke up hollow. I literally felt hollow all day, not knowing why until Fred's last Facebook Live video appeared in my feed, which brought my entire world to a screeching halt. I instantly became a sobbing lump of goo on the desert floor and immediately knew why I was feeling this way: I was mirroring Fred and how he felt. I put it all together, realizing that all my physical and emotional feelings since I last saw him four months prior meant I was empathically taking on how he felt. I know I wasn't feeling everything, but still, the pure exhaustion, the utter lack of drive and appetite throughout those months, the doom and despair, and the dread that kicked into over-drive on the eleventh—I had no idea why I was feeling any of this until I saw Fred in that video from the hospital bed saying goodbye to everyone.

I woke up feeling hollow in my torso. I couldn't feel my organs, felt nothing, wasn't hungry, and the thought of eating made me queasy. Couldn't understand why, but whatever, and got to work. That afternoon, around 4:30 p.m. MST, you posted your video, and my world was utterly shattered. My heart ached for you and all of your pain, and it ached over the fact that I would never see you again. I understood why you needed to go, but I was pissed off at the universe for cheating you out of a longer, painless life. I was mad because I would never get to hang out with you again. Truly a #FML moment.

The text bubble below was the last Facebook message I sent to him before he passed away.

Wednesday, Mar 12, 2025 · 4:58 PM

Thank you for being my friend & helping me out all of those times. You're truly a gem of a person. See you later down the road. 🖤

RCS chat with Fred Nass

I first called my mom, and she was devastated to hear this news. Then I called my daughter, and we talked for around an hour. She was in tears, and so was I.

Shortly after 6:00 p.m. MST, with my daughter on the phone, I noticed my solar panels were still outside and that it was getting dark. I'll add that the wind had been blowing really hard that day, and it was cold.

I asked her to hold on while I pulled in the panels. When I went outside to get them, the air was still and warm, with no forty-five-mile-per-hour wind gusts, unlike the entire day leading up to that very moment. Every-thing had stopped. There was a large gray cloud forming into a maple leaf shape from the NNW, and I had an absolutely overwhelming urge to remain outside and speak my truths.

I told my daughter I'd call her back, put the panels into the rig, then turned around, faced Yuma, and opened the floodgates of emotion, wailing and asking the universe why.

I was still empty/hollow—I had been all day. No hunger whatsoever. And toward 6:35 p.m. MST, I felt this forming, growing ball of energy bubbling up from the base of my spine and my inner voice telling me to tell you that "I love you." My over-analytical mind told my heart that it was foolish and that you wouldn't hear me, and my heart told my brain to shove it. That inner conversation lasted for two rounds while that ball of energy rose higher and higher within me. My soul took over, and I just opened my mouth and shouted, "I love you, Fred!" That statement surprised me; I knew it was true, but up to that point, I had never said it out loud, let alone formed that sentence in my mind. And since the world didn't blow up, I said it again, louder, and the tears started. Then I whispered it, then I shouted it, and stood there in the still and warm air. After standing outside for a few minutes, a big gust of wind hit the side of the rig. I looked up at the sky and went back inside, figuring the wind was starting up again as it had for most of the day.

I called my daughter back, told her what I did and what I had said. The crying continued, and at 7:20 p.m. MST, I looked on your Facebook page and saw that your sister-in-law had posted at 7:14 p.m. MST that you had passed away twenty-six minutes earlier—roughly the time the wind gust had hit my rig.

From what your cousin posted earlier, it sounded like you started comfort care at a little after 6:15 p.m. MST with a morphine drip, I would imagine. 6:30 p.m. MST, you were unhooked from the oxygen, and shortly before 6:45 p.m. MST, you were gone.

As I type this, I have the urge to tell you once more how much I love you. And that you definitely met your match for another soul who loves deeply, doesn't take things for granted, avoids conflict (but if there is some, I will go after anyone with a vengeance who hurts my friends or family, and you're definitely in that group.)

I scare the hell out of myself by realizing that I could have f'ed this up pretty badly with my cynical and jaded, grinchy self. But there was something about you that I just needed to know more. I'm so relieved that I followed the very quiet voice that told me to reach out to you for a lunch date, and in the big picture, I'm glad I got kicked out of the mean girl bunch, and I'm so happy that you welcomed me into your campsite. I can play every day over and over with you and me out there. I watched you like a hawk, trying to get a read on you and your intentions—definitely a tough cookie to read.

March 13, 2025:

I woke up sick: a screaming headache, couldn't open my eyes, stayed in bed all day, had a high fever, still wasn't hungry, and felt hollow. That entire day didn't exist except for the promise I made to one of my kids who lives in Minnesota for the lunar eclipse of the *Blood Moon* that evening. Since anything "celestial" that happens in Minnesota usually means the sky will inevitably be cloudy, I told my kid I'd go out and record it for him. I had no idea what would happen on the twelfth when I made that promise a week earlier.

My son told me the eclipse was at 10:30 p.m. So, as much as I would have loved to be sleeping and hiding from the world, I stayed up in layers of clothes because it was so cold outside and inside the RV (I hadn't gotten my furnace repaired yet, so I had no heat). With no appetite, my blood sugar was telling me to eat. Still, I didn't have it in me—absolutely no interest in food. I knew if I had eaten, I would have woken up, probably felt warmer and stronger—it would have been a good idea. But below my brainstem and above the soles of my feet, I couldn't feel my body. There was no point in eating.

While feeling absolutely horrible, I stumbled out of my RV ready to film this lunar eclipse. I figured it would be eighteen to thirty minutes, tops, then I could crawl back into bed. Instead, it started at 10pm-ish and lasted until 2:30 a.m. on the fourteenth. Great. Just great.

True to my word, and against every fiber of my being that day since I would have loved to be sleeping, I stayed up for the next three hours and got coverage every fifteen minutes through the part where the Earth's shadow started moving off the moon's surface. I timestamped it, created the YouTube video link, sent it to my kid, and haven't watched it since. *(video)*

I lumped the lunar eclipse video into the same category as Fred's video from the twelfth; I watched his "goodbye" video twice that day and will never subject myself to it again. I'm glad that he posted it so we all knew what was going on. Unfortunately, though, if I think about it, I can see the replay as clear as a bell in my mind. I do my best not to think about it; I can't allow myself to get into that funk again. It's taken me nearly a year to stop crying every day. Early on, it was damn near all day long, which subsided to a few bouts per day, which finally moved to crying unexpectedly. I could be completely immersed in work or watching a documentary about the most mundane subject, and my tear ducts would open on their own. I'd be back to my funk of doom and despair, tearing the hell out of this entire situation and threatening the universe with a lawsuit.

I also thought it was fitting to be out there watching this celestial event, since Fred and I had always done so. His trusty Google searches always kept him informed about what was happening in the sky on any given day, be it various moon phases, meteor showers, eclipses, rocket launches, planetary alignments, the ISS passing overhead, etc.

And then the name of the eclipse, the *Blood Moon…*

March 14, 2025:

I woke up around noon, all bright-eyed and bushy-tailed. Boy, did I have energy!!! It was like I had been sleeping for the past four months—which I had. My appetite started coming back. I felt like I had done a one-eighty from where I had been over the past few days, dating back to the previous November. Holy schnikeys! I was awake and energetic!!! Wow! Think five Red Bulls and the biggest sugar-high, ever.

On the afternoon of the fourteenth, which was a Friday, my daughter called. Her first question when I picked up the phone was, "Hi Mom! Guess what we're doing now?"

I answered with my first thought, "Coming down to Arizona to hug me and spend the weekend?"

I should have bought a lottery ticket that evening; I was spot on, which surprised my daughter and son-in-law as well as me when they confirmed I was correct. They called after they had been on the road for a while—they had escaped Friday night rush hour in Denver and were just south of Castle Rock heading to Colorado Springs.

As a mom, I immediately asked about the weather and road conditions and advised them not to bust their butts driving through the night. I didn't need more bad news that week. I also knew a blizzard was blowing through the northern half of Arizona that evening.

They did wind up turning off at Holbrook on I-40, since the gates were down along the interstate, and made their way south to Phoenix the next morning after an overnight in Payson.

March 15, 2025:

My kids made it to Quartzsite around noon to "mom-nap" me, and take me to the ocean as a way to console me and get me off the desert floor, where I had become a sobbing lump of goo. *(video)*

March 16, 2025:

I woke up in a hotel room in San Clemente, CA, that morning. The kids, the grandpup, and I checked out the beach in daylight, then headed back to Arizona, stopping along the way to visit a couple of family members in Southern California. *(video)*

March 17, 2025:

Filled with phone calls and emails from everyone on my end who knew of Fred, which was literally darn near everyone, since I couldn't shut up about him. Some people have never met him in person yet know everything about him, including random details about his childhood.

March 18, 2025:

A friend reached out to me early this morning to hone her skills and possibly connect with Fred. She wasn't sure it would work, but she would try. I immediately took her up on it, and she said she'd try either the twentieth or twenty-first. My three questions were:

1. Where did I stand in your life? Who was I to you? Friend? More? (I truly didn't know.)
2. Who was L.M. to you? (I was giving him another opportunity to tell me.)
3. Did he hear me tell him I love him from the desert the evening he died?

Well, Fred showed up that same evening, and she connected with Fred rather than waiting a couple of days as she had planned. Wow! It was a relief to hear from him. My energy got a boost, and I even went out for chicken wings that night. I really hadn't eaten much in the past six days. After hearing from her, my appetite came back with a vengeance.

Email from Kimberly Dawn,
who connected with Fred
on Tuesday, March 18, 2025, at 9:18 PM

Ok. Wow. He has strong energy and is the most prolific communicator I have ever connected with. I don't think he wanted to stop. LOL!

The back of my head is still tingling—it's like he's running his fingers through the hair at the base of my head. It is a helpful signal, though, because it strengthens when he shares emotional topics.

I didn't read your emails earlier because I prefer to review them with minimal prior knowledge. I appreciate you sharing them; it helps me trust what I'm seeing and ensures it's authentic rather than a preconceived idea.

I will also say that I have empathic/clairvoyant abilities (always have), so some of what he said to me is not a surprise after talking to you. Because there are a lot of raw emotions involved and he was such a strong connection, I verified what I gleaned from him before sitting down to type this.

Since he had a lot to share, I'll present it in chronological order rather than reorganizing it into a logical flow. Here goes:

Right away, the back of my head/neck began to tingle, followed by the back of my legs. Sometimes sensations like this can indicate a health issue the deceased may have had in that area. I suspect in this case it was indicative of a very strong connection.

One of the first things he conveyed was the notion of being a Grandpa or Grandpa-figure to a little girl. He adores her. She's the light of his life. To him, she represents lost youth, do-overs, hope, and light.

I'm also feeling a heaviness and some sorrow. He's not in pain (and thankful for that), but he still has things he wants to do. His time came too soon.

He's telling me that as a result, he's having trouble crossing–not yet.

I asked him what caused his passing, and he held his chest, which is typically indicative of a heart problem.

The color brown is presented, which, to me, means murkiness and inner turmoil.

I asked his last name and was given the letter "B."

Did he have a brother? I felt he was telling me he had a brother and that his brother's kids were almost like his own. Are there two? The little girls are his fave.

He's conflicted about L.M. She wasn't the love of his life, but she has been there for him for a long time. She's always been good to him, so he doesn't want to hurt her. And, since he's not with her often and knew he probably didn't have long, it was easier to leave things as they were. Loyalty, not love.

He acknowledges that there was chemistry with you, but he knew it couldn't/wouldn't go anywhere. He respected you and didn't want to hurt you. He's a gentle spirit, avoids conflict, loves deeply, and doesn't take anything for granted. He loved the companionship you shared. Maybe in another time (remember this) and another place. He reiterated that he loved your companionship.

I asked if he had heard you say goodbye. He said, *"Yes. She whispered. Our hearts are connected."*

He'll be in every orange sunset.

His wish for you is that you *"Learn to love. Don't hold back. Get out of your own way. It's okay to be vulnerable. That's where the greatest love is found. That was my role. To teach you what love feels like. Don't be afraid of it. I wish I could've returned your love the way you deserve. I see you. And, I will be there, in the sunset, when the warm breeze kicks up the dust."* And, something about crickets.

He knew he wasn't meant to be in your life long term. He was in your life to teach you something.

"I'm always around."

"Don't cry for me. Live and love."

I saw him fishing in a boat, and he said, *"Time doesn't stand still. Live life."*

He showed me fish, mountains, boats on water, trails, and high peaks. He was here for a higher purpose.

He showed me a road/route sign along a long road, like 707—something with a 7. He's shown me several configurations, but the 7 is the focus.

He showed me cranberries.

He showed me hot dogs.

He showed me a glass with ice and a lime.

He showed me playing cards.

He's showing me what I assume is his POV, looking down at a little table that's between two chairs.

There's a braided rug with colorful/reds, etc., beneath it.

I hear the song "I Can See Clearly Now (The Rain Is Gone)."

Then we got to the part that I was suspecting:

He admitted that he's an old soul. His energy is white, yellow, and blue.

He's showing me an intense orange sunset, the horizon, cactus/scrub brush, a balmy breeze, a campfire, and lights in the sky. Did you see orbs? I got the feeling that he might have been a starseed or an alien, and when I asked him, *the* back of my head surged with energy. I heard *"Arc...."* NOTE: Arcturian is a type of starseed. (I suggest you read the description and see if it fits him.)

He also acknowledged that your connection was a past-life recognition. You were his wife in a past life. He showed me the covered wagons heading west in the 1800s. And I heard, *"If I could turn back time."*

Then he showed me a Mexican-like blanket with shapes and colors draped over someone's shoulders-like it's cold.

At that point, I had the answers you needed, so I thanked him and closed the conversation. He didn't leave right away, however. ;)

If I may take the liberty of expanding on what he conveyed and what I picked up from our earlier conversation: You've been hurt in the past – both of those men were not worthy of you. No doubt. Often, however, it's easier to blame fortune than acknowledge that we don't trust our judgment. And to protect ourselves, we develop a strong outer shell designed to create a barrier against future hurt. Are you a strong woman? Yes. Can you be strong and vulnerable? Yes, but it requires faith and confidence in oneself. Fred knew who you were. He saw you. That's why your shield didn't phase him. He was in your life for a reason—it was his role/purpose to show you what the real thing should feel like. His purpose was not to make all of your dreams come true, but to help you see the subconscious beliefs that are preventing you from obtaining what you deserve. You take on the alpha-female persona, work tirelessly, etc., because it's safer there. Those are coping mechanisms. Set yourself free, girl. Truly free.

Hope I didn't overstep. And, I hope it helps you find closure. Let me know how much you can validate in the reading.

All the best,
Kimberly Dawn

After getting the message from Fred, I got my butt outside for the sunset, just in time. Two swallows flew right around the back of my RV and over my head, then, toward the end of the viewing, flew right over me again and disappeared past the back of my RV. (I did figure out a couple of days later that the tree in my spot was filled with nests—I had never noticed them before, though.)

I could see Fred's legs, crossed at the ankles, coming off the lawn chair I had set up for him during the sunset.

Every so often, since your passing, I catch glimpses of you—or parts of you—near me. This happens either through a partial full-body apparition or, more often, an energy-signature outline. I still see you, but it's not a solid vision; you're opaque. *(video)*

Verifying what my friend saw/heard:

I asked his last name and was given the letter B:

My friend thinks this refers to "Bowman County"; I think it's probably my birth surname. I did tell him everything about me, and I remember that conversation when I revealed all my identities to him. He'd only ever had one last name.

He'll be in every orange sunset:

*That's what we did. It's darn near a rite of passage and then tradition every following night out in Arizona and SoCal: You know exactly when the sunset is to take place, then set up your chair and gaze toward the western skies. If you're crazy enough in the morning to gaze toward the eastern skies, you can catch those sunrises, too. Of course, the *ONLY* thing that got me out for sunrises was Fred. Any other time besides sitting with him, I've simply assumed that a sunrise looks about the same, but the sun goes in reverse. I must have been crazy about Fred to get up all those mornings.*

"...And, I will be there, in the sunset. when the warm breeze kicks up the dust." And, something about crickets:

The sunset was every night unless there were clouds/inclement weather. We were all about the weather and the warmth and the breezes, the dust/dirt devils—it surrounded us wherever we went. That's the scenery everyone sits in for the entire winter in that area. I had also told him about my countless camping trips and where I had been, noting that the farther south I went, the bigger the insects got. I told him about all the one-inch-and-larger crickets I found underneath my tent in southern Kansas. I told him how I love the sound of crickets and falling asleep to their song at night, when it's still warm, and the stars are out.

He knew he wasn't meant to be in your life long term. He was in your life to teach you something:

He did. He showed me what true love felt like—I hadn't had that in my first fifty-four years on this planet.

I saw him fishing in a boat, and he said, *"Time doesn't stand still. Live life."*:

This is most likely him telling me I work too much. And I still hear this quite a bit from him, even now.

He showed me fish, mountains, boats on water, trails, and high peaks. He was here for a higher purpose:

He told me about most of his adventures, including his fishing trips in Alaska and other locales.

He showed me a road/route sign along a long road, like 707—something with a 7. He's shown me several configurations, but the 7 is the focus:

Ever since his passing, I see a lot of 7s every day: streets, highways, the clock, dates, anything 7-related will stand out to me. Also "17," "7:17," "7:27," "7:37," "7:47," "7:57," "71," "7," "70," "707," "77," "777." I won't even be thinking of numbers, and they nearly jump out at me. Today, the end of March 2026, I realized this is my seventh published book. I also see all the angel numbers and many number sequences.

He showed me cranberries:

I later found out it was the word "cranberries," which I figured would be the color of his vehicles. He did tell me about his cranberry-colored Trailblazer before he bought his cranberry-colored F-150.

He showed me hot dogs:

Although we had hot dogs a couple of times around the evening fires, I think this is because we both had involvement with fairgrounds.

He showed me a glass with ice and a lime:

Anytime we went out, I'd always order (at least) a glass of iced water with a lime, never a lemon, and that was something he had pointed out to me. I told him I was "special."

He showed me playing cards:
He played online Texas Hold 'Em on his iPad every day.

He's showing me what I assume is his POV, looking down at a little table that's between two chairs. There's a braided rug with colorful/ reds, etc., beneath it:
That's exactly what the area outside of his toy hauler looked like, and where we sat every morning to watch the sunrise.

I hear the song, "I Can See Clearly Now (the Rain is Gone)."
Music was (and still is) a huge connection for us. We listened to the radio wherever we went in the truck, we listened to music with our nightly camp-fires, we did three Monday night Music Bingo events over at Whiskey Road Saloon, we played different songs for each other, "Have you heard this one?" We liked the same artists and played all of those songs, and nowa-days, he sends me songs. I wake up singing them in the morning, he'll send me songs over the radio and through my music streams, I'll hear songs while out in public, and no matter where I am in relation to the speaker, I'll hear that song at the same volume level until the song is done. Then it'll go back to "regular" volume.

March 19, 2025:
Filmed the sunrise and posted it. *(video)*

    Wrote this on your Facebook page that afternoon:

A week ago, this world lost a beautiful soul.

    Although there is no funeral or memorial planned, please be sure to give a toast to Fred this evening for a life well lived and for the blessed fact that he counted you as a friend. To have the gift of his kind-hearted friendship bestowed upon each of us, in this crazy world, is immeasurable.

We all know that he loved campfires. I'm off to get some wood for the campfire I'll be lighting in his honor this evening. I know he would be astounded to see so many people sitting around campfires, sending toasts out/up to him. I bet he would be blushing.

I went out and picked up firewood for a one-week honoring campfire. My appetite was stabilizing, and I no longer felt hollow. While out getting wood, my back tire went flat. Pulled into a parking lot feeling defeated, and two friends showed up almost immediately and changed my tire. Got back in time to start talking after the sunset finished, which was roughly 6:45 p.m., and then I lit a fire for you. I made a video titled "A Fire For Fred" and posted it on YouTube. *(video)*

March 20, 2025:

Realized it was Ostara—a time for a new beginning.

My body no longer hurt as much as it had over the past few months. I'm not going to run a marathon anytime soon, but I didn't hurt, and my heart palpitations had gone away, too. I was mirroring your body and your pain.

March 21, 2025:

That evening, when going to bed, I opened up my mind's eye—I couldn't sleep through the night due to stomach issues from getting my appetite back. I was up this morning between 2:30 a.m. and 4:30 a.m.

Decided that I would try to meditate, and after five minutes, my body went numb, except for the massive tingle on the back of my calves. My mind's eye opened up, and I saw a two-lane highway of silhouettes crossing in front of me. The furthest line of people was walking to the left, and the closest was to the right. Of those people in the closer line, one turned to look at me, and it was Fred in full color—just his face, really.

Then I saw a cosmic explosion in space. Dark space with a screaming white ring around the explosion at the center.

I saw the letter "K."

I later saw various fonts/scripts of the letter "X" (Gyfu?)[*]

Saw the silhouette of mountain peaks against an orange sky.

Only four hours of sleep that night.

In the afternoon, I posted the fire video from March 19, 2025.

Sunset talk with Fred, and a staredown with a mourning dove[**] for nearly ten minutes. It stood still long enough for me to film it for six minutes. It puffed out its chest, staring at me. It looked toward the sunset a couple of times, but mainly at me, occasionally looking out over my head at the purple mountains on the other side of the valley. *(video)*

March 22, 2025:

Night with little sleep—you were definitely in the room, only three hours of sleep.

March 23, 2025:

Going to sleep, I saw lemons and bright sunshine. Five hours of sleep.

Otherwise, the brain won't stand still. I feel like *Jo Jo the Idiot Circus Boy*—all excited, but can't stand still long enough to get on the ride. (Reference to the movie, *Tommy Boy*.)[***]

March 24, 2025:

I tried meditating this morning. I got the physiological drop (woke up at 3:00 a.m., sweating something fierce but wide awake—so I decided to meditate.) I looked up and saw what I thought were clumps of leaves until

---

*Gyfu is one of the runes of the Elder Futhark, as in Fred being a "gift" to me.

**I had told Fred that one of my favorite birds is the mourning dove because of its call. I remember first really hearing them when I lived on the family dairy farm in West Central Minnesota—they lived in the barn. It was the same conversation as the cows in the yard after getting out of the sauna: opening the door and being greeted by a staring cow.

***He took me to the citrus stands in Yuma, and we hit other outdoor markets, too. Lots of sunshine down in Yuma.

they broke apart and flew away. Brilliant sun. A shallow-tread stairway up past a deep-colored Arizona sunset. Bears, mudskippers, fish, birds. Only had five hours of sleep this night.

Got up after an hour and went out to sit for the sunrise, and saw/recorded an orange tabby walking by. It looked at me, then hopped into the wash. The branch behind me moved and made a noise, but nothing was there.

The cat came back out of the wash, scratched its back, and sniffed my tire cover. I tried offering it a chocolate-covered blueberry, but it snuck under my rig and was gone, and posted that video. *(video)*

March 25, 2025:

Evening Zoom with Kimberly. When I shared my opinion (with Kimberly) that you shouldn't push people out of your (Fred's) life when you're ill or something bad is happening, Kimberly heard, "Yeah, yeah, yeah," and asked me if you had ever said that to me. I didn't remember that comment. (That comment came up again from you when she brought up the topic on the March 31, 2025, connection.)

I thought of you while drifting off to sleep. You were definitely there, and the room temperature definitely increased.

March 26, 2025:

Some days brought nothing, or I didn't notice anything.

March 27, 2025:

On the early morning of March 27, 2025, around 12:05 a.m. (I had just crawled into bed and closed my eyes around 12:03 a.m.—no antihistamines or gummies, lying on my right side and listening to ethereal music to go to sleep). My third eye opened up instantly, and I could see my iridescent gold and cream-colored shield. Then a fist came through it—also covered in gold. I could see the fingers, and the fist opened as if beckoning me to take hold and go with it (a 3-D movie in my mind). I even thought to myself, *Cool 3-D movie.*

Then the mind's eye fell to the background. I could then feel and hear this: From the top of my head all the way down to right below my rib cage, I experienced a severe, rapid shaking back and forth as if someone held each shoulder and shook me. Simultaneously, I heard a muted (not audibly, but I heard it) *thunk-thunk-thunk-thunk.* At first, I put music to it and thought this would be a good beat until my "conscious Kiersten" had to remind me that I am, in fact, in bed and not at a rave, and that something is happening that shouldn't be happening. The music disappeared, and listening to this muted thunking as I was shaken back and forth became a concern; I was trying to figure out how to escape it. My first idea was to lean forward and say, "Enough!" in my head, which did the trick.

Upon opening my eyes, my vision kept tracking down to the right—I was lying on my right side—and items in my view were racing up to the top left. My body had disconnected, and when I opened my eyes, I could start feeling my body again, slowly, starting at the top of my head and gradually making its way down—I had to check that I still had legs as those weren't coming online quickly enough. I never actually moved for this whole thing.

Then the music audio came back online for me, and I checked the time: 12:07 a.m.

WTF was that?

Then my entire body lit up with freaked-out chills. Initially, I wasn't going to document it, believing I'd remember in the morning, but I knew better and picked up the phone again to write it down. Sure enough, the next morning (March 27, 2025), I had no memory of it until I looked at my phone.

At 10:30 a.m. on the twenty-seventh, I reached out to a friend and asked her if any of that sounded familiar.

She gave me three possibilities of what could have happened:

1. I had an AFIB episode.
2. My soul ascended to a higher plane.
3. I had a bad dream down a very bumpy road.

Since I've never had AFIB before and I've slept on my right side a lot throughout my life, I doubted that. The bumpy road was just for fun, so I'm going with ascension. Wow!

At 3:30 p.m. that same afternoon, I called her back and asked, "What do I do next?" She told me to perform a cleansing ritual for the bedroom, closets, drawers, and under the bed.

Around 5:00 p.m., I performed a cleansing ritual not only in every nook and cranny of the bedroom but also throughout and around the outside of my RV— and carried it out along and around my car. I also included the space underneath the tree in my campsite.

In the evening, I mentioned that you touched my lower back (the small of my back) and that it sent pure, absolute energy through my body at the Texas Roadhouse on March 31, 2024. Wow, and holy monkeys! Never had that before, and especially to that degree. I then added that my two erogenous zones are the small of my back and the side of my neck.

March 28, 2025:

I showered and did some work before hitting the road for Palm Springs. While doing that work, I noticed my legs looked dry and scaly, so I started applying lotion. I raised my right leg, put lotion on, and as I started rubbing it in with my right hand, the sensation in my hand disconnected: my leg could feel the pressure of my hand, but it was a different, warm, tingly energy rubbing the lotion on. I couldn't feel *my* hand, but my leg could feel pressure and definitely a different energy that was not my own for a couple of strokes. I think you were being a cheeky monkey, weren't you?

I drove to Palm Springs that afternoon.

That night, before going to sleep, I did my evening talk and brought my legs up so you could sit on the edge of the bed if you wanted to.

March 29, 2025:

I woke up that morning and sat in bed with my back against the wall, talking with you. The rest of the household was still sleeping. I moved over so you could sit if you wanted to—my morning talk. While I was silent, I barely felt two or three strands of hair move aside along the right side of my neck, followed by a warm tingly sensation about two inches right under my ear. I sat there wide-eyed. I asked if you just kissed me? And got the feeling of *yes*. Holy monkeys! (Damn, you're good.) Tingles everywhere, and OMG! My heart skipped a beat.

That afternoon, my sister performed EMDR (Eye Movement Desensitization and Reprocessing Therapy) on me. I was wary going into it, but I thought I'd give it a chance, so I'm not a weepy mess 24/7. I asked every imaginable question about not wanting to forget you, and I was assured that everything would be fine.

After it was done, I felt different. I felt an energy shift toward the end of it, which caused me to be horribly worried that I did indeed lose you. *Oh, NO!!!* I didn't feel the safety blanket of devastation and sadness anymore. I knew about you, the situation, and my feelings for you, but they weren't right in my face. Even though that safety blanket was filled with tears, it was something for me to hold onto.

EMDR thoughts during each swiping:

1. Nothing—concentrating more on the process rather than letting go
2. El Centro, hot dogs, crying
3. Focus, Yuma, time
4. Time spent, desert, sunsets
5. Time spent with Fred, Pilot Knob
6. Whiskey Road Saloon, places, Mexico
7. Life's unfair, heartache, time missing, crying
8. Places visited with Fred, sadness
9. La Posa South, desert, getting there
10. Traveling, North Dakota and Minnesota, anticipation
11. Lonely
12. Married, time spent together, cats
13. Calexico, movies, marriage, time
14. Interrupted by an exterior conversation about Lake Tahoe being the coldest lake
15. Las Vegas, I-15, Utah, western North Dakota
16. Decades before, driving in North Dakota
17. Harbor resentment @ universe
18. My mom, two kids, Los Angeles, ignored, lonely
19. Moving to Minnesota, route taken, Minnesota
20. Being ignored, bullying, family, farm, Minnetonka
21. A life stolen, heart palpitations, high school, forced to live others' ideas
22. California, surf and sun, warmth, sherbet

After that, I went in and talked with my twelve-year-old grand niece. I asked her to pause the TV and put her phone down because I guess I needed some pure good-feeling energy. I remember coming out of the bathroom and feeling an urge to sit with her and talk. So I did just that for about twenty minutes—asking open-ended questions. I found out that her best friend's name is Daisy, and I told her daisies were one of my favorite flowers. Then I had her look up Gerbera Daisies, and she agreed they were pretty. I also had her look up hollyhocks—she liked the daisies better, and she likes white roses. I ended the conversation by informing her about TED Talks.

We all then sat in the hot tub (my sister stayed inside cooking dinner). I told my niece what her daughter and I had discussed, and then we went in to eat. After dinner, the kids returned to their activities; my sister and niece sat on the couch watching TV, and I worked at the table.

Eventually got up to go to sleep—talked with you in the process of getting ready for bed.

March 30, 2025:
Talked with you in the morning and at night, thought of you all day, told my sister about the energy shift I felt, not waking up teary-eyed, and worked all day. My niece and her kids had left around 6:00 a.m. that morning.

March 31, 2025:
I got up and talked with you. Went out and did some work/watched YouTube while having coffee. Then my sister mentioned that it was approaching noon, and neither of us had gotten dressed for the day/done anything productive. I told her I'd go take a shower.

At 12:00 p.m. PST, I took a twenty-minute shower, then got dressed. I originally pulled out my lavender shorts and a lavender shirt, but then muttered I didn't want to look like a big grape, so I dug through my clean clothes and pulled out the first tank top I saw—a fuchsia-colored one (although I was thinking the green one, and again muttered that I look like a flower garden). However, I knew that was my wrong saying—had to really put effort into my ice cream shop* comment—the flower garden comment came out first. I got dressed, packed up my room, and put stuff by the garage door to load into the car, then came back into the living room to get my phone and computer and put them by the door, too.

After that, I went back into the living room with my phone and told my sister I was going out to take a selfie by the pool because it was my last day

---

*My joke is that my wardrobe is either all black, or I look like an ice cream shop threw up on me (I wear bright colors and mix them, sometimes obnoxiously.)

in California this winter. She said she hates having her photo taken. I told her I was the same way before being out on the road—I saw it as a way to boost my self-confidence. She looked at me like I had enough self-confidence to last lifetimes for everyone in all of the universes, and she then said as much. I smiled and started walking out the door.

I had my right foot out the door, and before pulling my left leg out, I leaned back and said, "Actually, I've gotten used to doing the selfies and posting the Facebook Livestreams because I purposely did those to get Fred all hot and bothered. Now, it's just a habit."

Outside, I took a picture of my hair up, then one with it down. In my third picture, with my hair down, the wind kicked up and blew it across my face, even though it hadn't been windy out there before that.

I left her house at 1:00 p.m., filled the gas tank, and then went over to Islands Restaurant in Palm Desert. In all of that time, Kimberly connected with you. Maybe thirty minutes or so? When I arrived at the restaurant, I saw her message about connecting with you and checked my email.

Email from Kimberly Dawn,
who connected with Fred
on March 31, 2025, 1:26 PM

Hi, Kiersten,

I just connected with Fred. He definitely came in, but with less energy than last time, which, to me, is a sign that he's at peace and comfortably transitioned, vs. before, when it was his first opportunity to reconnect with you/anyone.

Here's what was communicated to me:

He showed me the letter K.

He showed me two collapsing lounge chairs...the kind from the eighties with those tube-like straps that wrapped around them. They looked kind of weathered.

He showed me a small fire ring of rocks with a large

metal can or cooking pot on top...makes me think of cooking while backpacking.

He showed me worn hiking boots.

When I asked if he had any messages for you, he said, *"I see you."*

I relayed your message about letting people in vs pushing them away when he was ill. He said, *"Yeah, yeah, yeah"* (which I heard the other night when we were talking, too), and sheepishly said he didn't want you to see him/remember him that way. *"It's a guy thing."*

He showed me a hot dog again, in one of the red-and-white heavy paper holders.

He showed me a bull, presumably at a rodeo.

I asked if he was ok. He said, *"I am. I'm free. I'm flying. I'm in the breeze. I soar."*

He showed me Saturn and something related to planets/solar system.

I asked if he felt the zing you described when your hands touched. He conveyed that he did. It was similar to being shocked by static electricity. It startled him, but in a good way, and caught him off guard.

I asked if he had a message for you, and he said, *"Live your life. I'll be around. We'll meet again someday."*

Then he showed me some crystals/stones. There was a deep pink one that stood out.

I asked him for a sign to validate our conversation, and he showed me two scenarios.

1. A bumblebee crawling in the center of a daisy. There's some deep pink/lavender nearby, like other flowers in a garden, maybe.
2. A honeybee crawling on a clover flower. I feel like it'll be right at your feet sometime if you look down.

At that point, he was satisfied. He seems very at peace.

I hope this helps. Let me know if it makes sense to you.

\- Kimberly Dawn

Verifying what my friend saw/heard:

He showed me a bull, presumably at a rodeo:
The videos and pictures he saw of me attending rodeos in Cody, WY, the previous summer (2024).

He showed me Saturn and something related to planets/solar system:
We have always looked at the night sky, and over the past year, I have had numerous random mentions of "Saturn." I also shared the Stellarium and SkyView apps with him in January 2024.

I asked if he felt the zing you described when your hands touched. He conveyed that he did. It was similar to being shocked by static electricity. It startled him, but in a good way, and caught him off guard:
This was the time I tapped his hand while sitting in the hot springs, and when he looked at me abruptly, I told him not to worry and that I wasn't giving him cooties. (I didn't know how to read the look on his face when he looked at me.)

Then he showed me some crystals/stones. There was a deep pink one that stood out:
He knows I'm a rockhound and have an extensive collection. I showed him pictures and told him ALL about that, too.

I asked him for a sign to validate our conversation, and he showed me two scenarios.

1) A bumblebee crawling in the center of a daisy. There's some deep pink/lavender nearby, like other flowers in a garden, maybe:
The bee for either the electric shock or the movie we both really enjoyed,

"The Beekeeper." Deep pink/lavender would be the color of the clothes I was wearing that day. Daisy is one of my favorite flowers—especially the colorful Gerbera Daisies.

2) A honeybee crawling on a clover flower. I feel like it'll be right by your foot sometime, if you look down:
I haven't yet seen a bee on clover, but you had better believe I look at every clover plant I see since being told this.

The daisy reference, the color of my clothes, the wind around the pool—all of that—impressive. I will add that once I got on the road back to Quartzsite, the first song that came on was Rihanna's *Only Girl in the World*, and the next was Modern English's *Melt with You*. A commercial came on after that, so the next station the radio scanned to was a repeat of the *Melt with You* song.

In the valley between Coachella and La Paz, where there are absolutely no radio stations, the only thing playing (with a strong signal, too) was Kenny Chesney's *She Thinks My Tractor's Sexy*, which I did tell you was one of my favorites before we launched into another conversation about (sexy) farming equipment. You thought I was funny when we had that conversation about 1970s farming equipment vs. today's equipment—need I say more? You knew I had a point.

April 1, 2025:
I worked and talked to you throughout the day. I realized the hiking boots were a way to say I need to put them on more and get outside. And that your instructions to "live" were possibly to go on more earthbound nomadic adventures with me, which I'm more than happy to do—to take you on my adventures. I will be speaking as if you are with me, so a lot of "We're gonna do this," and so on.

April 2, 2025:
I worked. I asked my daughter to design a tattoo for me of a daisy with fuchsia inner petals and a gradient out to lavender, with a bee, and your initials

and the date of December 6, 2023, on it or near it. She said she would, and I'm planning on placing it on my neck* where you kissed me. You still can light me up. That's for sure, and again, impressive.

April 3, 2025:

A stunning sunset tonight—I have been dutiful about getting my butt outside to watch the sunset and record it. Eventually getting it posted, too, picking out songs to go with the sky's palette that particular night. Before, and especially during and after sunset, I felt like staying outside more. Whether it was the colors, the clouds, the moon, you—all of it—I needed to be outside longer. I took several pictures and then went inside. It started getting cold out. *(video)*

Started watching videos about connecting with you—I have a good grasp on things, or am at least open to it. But I need to know everything before trying it—back to my OCD perfection habit. I did try to meditate, but I seem to fall asleep more than anything. Whenever I need a pick-me-up, I watch videos of you and listen to your voice.

Around late morning, early afternoon—and as I'm always thinking about you—a short but strong burst of wind hit the RV out of nowhere, there was no wind before it, and no wind after it. Nothing was moving outside. I'm going to take that as you, and with that, huge props for being so impressive.

I imagine you're fairly busy stopping in to visit everyone. I'm trying my best not to be annoying. I know I did work myself into a tizzy at one point today—can't remember if it was before or after the wind gust, though. I want to say the weepy tizzy was beforehand because I was sitting when the gust hit, and I was working—fighting with my stupid printer.

April 4, 2025:

Got up this morning, talked to you—you might have a point about me talking too much. At 8:15 a.m., after breakfast, I went to take my morning nap and fell asleep. Upon waking shortly after 9:00 a.m.—probably 9:10-ish a.m.—before opening my eyes, my entire body lit up with energy, and

---

*The neck tattoo has now turned into little stars in that area, while that flower tattoo will be on my lower back, where he touched, and that massive amount of electricity went through me.

you showed up smiling at me with your baseball cap on, then looked over my head into the sunshine. And I started talking—a lot. Thank you for being here and visiting me. You had a couple of different looks—one with the fuzzy (unshaven) bear look, and then one with your face having a trimmed beard (sort of what you looked like at Slab City). You kept looking at me, then over my head toward the sunshine. I'm taking that as meaning you're anxious to get out of Quartzsite and get on with our adventures, which also leads me to believe you were, in fact, in my car on the way back from Palm Springs this past Monday. I told you as soon as the kids pick up the car, we're out of here.

After getting out of bed and doing the dishes, I posted a small feel-good "love note" to you on Facebook. Nothing glaring and no tagging, but I just feel so wonderfully warm and fuzzy, and again, I thank you for that.

Also, doing the dishes, I remembered once again that I tend to see and feel you more nowadays than before. But I know you were busy, not feeling good, and such, and I don't blame you. Know that I loved you then, and I still love you now. Not much can tick me off with you. I am so unbelievably grateful that I passed over the split-second thought of blocking* you on Facebook. I just couldn't do it. Not to someone I love. (One of those near misses that will haunt me for eternity.)

April 5, 2025:

Woke up at 3:00 a.m. and started stalking him, and then began carrying on about how we both fucked it up, communication-wise. That haranguing from me went on until about 11:00 a.m., on and off, followed by crying in the afternoon. I kept apologizing to him that I wasn't yelling, and then I would yell again. I did get the sunset and went into town for chicken wings,

---

*After Fred drove away from the November 18, 2024, campfire, I had no idea that was the last time he would make the effort to talk to me or see me again. He began ghosting me, and I had no idea what in the world I had done wrong to cause that reaction. If literally anyone (besides my mom, my kids… and apparently Fred) treats me like that, they are gone and blocked forever. I don't take kindly to being treated disrespectfully. But for some odd reason, my thumb hovered over "Unfriend" and "Block," and I just couldn't do it. My inner self screamed, and my brain hurt… it wasn't going to happen. So, I put the phone down to think about it. I really never got back to it, but I did start noticing that he was still hopping online every time I posted and always watching my Facebook Live videos; he was still stalking me. So, I let it ride.

sitting on his barstool. I only slept a couple of hours before waking up at 3:30 a.m. with a sore neck and head from the rig's position. (I need the rear springs replaced in this RV.)

I started taking a nap around 1:30 p.m. I knew he was listening, but he wasn't saying much, and I can understand why. I wouldn't say much, either, if I were him.

April 6, 2025:

I woke up around 3:00 a.m., but opened my eyes in defeat with a headache at 3:38 a.m. I started talking to him again (he might have a point about me talking too much…), apologized for the previous day's meltdown, then spent an hour or so stalking him on Facebook, and finally apologized for being so damn-ass needy. I guess one of the "perks" of being in my inner circle.

I also told him that I'm not being trivial when I declare him the "greatest love of my life," even though nothing physical (tactile) happened between us. The connection, the calming, and the comfort are what hooked me. His intelligence, and the fact that I am sapiosexual—intelligence is a huge turn-on for me. And he was extremely intelligent, although he tried to tell me he wasn't smart when I first got out to Pilot Knob. I told him something along the lines of, "If I didn't think you were intelligent, I wouldn't be sitting here right now." (Another failed attempt to be rid of me.)

While stalking him on Facebook, I finally realized what the constellation thing he showed Kimberly on March 31, 2025, was. I wasn't aware that he had made a short video of a few pictures of his Sky View app after I had shown it to him. All of his videos start with him and his face—and apparently, I had never looked at that specific video, or if I had, didn't put two and two together. He had posted a video similar to the one I posted on my YouTube channel after I had shown him the app.

The other funny thing I figured out was that when we went to see *The Beekeeper* movie, we stopped at Walmart so I could pick up a few things. While I was inside, he reviewed the movie on a short Facebook Live video, and said he was at the laundromat waiting for his clothes. Toward the end of his review, both of his eyes look off to the right, and he suddenly wraps it up in a hurry, suggesting that his clothes are done. It was actually me getting back to the truck. I laughed at that this morning. (Seriously, who is ever that excited and in a hurry to get his clothes out of the dryer?) Plus, you can see that he is in a larger parking lot—none of the laundromats down here has that big of a parking lot.

Anyway, after all of that, it was nearing 5:30/6:00 a.m., and I thought I should try for a bit more sleep, if possible. Shortly after I lay back down, the full body "light-'em up" began, and then the disconnect from the body and my head filled with visions of him and all that he showed me:

A couple of shots of his face, smiling coyly (his sneaky look—the same one he gave me after getting into Cocopah on a Senior discount), different outfits with and without a hat, full beard, or trimmed, or none, various smiles. He showed me a variety of pictures that morphed into one another: sunshine, sunsets with mountain silhouettes, the desert, flying, lemons, constellations, fields, his POV while standing and while sitting, looking down. I saw his hands cradling something or working on something—his fingers turning something over in his hands. And darn it - a lot more that I can't remember. I'll add it as I remember it. I also asked him something, but for the life of me, I can't remember what.

Got a couple more hours of sleep, and then set about typing this. Now for a busy day of getting stuff done so we can hit the road in a few days. Yes, I say *we* because Fred is traveling with me. Actually, typing that reminds me of last April, when I suggested that we travel together on the way up north—I'd splinter off to go to Wyoming, and he'd continue on to Montana and then to North Dakota. He gave me a look of shock/surprise/caught off guard. Again, he's got looks that I can't figure out. But he did feel the zing (in the hot springs).

10:11 a.m.—Looking out my door at the ground, thinking of whether or not I should take a run up to Sedona on Thursday morning, a chipmunk hopped out from underneath my rig, looked at me, then hopped away. I thanked Fred. (I'll add, prior to Fred's death, I never saw animals out here—even lizards. Since his passing, I see animals everywhere, and I'm not looking for them, either.)

Around 5:00 p.m. today, I told him the only way for me to handle all of this is to treat him like he's on an adventure, and he's got lousy cell service, so I can't text or call him. To avoid a long tangent about our situation, I'll simply refer to him as "my other half" since he's been on my mind every minute since December 6, 2023, when we zoned in on each other.

I would also say I was never too far from his minute-by-minute thoughts, since we both had a habit of stalking each other. So, there you go: sixteen months later (to the date)—he's now being referred to as "my other half." I told him that even though he pulled this stunt, he still can't get rid of me.

I had a fire this evening after sunset. Just got back inside at 8:40 p.m. The Bluetooth speaker* dictated how long we stayed out. Nice evening. Burning ironwood, so I can finish the fire tomorrow night if the wind stays down.

April 7, 2025:

I had a couple of views of Fred's face early in the morning—a variety of looks, and of course, I woke up at 3:00 a.m. and set about watching his videos for a few hours before going back to sleep at 6:00 a.m. and waking up at 8:00 a.m.

I did video work and mentioned to him that I remembered when he stopped by to jump my battery in December 2023, which, of course, made me weepy. A strong but gentle breeze came in the door from out of nowhere, and I thanked him.

This afternoon, at 3:35 p.m., I asked him for a little gust of wind. Instead, he gave me a momentary gentle breeze—not as strong as this morning, but still a little something. I'm smiling, and I said thank you. Other than that, this day has been quiet.

This evening's Facebook entry:

> In the last few days, I've watched seven tarot readings from various content creators who are unknown to me—never watched them before, and every single one has dwelled on the fact that a lot of love is coming my way. The headlines of these videos don't say that, but that's where the reading winds up going, they pull close to the same cards, then perfectly describe Fred on all sorts of points, and describe what happened and is now happening, then put the

---

*The Bluetooth speaker doesn't have a lot of battery power, so spending time outside tends to be short when streaming music.

bow on it of, "this is the person meant for you–your soulmate."

Oh, FFS!

I was wondering whether my business would remain unscathed in this shitty economy, or if I'd win the lottery (of course, I'd have to remember to play), or something. But instead, I get him described along with all sorts of details and situations/happenings perfectly pinpointed.

I will say, I see him and spend time with him a whole lot more now than I did over the past few months, for which I'm very grateful. But back to the ongoing synchronicities experienced every day, it is absolutely uncanny–it's beyond "mere coincidence."

Of course, with all of these situations, I've been returning the grace by giving him crap about not reading the invisible warning label I have, which urgently warns people that once Kiersten zeroes in on someone, there is no getting rid of her–even if you exist in a different realm.

And strangely enough, I'm really good with my situation, considering not being able to have control/have input with what happened health-wise with him. (I do, however, have a large bone to pick with Sanford Health & Mayo. As far as I'm concerned, a lot of negligence caused this outcome.) It gnaws at me that I can't go into those hospitals with the proverbial guns a'blazin' and a lawsuit in tow, to advocate for him. It won't change our current reality.

In fact, he said in his last video, "Don't try to figure out what happened." I know a large part of that statement was probably geared towards me. He knew that I've advocated on behalf of several people regarding their health issues, and that the "mama bear" in me can go on full display (zero to six hundred miles per hour in seconds) should anyone fuck with my loved ones.

    So now in my current reality, I'll join
    Fred outside to watch the sunset in a little
    bit. It should be a nice one tonight with the
    wispy clouds.

I came back in and watched one more tarot reading from an unknown reader, and it was the most intense and complete reading I've ever viewed.

After this one, I had another discussion with Fred. Poor guy—can't get rid of me. I suppose he could shut me down, but that was part of the discussion. I told him that he did love me more than he knew and that love isn't all about sex. While that's great, true love is about touching someone's heart and soul. What I had from/with him was something I have NEVER experienced with anyone else. I asked him not to disconnect from me. I'm, in fact, perfectly okay with having a relationship with someone on a different plane of existence.

Regarding sex, I informed him that tantric sex is an intimacy without putting one body part into someone else's body part. Essentially, sex is carnal pleasures and can be kept at that—simply physical without love. Love, on the other hand, is much more meaningful and deeper, and it's the connection I crave. I'm sure he understands now.

Again, I will follow his lead. He's on a higher level of consciousness and can "see" what's coming and/or how this setup may operate. I've also told him that if this arrangement isn't going to work, I'm leaving it up to him to put an exact duplicate of him in front of me. Otherwise, I'll go bounding through life not even noticing. This new individual will need to consistently remind me of Fred and say things that remind me of Fred; otherwise, it will be a no-go, and I'll most likely dismiss that new person as trivial.

I'm about to go to sleep and will be taking two antihistamines this evening to hopefully get a good eight hours of sleep. The last week or so, or more, I've been getting roughly four to five hours of sleep each night. I need to get back to at least six hours per night, especially with a lot of driving coming up.

By the way, the hummingbirds were out during the sunset, and I have a little chipmunk that shows up occasionally.

April 8, 2025:

Got nearly ten hours of sleep last night, thanks to the antihistamines. Drove into town to get the tires balanced, and still weepy and regretful. Didn't spend a lot of time learning more about Quartzsite this year, didn't go to a lot of restaurants and bars, and never checked out all of the rock shops, which is actually a blessing in disguise. Perhaps one day, I'll come back for a visit.

Drove into La Posa South to get five gallons of water for the black tank. Driving in there brings up a lot of mixed emotions for me—probably more sadness than anything. All of the BS in 2023, and of course, Fred's pushing me away from November 19th through March 12th. I understand why he did it, but my heart was/is crushed. I'm not mad at him now that I understand why. But it's time lost, and that still hurts. I am happy that he is near me, though.

April 9, 2025:

3:33 a.m. - Woke up hungry, and then was shocked into full body tingling, realized it, and opened up my third eye: Fred turned into a bear > mountains > butterflies > insects > monkeys crawling up a cliff > turned into Fred on a ladder, then got to the top and turned into a bee and flew off.

Right side of my body is still buzzing/tingling, and my entire head is buzzing/tingling.

Then it went to a profile of a man turning to his right. This person became Fred, and then, after a couple of seconds, morphed into a female with brown hair, sitting in a lawn chair, leaning over to tie her shoe, then looking up quickly, smiling at the man who was Fred, looking at him with happy eyes, and laughing/smiling.

I believe that was me seeing Fred, and then what I looked like to Fred. Both of us were in the desert out at Pilot Knob. I saw his toy hauler behind the chair I was sitting in, and he was standing to my left, about eight feet from the front of his trailer.

Then that scene misted away.

3:42 a.m. - Head and right shoulder are still buzzing. Then a bunch of morphing animals > turned into a skull > turned into sand > dark > done.

I tried to keep both the buzzing and the visions going. Lasted another minute or so, then, as it started to dissipate, I got up and wrote everything down.

3:45 a.m. - Head and right shoulder are still buzzing.

3:48 a.m. - My body continued buzzing, then sloughed off to the head, down the neck, and the right arm. Sat up, writing from there on, then fell asleep around 4:30 a.m.

7:11 a.m. - I woke up but remained in bed. I was lying on my right side, and buzzing returned to the right side, wrapping around my feet and enveloping my body (as I write this, my heart has a faint, dull ache).

He appeared and smiled, then showed me a couple together now, then reversed them through the decades, then the centuries, then the millennia, then the Neanderthals, and then it went dark.

And then again, the visions started in the early twentieth century, going back in generations to the early European countryside.

Then Fred appeared again, current age (my heart still hurts), and then he began a regression through his years, back to toddler > baby > infant > dark.

And then he appeared again, and it was his profile turning to his right and me turning to look up to the left—the original scene of us out at Pilot Knob in front of the toy hauler.

He then gave me a picture of a polar bear. Actually, it started as a brown bear that morphed into a black bear that morphed into a polar bear, quickly, and then was done.

The buzzing then subsided, but then came back in two and a half succinct waves with pictures of him, and then was done.

The first wave was the longest, and I told him through my thoughts that I was and am happy that he's free of pain and is happy, himself. Then the entire area was filled with a white/white-blue glowing energetic light. A happy, content light.

But then I said I understood why he treated me the way he did, and I saw a solid, translucent olive green, slightly clear and full.

Then I said it hurt me, though, and the color turned to a ribbon/wave—similar to northern lights of dark olive green, edged with varying shades of brown energy flowing through the band of light.

I immediately told him I wanted to stand up for myself and get answers, but purposely didn't want to put undue stress on his heart, and knew he had other pressing things to worry about besides me being needy and whiny, so I backed off.

And it went dark; the energetic buzz began to subside.

I said thank you, apologized for talking so much, and wanted to let you know how much I love and appreciate you.

With that, the buzzing surged back into my full body, and his face in his late forties appeared in my mind, then faded off, and I thanked him for visiting me. Then he faded back in with a more current face and smile.

Then the vision and buzzing faded, and I slept soundly for another four plus hours.

The giving side of me wants him happy, free, and having fun.

The selfish side of me enjoys his various visits. I hope I'm not being perceived as needy and a pain in the arse.

As I write, "If that's the case, I'd rather not be a burden," I hesitate to finish the thought, worried that it might cause him to disappear. But I also don't want to seem like a needy problem.

I continue to tell him that I'll take his lead as I did when he was in human form.

I continue to thank him for his time, kindness, and friendship.

I also acknowledge that this is not the only reason I'm head over heels in love with him, but it was a definite foundation and caught my attention.

I continue to kick myself in the butt for misreading his response to my "lengthy text"—I took it as he's got L.M. and they have some dynamic, and my observations were *wrong* and *way off base*. My mom suggested it might be the opposite of what I was thinking, but I argued against that because my track record tends to lean on the "shit side" of a situation—so, I thought the worst. And with mixed signals, observations, and vibes, I didn't drive over that morning for a chat about life, and also because I didn't want you to get mad, put stress on your heart, tell me to permanently get lost, and cause a health episode for you.

Essentially, I gave him the perfect "out" to hide behind while screwing myself over in the process; I didn't want to cause him harm.

Last night, before going to bed, I pulled up the photo montage his nephew made and told Fred that it's my daily litmus test to see where I'm at in the grief process. I'm near a one-eighty from where I was a few weeks ago: I only get weepy with the last five or six pictures and the final video—the time I was in his life, and the one picture I took of him, in the truck, at Slab City.

I remember back to the times he saw me changing clothes, and had to take a deep breath and look away. The time I had to change behind my rear driver's side door to avoid the neighbor sending up a drone to spy on me. The time (January 27, 2024) when I had an oversized tank top on with no bra while we lazily hung out at our campsite, and I helped him by pulling down the legs of the campstove as he stood to my side. When I looked back up at him to tell him it was set, he was smiling. I didn't understand why until I looked down at myself and understood what he was looking at. What could I do? He'd already seen the "goods" and, quite frankly, I didn't care.

That evening, I randomly remembered how he liked cucumbers and cucumber-flavored items, including Cucumber Gatorade.

I remember going grocery shopping with him, and I was impressed that he liked green bananas that were just on the cusp of turning yellow, but not quite yet. I remember commenting to him that I prefer and buy that same type of banana—we both agreed that those were the best time to eat them and would not eat bruised bananas, which were only good for banana bread.

He ordered his steaks medium rare, just like I did.

I have had men flirting/hitting on me since I was nine years old (which I told him). But between the two of us, with the mixed signals and lack of communication in this area, I couldn't get a read on him—another thing that held me back from reciprocating his advances and discussions. Back to him asking me, "How do I flirt with men?," and I really had no idea, which left him floundering and confused about me.

April 10, 2025:

Third eye was a pitch-black negative of his form; then his body would fill in full color, then wisp away. Chest up to the top of his head. A variety of looks with hair, smiling, or just looking.

Then I fell asleep. I can feel him, but it's been quiet.

No sunset as I was driving around Phoenix and picking the kids up from the airport. The kids had flown in to pick up my car. I was giving it to them since I couldn't flat—or partial-tow it. I need to get a different car in the future.

April 11, 2025:

Moved over to Fred's spot for my last night in Quartzsite. Got the sunset and made a video. *(video)*

I sneezed once out of the clear blue. Had no reason to and didn't again after that. I looked up a possible spiritual reason. I have sneezed twice and three times before, on different dates.

- One sneeze: Someone is talking about you, or you'll experience good luck.
- Two sneezes: Good fortune, protection against evil spirits.
- Three sneezes: Good luck is on the way.

Parker, AZ - Blue Water Casino

April 12, 2025:

Today marks one month.

Did errands and went up to Parker. Captured a sunset over the Colorado River and talked with Fred. *(video)*

April 13, 2025:

Spent a day out at the boat races with Fred—got a lot of footage. Fairly sure he was with me for the two sunsets and the boat races—I felt very serene and happy out there. (We had made tentative plans to get out to see the boat races during that November 2024 campfire before he started ghosting me.) *(video)*

April 14, 2025:

Upon waking up this morning, I looked up toward a large, five-point, dark, muted gold star while my eyes were still closed.

I heard inside my head, (Jefferson) Starship's "Nothing's Gonna Stop Us Now"—primarily the chorus.

I smelled not exactly burning toast, but something for breakfast burning—although nothing was happening inside my RV or nearby.

I briefly saw a wisp of his smiling face.

After opening my eyes and making the comment of wondering where the "Nothing's Gonna Stop Us Now" song came from, and how much I didn't like that song since it was so overplayed in the eighties, the song immediately switched to Lindsay Buckingham's "Trouble" chorus. Again, no idea where that song came from since I haven't listened to that song in forever. Can't remember the last time, actually, but it was playing loudly inside my head.

Not much of a sunset tonight—got pictures instead.

Morristown, AZ - Boulder OHV (BLM)

April 15, 2025:

Caught the sunset tonight. *(video)*

Was thinking about the worn-out boots. Get out and break them in, meditate while I walk/hike.

Put two and two together with the thought of Fred never making a promise that he can't or won't keep, then merging that into the comments of "seeing me" and "being around" would hold because of his view on promises.

Figured out the promise thing at 5:55 p.m.—look up angel number spiritual importance.

I've really noticed that I keep seeing angel numbers everywhere. Until this whole situation happened, I really never saw them, or if I did, they certainly never stuck out to me. Now, that's all I see. It's also the only time I tend to look at the clock. Or I get 5:17 (which is 17:17 military time), or 7:17 on the clock. Also, 1:01. 2:02, 3:03, 4:04, 5:05, etc., and a lot of 1:11, 2:22, 3:33, 4:44, 5:55, and 12:34s on the clock, too.

I was told to look for black feathers in a tarot reading today. It would appear there's a black feather around the neck of the guy who did the reading.[*]

April 16, 2025:

Early morning, I woke up at 12:30 a.m., went back to sleep, and that's when the electric tingling came back on. Full body. My mind was chaotic, and I

____

[*]I did look up Angel Number meanings, and although they are in my personal notes, I did not include them in this book. I encourage readers to look them up if this is unfamiliar.

couldn't hold still, but I got the crash course of some personal information about Fred, as well as his retiring early at fifty-six because of health issues/mobility issues. More than likely, he slept in his chair rather than crawling up onto the bunk, even if it was down. (??) I'm not sure, but those are the feelings and thoughts I received.

I got all of this info or had these thoughts in one fell swoop. But my mind was chaotic and wouldn't settle down. The electricity lingered but was also muted at its peak. Then I fell asleep again.

A couple of types of birds have been stopping by my door to say "hi" and stand outside squawking during the day.

I've been working on my tarot homework—getting more attuned to that. I'm hoping to quiet my mind this evening.

Going to sleep, I remembered that it has now been five weeks as of the weekday. Perhaps that was why I was in a shitty mood today—trying to calm my mind so I could sleep or meditate. We'll see how it goes.

April 17, 2025:

Early a.m.—still dark out—probably 4:45 a.m. to 5:00 a.m. - I was jolted awake thinking I had heard a motorcycle outside—just a brief soundbite. Slipping back to sleep, I questioned myself—did I just hear a motorcycle? It was in my short-term memory, but my logic came in and said I was making things up because a motorcycle isn't out here riding around on gravel in the dark, plus I would have heard more of it rather than a short second or two. Then I closed my eyes.

I was on the back of a motorcycle, holding onto Fred. We were riding at night along the Needles Highway, and I looked up to see the stars, and the spires and mountains were pitch-black against the sky. We drove through the tunnels, down the dark highway, with the forest on either side of the road and the moon off to the side lighting our way. I saw the headlight on, and the dashboard lit up. I rested my cheek against the back of Fred's shoulders, looking off at the dark passing scenery.

We were out at Sylvan Lake during a cloudy afternoon, walking that path and through the walkway tunnels. I turned around to see him smiling and standing along the pathway.

As quickly as it started, the visions were over. I tried to get them back, but between my bladder and my racing mind, it wasn't going to happen.

Total of five hours over the course of nine hours—not good sleep.

"My person" may just be my way of describing you rather than "my other half." I'll figure that out as time goes on and how it comes out. I ran it past you… I definitely don't want to offend you, and I want to be respectful.

I will say that the tarot readings I'm following as of late are spot on for the relationship I have with Fred.

April 18, 2025:

I woke up around 1:30 a.m. and stayed up until 3:00 a.m. My mind was still racing over political BS, work, money, water pump issues—the usual. Throw Fred into the mix, and I start crying—so many things left unsaid, undone, and uncommunicated. I closed my eyes, and the best I got was detaching from my body and seeing the head of a grizzly bear poke out of the darkness at me. Then, I saw a view resembling Crater Lake (OR), and to my right, Fred stood overlooking the lake. At one point, he turned his head to the left and smiled at me. Then the vision was gone. I fell asleep.

April 19, 2025, Facebook entry:

It's been a little over five weeks since "my person"* moved onto a different realm.

This situation has put me on every level imaginable, flung between one extreme and another, questioning myself and outwardly screaming at the universe for doing this to me.

But I have also learned a few things along the way, had some thoughts confirmed, and received answers to many lingering questions that had remained while he was still here in this plane of existence.

---

*Yesterday, I told him that rather than referring to him as my partner/cohort/other half, I'd call him "my person." I haven't heard any rebuttals, so I'm going with that until further notice.

I document every day and intend to continue until he says otherwise, whenever that may be.

As I've mentioned before, one person stepped forward to help me immeasurably in the wake of Fred's passing. I truly believe if it weren't for them, I'd still be a sobbing pile of goo on the desert floor. I'll also throw my kids into the mix with personal and virtual hugs, constant "I love you"s, and their overall support for anything I need from laughing/crying with me on the phone to listening to my same stories over and over again while asking the same questions as I methodically work through everything logically/doing my over-analytical thing that I'm so good at, to "mom-nappings," and the camaraderie I share with them–knowing I can call them whenever and depend on them to make any of my days a little brighter.

But what I've learned from Fred and his situation has been eye-opening and mind-blowing, to say the least. And I don't put any of this out there in jest. In the very short time I knew him, and even less time I spent with him, in this plane of existence, he managed to move himself into my very exclusive circle of "inside" people (the only other people in that circle are my kids and my mom). I did tell him about these circles I placed people, in terms of "rankings in my life," around one of our many campfires.

For the most part, I know what happened–the sequence of events that caused all of this–and yes, I have a huge bone to pick with Sanford Health and Mayo. Still, seeing that I'm not a relative and that he specifically requested that people not try to figure things out, I'm going to let it lie (but he knows I know, and he also knows I'm pissed off.)

I also know that he no longer has pain, is feeling quite youthful, is soaring, and is free of all cumbersome worries, for which I am incredibly grateful. You never want to see a loved one in pain and in fear, and in all-around hurt.

I knew the timeline of his last hour, and I know exactly when he passed.

The morning of March 12th, I knew something was off, and that afternoon and evening confirmed it. All of the pieces I had been personally experiencing fell into place.

Since meeting him in December 2023, and especially over the last few months of his life, my body has mirrored his. I felt part of his pain, I felt his exhaustion, and I got sick (to a lesser degree) when he was ill. I may have been mimicking what he was going through, or helping him lessen what he was experiencing. Not sure which, but I haven't brought it up to him or asked him, and at this point, it doesn't matter.

I've always been able to read/work with energy, and to a point, was aware that I had psychic abilities (actually, everyone does—it's simply whether or not a person wants to open their mind to it.) Since March 12th, my abilities have exploded by a hundred percent, and I'm so happy about it because that's what allows me to stay in contact with Fred, which is an absolute lifeline for me. I tease him that he was trying his best to get rid of me by going to this extreme, and he *still* can't shake me... I would tell him, in this realm before March 12th, that I was "bothering" him, and to this day, I still tell him I'm bothering him. It's my mission in life, and I take it very seriously.

Between March 12th, when he heard me say goodbye from ninety-five miles away, and when he made me aware of his departure from this realm through March 18th, when a friend connected with him, I was a blubbering lump of goo on the desert floor. But upon hearing from him the evening of the eighteenth, with so many things only I/we would know, and confirming/answering questions I had, etc., my faith in and the various beliefs I hold about what happens when death arrives, were cemented, and my soul became somewhat at ease.

Sure, it's taken a good handful of weeks to get better about not bursting into headache-inducing, crying tirades every hour—now it's only a little bout of weeping, once per day. But I also know that's my selfish side, wanting everything back the way it was, and then I yell at myself because the situation now is better for Fred, to a point. I know he didn't want to go at his age, that he had a lot more he wanted to do, and he confirmed that he would have liked to take our relationship further had he been in good health. (A large reason I'm so gd ticked off with the universe; to finally find someone I vibe with and is positively responsive toward me, and the universe is like, "Psyche! Not happening... You wish. LOL!")

Along with knowing the exact time of his moving onto a different realm, I also know the exact day and time he transitioned. I felt the energy shift, and was afraid that I had lost him. He proved otherwise a couple of days later.

In his contact with me, whether through my friend or directly between us, he has described the clothes I'm wearing on certain days, the conversations I have with myself and others, and the little nuances he observed about me when we were together, as well as references to tidbits of conversations we had in '23/'24. I still feel him, and I've "heard" him in my thoughts; I see him all the time, either in my thoughts or in his energy signatures at various degrees out in this "real world." I've had experiences of smell, touch, and hearing his motorcycle—again, in my head, but very obvious/significant (can't think of the right word here.)

The synchronicities I experience on any given day are incredible. Sometimes I'll be doing something that has nothing to do with anything, and my brain will click with a "two plus two" moment. A clarification on something I hadn't even thought about. It's crazy what these last five weeks have brought.

He had a motto: He never made a promise he couldn't/wouldn't keep. I told him that it was admirable and a good way to live. With that theory in place and from what he has said to me since March 12th, I am comforted by the knowledge that the promises he has made to me will continue.

As I mentioned earlier, I have a month's worth of documentation from my experiences with him and this whole situation. I'll continue documenting as time goes by, or until he requests otherwise. Our connection is what is keeping me sane. Yes, I do miss his physical being so very much, but I'm grateful that he is in a much better spot, doing a whole lot better than sitting here on Earth in pain, and worrying about so many unknowns.

I appreciated and loved him while he was physically on Earth, and I still appreciate and love him as he soars on the wind, feeling great, in the spirit realm.

Black Canyon City, AZ - Mesa Table Trailhead (BLM)

April 20, 2025:

Nothing noticeable or that I can remember. I switched spots today by about forty-five miles. I have found myself randomly saying "Hi" or "Hello" to him, especially when I have nothing to say but still want to talk to him.

Perhaps that's an attempt to keep him near? I'm probably annoying him by constantly saying "Hi."

April 21, 2025:

Sometimes it's so faint.

Today, I think my eyes leaked at least seven times, in varying amounts. I put together a manifesto of thoughts and questions for Fred and read them back to him for what Kimberly will bring up on their next connection.

Earlier this afternoon, his cousin got back to me and showed me the bowl set his brother had sent her, which she was now forwarding to my mom's house. I cried again and, of course, posted on Facebook along with the videos of how he made them. I lifted those videos off his Facebook page.

Afterward, I was drawn outside, and sure enough, a couple of sundogs disappeared as soon as I took their pictures.

While sitting out there waiting for the sunset, my body chilled out. My mind was free, I stared at the clouds and thought of Fred and the life he had experienced, hoping I could one day even do a fraction of what he's done.

As the sunset unfolded, I had a faint realization that Fred had come back to Arizona specifically for me. Of course, I added that it was also for him and all his experiences, once more. Still, as I sit here a couple of hours later, I'm realizing I always knew he had fun down here and such. For it to just enter my thoughts out of the blue, I'm going to go with that gut feeling that originated that thought, and go with the fact that (at least) one of the top reasons he came back down here was for me. (It wasn't like I was secretive about the way I felt about him with my Facebook posts over the summer.) It was quite obvious when we were together, and it was obvious in my heart-and-soul-baring text to him, the subsequent texts, and my final text.

After this thought, two swallows came up from the valley and flew over me for one lap and disappeared back down into the valley.

Afterward, sitting inside, I had an overwhelming feeling of heat, uncomfortably hot, hot enough to turn on the fan to cool off. This happened when I was watching a tarot reading on YouTube entitled *Aquarius, WTF did you do to this person?* (Posted at 3:33 p.m. PST on April 21, 2025). I looked up the angel number. This was around the time I got the info from his cousin at 3:16 p.m. PST.

April 22, 2025:

I'm sure I was amusing Fred with my burro adventures. I did talk with him last night—asked a couple of questions and "felt" answers, which I responded to accordingly. Nothing massive, just bantering conversation.

April 23, 2025:

8:30 a.m. - Caught a faint sight of Fred (needed a haircut, full beard—*Grizzly Adams* look—sitting and watching me with one of his amused smiles) before getting out of bed this morning while my eyes were still closed. I think it would have been stronger if my mind wasn't everywhere else, thinking about what needs to be done today.

11:25 a.m. - Sitting here, before I get to work, I told you that every time I feel just the faintest warm breeze—I'm reminded of you. It's so comfortable. But I am also well aware that you can hit the side of my RV with a very forceful gust of wind—rather impressive, too.

I also told you that I'd like to think I'm not completely off my rocker, sitting here talking to myself. I truly believe you're here, I can feel you—it's very comfortable—I don't feel alone, at all. I talk to you non-stop. You may be right that I talk a lot, but you're so comfortable to talk to. I am comforted in the fact that you're here. I feel loved. I know you said you didn't love me the way I deserved, but you did. You made a helluva dent in my heart, cracked it open. I'm on my second bout of tears today—I have the cleanest, unclogged tear ducts of anyone on the planet.

12:40 p.m. - Just watched a tarot reading that popped up in my feed. This guy is good and explains it so well. The validation I get everywhere is just uncanny.

Fred, you have nothing to worry about; my heart belongs to you.

1:45 p.m. - Took a one-hour nap and woke up to Fred smiling at me again.

6:36 p.m. - I'm to the point of damn-near hysterical laughter. Over the past few days, I've been trying to catch video footage of these "invisible" burros that cycle through this campground every ninety minutes between 6:00 p.m. and 6:00 a.m. I hear them braying, I hear them clip-clopping, I hear them literally right outside my windows, but for the life of me, I can't seem to see them through the window, and when I fling the door open to catch sight of them, there's nothing. They are nowhere to be seen, even with all of my handheld flashlights. I literally said to myself out loud that I felt like one of those stereotypical white chicks in a B-rated horror movie, hanging out the door in her underwear and a tank top, in the dark, looking for a phantom burro.

So, tonight, I was dressed and wearing my shoes, and fashioned up a contraption that held my camera grip and my thirty-foot motion-detecting ground lamp. I left the door slightly open and listened for the telltale clip-clopping, ready to pounce in stealth fashion to get these elusive burros on camera.

The time finally arrived. I heard them approach and snuck out the door, and… not a damn thing out there. WTAF? There were piles of "evidence" of their existence out there, so I knew they were real. But for whatever reason, I could not film them. They're the fastest burros who make no noise when they run away and are skinny enough to hide behind a Saguaro. But you know darn well, Fred was laughing. I could see him in my mind having a good time with this entertainment.

April 24, 2025:

Two different times, this morning, around 1:00 a.m., and around 3:30 a.m., Fred's face showed up a couple of times, more so at 3:30 a.m. I said, "Hi," then fell asleep.

Regarding this burro adventure, I'm beginning to think it's Fred giving me grief. That darn thing crawls up the side of the valley, brays as loud as it can, then runs by. An hour later, it creeps up to the side of my rig, brays loudly for a second or two, then disappears. Not to be seen under the cover of darkness. Fastest burro. *(video)*

Twice, I watched a hawk float on the currents right outside the rig today, right at where the mesa meets the canyon wall. It happened both times, either when I was talking about Fred to my mom or when I was thinking about Fred. Okay, I always think about Fred, so…

April 25, 2025:

I tried a few times this morning to connect with Fred, but I've been juggling work, travel, financial issues, and political issues. Got a few shots, but then my mind marches in and ruins everything. Got a few body detachments but no electricity.

Talking with you out loud this morning, I realized that with you, I felt safe and all-encompassing. I've never felt that with anyone before; I usually have my "spidey-senses" going at all times. But when you were nearby, and for the most part, I still experience this—I'm not really worried about anything. Essentially, I felt safe with you and was in a bubble with you. When we went out to the Desert Bar and had three other people in the back-seat of your truck, if they hadn't spoken, I would have forgotten they were there altogether. When everyone walked up on December 6th, although I saw everyone, I really only saw you. When you stopped that morning to help me with my battery, it was "home" to stand next to you, looking under the hood of my car. It was so oddly comfortable. Sitting anywhere with you, the rest of the world melted away—in my mind, it was just the two of us. A nuclear bomb could be going off behind me, and as long as I could see you, I was good.

I talked with my mom today. She suggested I get over it all and start living in the present and future. I know she means well, but I'm grieving and would like to take my time. It hasn't been two months yet, and she's suggesting I get over it and move on. I would never have thought to tell her this, with all of her close relationships. And although I knew Fred for a short time and wasn't married to him (in this life), I just can't shrug and say, "Welp," and then get back on a dating site. I will not diminish our relationship or my experience with this cavalier suggestion.

Watched a YouTube video of a tarot person who suggested I would see sunflowers and "2"s to confirm the message given—which, as usual, fit Fred perfectly. (Look at the April 26th journal entry.)

6:30 p.m. - Setting up the camera for the sunset, a moth showed up and fluttered around in front of the camera, inches off the ground. It landed on the phone and tripod, and when I said "Hi," I held out my hand, it landed on my thumb and sat for a while.

At 8:30 p.m., the burro showed up at the back of my rig and brayed extensively. I did go out to try to find it, but I got nothing. I'm doubting I'll be able to get footage. Starting to wonder if the braying isn't an audio time stamp for this location? A haunting of sorts.

Phoenix, AZ - RV Resort

April 26, 2025:
Checked into the resort. Spent the day sitting in a lounge chair around the pool thinking of Fred.

The dance I went to this evening was a birthday party for one of the resort owners, and it was decorated with sunflowers!

I can't remember exactly where, but a "2" showed up a few times, as well.

April 27, 2025:

More sunbathing, thinking of Fred.

April 28, 2025:

I explained to Fred that he is the one I love, no matter how promiscuous I might become in the future, although I'm not exactly someone to be categorized as "promiscuous." Not that I have any responsibility toward him, I felt bad for having that conversation with him. However, sex doesn't constitute love. I love him, but I can't have him physically, and I'm not sure whether fantasizing about him is disrespectful to his soul and presence now.

April 29, 2025:

Nothing from Fred. I told the universe I'm rather miffed at taking a good thing away from me—even if we didn't end up together, I only want the best for Fred. I also told the universe that I have serious doubts about *better* things coming down the pike for me. Sure, that may be a cheap thing to say now, but I had found something good, and it was yanked away from me (in the usual fashion).

April 30, 2025, Facebook entry:

```
Here's today's question for the hive-mind:
    I've done this before, but now more frequent-
ly since Fred passed away.
    Has anyone else experienced looking at some-
thing and then realizing/feeling that you are
looking at it as if you were that person?
    You still know that you are you, and you are
sitting there looking at whatever it is (and
you know what planet you're on), but you just
```

have a feeling that someone else is in your cranium looking through your eyes?

I've felt other energetic things with Fred, but more and more, it's as if I feel him looking through my eyes. I can feel my facial muscles changing to the way he would look if he were actually there, but my face doesn't move.

Typing this out–I'm sure half my friends are going to disappear, and the other half will stick around just to find out what weird thing will happen to me in the future.

I'm not watching myself (although I have done that frequently by moving out of my body and watching myself in the third person–it's the worst when you are on a stage giving a business presentation and you have to snap yourself back together before something goes awry.) But with this, another energy signature moves in, and I can feel another pair of eyes watching with me. The main intake is through their eyes using my eye sockets, and I can feel their "look"/ facial muscle disposition. It's fleeting, but long enough to be noticeable. I suppose if I didn't question it, it would stick around. ???

Does anyone get what I'm talking about?

Got affirmations from a few friends. The one friend I asked about soul ascension wrote back and provided more information, confirming what I was experiencing.

May 1 - May 5, 2025:

Nothing noticeable—I will say, at this time, a hopeful suitor was following me around the resort. I left on May 5, 2025.

Marana, AZ - Cactus Forest (BLM)

May 7, 2025:

Arrived at a Cactus Forest just NW of Tucson, in Marana, AZ. It's beautiful out here. Got here just as it was about sunset, with heavy cloud cover. Low-hanging gray fluffy clouds with the clear sunset gold lining on the horizon, but still quite bright under the clouds, too. *(video)*

I pulled into my spot, and after I finished backing up, I looked out the front to see a black vulture, crouched on the ground—hopping in from the right and exiting into the brush on the left, looking at me like I had "caught it in the act." We were maybe forty feet from each other and locked eyes for just a second. I looked down and back up, and it was gone. The first thought was that it was Fred/Fred sending me the bird. It was that same zoning that I had with Fred, except I was obviously not attracted to the bird. But that bird locked eyes with me, and in that second, it was like we were looking into each other's souls. The weirdest thing. And typing this, I can put myself in that area, on that day, with that weather, seeing the bird, getting that connection, I looked down, and then it was gone. Seriously strange.

Did some meditation: Mind won't really settle with money and work and uncertainty, but this is eventually what came through:

Robotic black wet hand coming out of twisted space, flexing.

Turned into a swallowtail butterfly—followed it with my eyes.

Got into a wormhole and broke through open space. Headed into and surrounded by comfortable greenish-blue light.

Eventually, I swerved off to the right through another door.

Did see some shots of Fred's face smiling at me, then looking over me to his right with light shown upon his face.

A couple of other times, he looked at me.

May 8, 2025:

I've been really distraught that I can't picture you as quickly or as completely as I used to. That's really ticking me off and making me sad all at the same time.

May 9 - 13, 2025:

Not much that I can remember—have been driving, working, and talking with him. Not hearing much. I am guessing he's done. I hope I didn't scare him away. Probably did.

Email from Kimberly Dawn,
who connected with Fred
on May 14, 2025

Kiersten,

Fred says, *"Hello."*

In the past, he's shared more evidential images, etc., first and his message/wisdom second. This time, he was providing overarching answers for you rather than a specific answer to each question (I read your email before opening up).

Below is what I received:

"I see you. I am always around. Sometimes I listen/ observe. Sometimes I send signs in the wind. Birds.

I know that you love me. And you know I love you. Time, space, and dimension will never change that. But you need to live your life on Earth. It's a place to learn, to grow. I am not the happy ending. I was in your life to teach you.

Love yourself, genuinely. Slow down. Dissolve your wall. You're safe in yourself. Trust yourself. I will guide you–but all the answers are within."

In response to my clarifying question about "hot dogs," Fred showed me a hand holding a red-and-white gingham paper tray with a hot dog in it. The background seemed like a fairground. And, I heard *"All American. Family. Happiness. Contentment. Seek it. You deserve love, but you have to love and trust yourself first. People don't happen to you."*

Fred showed me red grapes on the stem in a container on the table between two chairs. I sense desert brush. Quails.

I heard: *"Do not second-guess. Everything happens in its own time as it should. Look forward, not back. Clarity isn't in the past but in the future. Look forward."*

He showed me three Burros amongst the brush. It's night. They're calling. One has a bright green pack on. ...for me means rebirth/growth/nurturing. It's also representative of the heart chakra. Given the preceding portion of this message, he seems to be encouraging you to focus on yourself, specifically on trust and love.

He showed me a road runner and power lines in the desert.

I heard about your visit to his family. *"Go where you need to for you. But I'm not there. I'm all around, every/anywhere."*

"I'm one with the Earth."

"Breathe. Open Up. Feel. Release. Live."

I see him in baggy jeans and a red tee.

I also see a gas station in the desert with several motorcycles near pumps—one is clearer than the other two.

He's showing me a long cardigan sweater with big buttons...beige/brown.

He's showing me a cantaloupe behind some newspapers...seems like there's a small stove to the left and maybe a toaster to the right.

To confirm this message, I'm told that you'll see a large dark bird (vulture?) cross in front of a blazing sun and/or hear a chorus of crickets at dusk.

-Kimberly Dawn

Verifying what my friend saw/heard:

Fred says, *"Hello."*

The deadpan delivery of this opening had me laughing since that was all that seemed to come to mind to say to him over the past month. I believe I mentioned earlier in this book that I was sure he was getting tired of my constant greetings of "Hello" and "Hi," and it appears I was correct.

Fred showed me red grapes on the stem in a container on the table between two chairs. I sense desert brush. Quails.

He was clearly spying on me. This would be a setup at my campsite on any given day. Usually, at 1:00 p.m., with the quail wandering by.

He showed me three Burros amongst the brush. It's night. They're calling. One has a bright green pack on. ...for me means rebirth/growth/ nurturing. It's also representative of the heart chakra. Given the preceding portion of this message, he seems to be encouraging you to focus on yourself, specifically on trust and love.

But were the burros really out there? Or was I simply hearing things?

I heard about your visit to his family farm. *"Go where you need to for you. But I'm not there. I'm all around, every/anywhere."*

I was going to try to stop by his family farm in Cando and visit the bar where I bought his birthday dinner—to say thank you in person. But with the RV repairs I was experiencing on my way up to the Midwest in May and June, I never got up that way due to time constraints.

I see him in baggy jeans and a red tee.

What he was dressed in the morning of November 16, 2024, when he got back down to the desert.

I also see a gas station in the desert with several motorcycles near pumps—one is clearer than the other two.

I had just arranged to be out at Sturgis for the Bike Rally—this was later determined to be his sign for the Bike Rally he attended each year.

He's showing me a long cardigan sweater with big buttons...beige/brown.

I still haven't figured this one out. Unless he's talking about my winter coat, although he never saw it. He did have a zippered brown hoodie. ???

He's showing me a cantaloupe behind some newspapers...seems like there's a small stove to the left and maybe a toaster to the right.

He told me where my cantaloupe was in the RV. I had bought it, put it in a safe spot, and never saw it again. So for fun, I asked Kimberly to ask him where I put it, and he knew.

To confirm this message, I'm told that you'll see a large dark bird (vulture?) cross in front of a blazing sun and/or hear a chorus of crickets at dusk.

I saw the vulture two days earlier when I arrived at the Cactus Forest; granted, it wasn't flying, but that bird and I definitely locked eyes. As of the date of writing this book, though, I have seen countless large birds fly over. In regard to the crickets mentioned, that's coming up at the beginning of June 2025.

May 14, 2025:

Well, between not hearing much from him and reading Kimberly's message, my guess is he's done with me. I managed to scare one more person away. Great.

I read the email to my mom, and I gained greater clarity on the info. I didn't scare him away, but the info is broader than evidentiary.

May 21, 2025:

7:17 a.m. - Upon waking, I got a heavy sinking feeling in my chest, my body let go, and I saw the outline of a person (guessing Fred—had his stature and height). It transformed into a huge black bird, flew in front of me and up over my right shoulder, and then looped around at a higher altitude and disappeared to the left/behind me. Then the vision turned into a close-up, big black ant on a light brown ground—similar to what I was taking video of at the *Art City* installation north of Tucumcari, NM, a couple of days ago. Then the pressure on my chest abated, and my body came back.

May 22, 2025:

Talking with Fred, a spider web floated out in front of me, and it landed. (Since then, I've been very aware of cotton seeds and other light substances floating on the breeze.)

May 24, 2025:

An eagle swooped up on one side of the road, flew across, and then down on the other side. Talking to him and then saw the sign for Fredonia, KS.

Des Moines, IA

May 26, 2025:

Opening up my third eye before going to sleep, I saw the wind blowing left to right. Brown and dark green wisps over a gray background.

May 27, 2025:

Literally 11:11 p.m. - Instantly when getting into bed, the heaviness showed up in my chest, my body disappeared, and the (full body) tingling came in full force, starting at my stomach and flooding my body—complete with what looked like sparks from a fire flying up and sideways. I felt a presence and "walked" into it for a hug. There was a bit of an enveloping, but not exactly a hug. I started talking and thinking as fast as I could since I didn't know how long it would last—missing you, giving compliments, and thanking him for visiting and staying with me.

The visual sparks dissipated. He then stood in front of me, off to the right, and looked over his left shoulder at me with a smile—the "bear butt" picture smile (a reference to a photo in the montage his nephew made, where he was smiling in front of a bear's rear end)—silently asking, "Are you coming?" So I walked up to him and followed him through a rapid series of his different looks. Old to young and a variety of older pictures/flashes. Did that one and a half times, then the tinglies started wearing off. I asked him not to go, and he re-tingled me maybe twice. Afterward, I was feeling warm, comfortable, and loved. Then I fell asleep.

May 29, 2025:

Early morning visions and body numbing out—no tinglies, though. Didn't last long since the bladder was whining. Visions of black and white snapshots. Nature scenes and horizons—a couple of short ones of Fred. My mind was more on my complaining bladder.

12:12 p.m. - Saw your name pop up on the sidebar of my Facebook page. Got all excited for a fraction of a second and then remembered reality.

12:36 p.m. - I told you how much you are missed and, once again, said that I may have been stalking you. Then laughed and commented that we had at least one thing in common: We mutually stalked each other. Laughing with tears.

Admitted once again that I posted selfies solely for your benefit—definitely not for me. I posted Facebook Live videos to check that you were still stalking me. On the rare occasion that you liked one of my posts, it felt like getting a gold star—that I was still somewhere in your orbit.

May 31, 2025:

Trying for one more round of sleep, a quick blip this morning upon getting out of bed. A picture of who I assume was Fred (body and stance looked like Fred's), sitting in a chair, leaning forward, looking at me. I was sitting across from him, my hair down and my new hat on, smiling at him. There were two other guys in the room walking toward him, but they turned around to look at me (glanced over their shoulder) when he said this to me. "You're so pretty, but I have nothing to offer you."

I did inform him that, if that was him, thank you for the compliment; your time, company, and love are more than enough for me.

June 2, 2025:

Before calling it a day and going to sleep, taking this conversation into June 3rd to 1:30 a.m., I finally came clear on something that had been bothering me, full-blown crying and all, making myself understood.

Whether it's your words or Kimberly's words, or a combination of both, when I'm told that I need to be vulnerable and dissolve my wall, etc, to find the greatest love… I finally put into words what had been bothering me about that.

Over the course of June 1st and 2nd, I pointed out that although I respect(ed) you and your suggestions, I'm not going to be vulnerable for everyone in hopes of getting a man. The world is too dangerous for that naivete.

But last night, I made it clear that I have no problem finding someone else if they happen to wander by and I pick up on something. And yes, I showed my vulnerability with you. However, over the course of 2024, and especially after being ghosted on November 19, 2024, and on, my "vulnerability" got me exactly what it's gotten me every other time I allowed someone into my life: a big fat nothing and a whole lot of hurt.

So, it's not that I'm ignoring your suggestion, but I find it interesting how I did just that with you and wound up getting screwed over anyway. I now understand why that happened, and I appreciate the acknowledgment and the semi-apology. Still, that experience once again shows why I don't let many people in and why I operate the way I do. I have no problem with vulnerability (and whether that's your word or Kimberly's version of the Hallmark Channel word, I don't know.) But even you wound up proving my point with the whole "dissolving your wall issue."

Now, I'm not upset with you. I find it rather interesting that I'm getting advice from someone who ghosted me, but I understand.

I also have regrets that keep coming back to me because I was dense in December 2023, should have gone back to you in February and March 2024, regret not having the opportunity to put something together with you, or at the very least, had continued our friendship throughout the remaining months you were physically here, rather than the confusion and hurt experienced on my end.

Shoulda, woulda, coulda... no amount of regret is going to get that time back—no use in crying over that.

But yes, I may have chewed you a new one last night for hurting me the way you did, and now throwing the possibility of vulnerability into my face after what was done. Still, understanding the situation then and now, realizing you (now) are not what you were in human form, when you used your free will to push me away.

I finally fell asleep around 2:00 a.m. on June 3rd and experienced a sinking pressure in my chest then, and again when I woke up in the morning. Perhaps you were with me. I'd like to think you were.

I also requested that you don't leave me because I value your company and friendship—as I did when you were on Earth—and I admitted that we seem to spend more time together than we did in 2024, and definitely more compared to when you started ignoring me. I don't want to lose you again. (Ghosting, dying, and if you abandon me now...)

June 3, 2025:

7:30 a.m. - Upon waking this morning, and of course, thinking about you instantly (habit), I heard a light rock song from the late seventies, then it switched to Chris Stapleton's "Think I'm in Love With You," along with that heaviness in my chest, creeping in (you visiting). No tinglies, though.

I felt a quiet energy this morning, and I reiterated to you how much I love your company, even though I needed to get all of that off my mind last night. Still quiet throughout the day, but this afternoon (after you were missing from the sidebar of Facebook Friends online feed in the morning), you popped back up with everyone online. I made a post about it and how appreciative I am. I'm sure you probably know that. I do feel you near-by—and I'm sure you are just waiting for me to start talking to you again… (*Does she ever shut up???*)

I opened the door to get a little of the sunset—I had an urge to do the picture properly, and when I opened the door, I thought I heard tree frogs off in the distance. I commented on it and shut the door. Not five minutes later, they weren't tree frogs, they were a handful of crickets all right outside my door, wildly and loudly rubbing their back legs together.

I will add that I get quite a few birds out here and always watch them. I have some crows/grackles? They feed in the yard, right off my door. I talk with them. The breeze is light and welcomed when I'm sitting here.

You are always on my mind. Always.

9:30 p.m. - The synchronicities are freakin' wild and/or he's got "mad skillz" for pulling it all together into a tight web of hints and coincidences.

I just remembered one of the songs that popped into my head this morning while I was waking up and experiencing his energy (the heavy-chest kind, not the tinglies kind). So, I looked it up and watched the video. Back to full-blown tears with what I saw on the video (I've never seen this video, either—and it popped up at the top of the feed.) The song is Chris Stapleton's "Think I'm in Love With You."

The thing that really got me was when the little boy looked up and saw a "big black bird flying across the sun" with its shadow on the ground.

Combine that with having the urge this evening to get up and actually take a picture of the sunset out the door rather than through the window, then opening the door and thinking I was hearing treefrogs, only to voice that out loud (to Fred—he's the only one I talk with regularly... I'm sure he's thrilled), and not five minutes later, what I thought were treefrogs off in the distance was now a chorus of loud crickets right outside my door. I then told Fred that, and within five more minutes, the crickets subsided.

Why am I talking about crickets, sunsets, and large black birds flying across the sun? Because Fred told me he's in the sunsets, and I would see him as a big black bird flying against the sun, and he'd be in the chorus of crickets.*

Every day is something magickal. My life, in general, is rather magickal for many different reasons and in many different ways. But Fred brings the game. There's no doubt about that. He's impressive.

June 4, 2025:

Woke up to Moby's "Porcelain" playing in my head. I woke up to crickets and fell asleep to crickets. There was also a beautiful sunset this evening.

June 6, 2025:

Along with my belief that the universe likes to kick me when I'm down for its pure amusement, I will say these are the three things I learned from you:

1. That true love actually exists, and it's not a tagline to sell more Hallmark cards.
2. Teaching me about (physical) death and offering insight into the whole process and beyond.
3. Awakening the in-depthness of my spiritual journey.

It's not that I didn't know who I was or what I was capable of. It was that I didn't have many opportunities to meet others and open my heart. I know this exists, and my standards have naturally become higher. I know what is capable of happening, and unless someone crosses my path and exhibits those signs, I'm not going to think twice about whoever that person happens to be.

Rochester, MN

June 13, 2025:

Dream: I took a job/worked in the same area—near a park—Fred was nearby (working or not—not sure.) I knew him, and we had already hung out in

---

*These were the first crickets I've heard since meeting him, and I've been looking for a large black bird since he said this a couple of weeks ago.

some capacity. I had a sunburn on my shoulder, and Fred applied chocolate syrup to it. One of my kids also had a sunburn, and chocolate was applied to it. It worked.

Later, the first layer of skin on my pointer finger came off, and he cleaned it, applied salve, and bandaged it. I said thanks, but cut myself off before saying "Babe." While tending to my finger, he explained everything, plus a bit about physiology and cause and effect. I heard him talking, but was more in my head about him than what he was actually saying. I heard him, but was more into his presence—heard a few words but was more about looking at him and being with him.

He went about his job, and I decided to tell him I was about to call him "Babe." When I finally had the chance and did, he didn't say anything back and went for a walk to think things through.

I did tell him that people who mean a lot to me often are referred to as "Babe." He understood it, but I could see it freaked him out. The kids were with me, and they explained it, too.[*]

June 15, 2025:

After dropping off the RV in Oronoco, MN, for repair work, my daughter was driving when I happened to catch a hawk flying above the car. A couple of miles down the road, a lifted Lexus SUV passed us, and I was reminded of the lowrider picture Fred sent me from the Harbor Freight in Yuma. Not half a mile down, we passed Harbor Freight in Rochester. (Early on in January 2024, he texted me a picture of a low-rider parked at the Harbor Freight in Yuma; we had been talking about cars and car shows the night before.)

June 16, 2025:

4:40 p.m. - On the computer, the video for "Think I'm in Love With You" came up. Of course, I watched it and teared up. I noticed it was then 4:44 p.m. on the computer. Then, at 4:47 p.m., another cottonseed floated by as I looked out the window.

---

[*]My kids and any significant other I've ever had in my life—I've always referred to them as "Babe." It's a lifelong habit for me.

June 17, 2025:

Going to sleep, ran through hundreds of faces, then turned into Fred's face, both young and old with and without facial hair, a woodland/prairie area with an old barn/shed, 1800s, hiding inside while people outside—someone in a flatter cowboy hat came in and got me out. Looked behind me, and the building was on fire.

June 24, 2025:

Lots of synchronicities and black birds flying.

June 25, 2025:

I wrote this on your Facebook page for your birthday:

Kiersten Hall>Fred Nass

Happy Heavenly Birthday, Fred.

June 26, 2025:

A couple of flashes of light in my peripheral vision.

June 27, 2025:

A short cool breeze on the back left side of my neck while driving out of Rochester. No fans, but the window was cracked, and there was no wind while driving; the windows opened in front of me, not behind me.

June 29, 2025:

Astral traveled to my mom's house and saw her walking past the grandfather clock at 7:10 a.m. (later confirmed that's what she did at that time, that morning).

June 30, 2025:

This morning, I woke up to "Little China Girl" by David Bowie, then flipped to "Birds of a Feather" by Billie Eilish.

A genetic disorder that I believe was the root of Fred's many health issues popped up in my YouTube feed. My best friend in high school has it, and I briefly dated a guy in Illinois who has it. Fred exhibited a number of the markers. I never brought this up to him, and he never said anything, either. We mainly spoke about his heart issues, which is another marker for this genetic disease I'm pretty sure he had.

La Farge, WI

July 2, 2025:

I'm spending the week on sacred land. An eagle just showed up in my line of sight, soaring over my rig, riding on the currents. I'm listening to the blues, remembering the good times and the good company.[*]

July 4, 2025:

My third eye opened. Fred showed up, and I saw his memories/what he saw. Can't remember specifics.

Email from Kimberly Dawn,
who connected with Fred
on July 7, 2025:

Kiersten,

Apologies for the delayed follow-through. This week turned out to be a doozy. I did have some quiet time this morning and channeled Fred.

---

[*]Recently, Fred told me he'd appear as a large black bird soaring past the sun overhead. Can't get any bigger than an eagle in WI, unless I was on the west coast looking at a condor.

Initially, he showed me images I'd seen before: parked rigs, chairs, the desert floor, scrub brush, and a breeze. Warm breezes seem to be a recurring icon in his communications. He also showed me the large dark bird soaring across the sun. I take these images as confirmation of our connection.

He showed me you, and I felt a gentle love. He's always with you and also sees you living your life and is pleased/content, but I also felt some apprehension, then was shown a scorpion...like I was ground level with the scorpion. I found it confusing and jarring. Then, after a moment, a boot came down and squashed the scorpion. Still perplexed by the meaning, I asked Fred to clarify. He conveyed that he is acting as a guardian angel. You can live your life without feeling the need to keep your guard up. Trust yourself and know that you are protected.

This one I can't place, since it was blurry/out of focus... but the color purple and a spot of bright orange were very clear to me – no tangible imagery, though. Does that resonate with you at all? Or maybe it's symbolic.

From there, I asked him about the motorcycle gas pump scene and heard *"Sturgis."* If memory serves, you've been there before. Any memories with Fred from there?

I also asked for clarification about the hot dogs and saw both a fairground and an image of the two of you eating hot dogs. So, I don't think it's meant to be taken literally, but as a context for memories.

In many of the desert scenes, there's always a breeze that washes through from left to right. Often, the left is considered "the past" and the right "the future" – so there are several ways to interpret this. 1) Fred has already told us that his presence can be felt in the breeze. 2) The sweeping movement from left to right could connote the timeline of life. From the past to the future. Moving forward.

I hope all of this resonates.

Thanks, Kiersten. Hope you're well!

```
-  Kimberly  Dawn
```

Verifying what my friend saw/heard:

This one I can't place, since it was blurry/out of focus... but the color purple and a spot of bright orange were very clear to me — no tangible imagery, though. Does that resonate with you at all? Or maybe it's symbolic.

All I can think of are flowers that I have seen or spoken about.

From there, I asked him about the motorcycle gas pump scene and heard "Sturgis." If memory serves, you've been there before. Any memories with Fred from there?

I had not been to Sturgis yet, but had just arranged my trip for the 2025 event.

Sturgis, SD - Sturgis Bike Rally (pre-rally and during)

July 10, 2025:

On the first day at The Buffalo Chip, I was busy with something. Your photo montage song started in my head: "Dancing in the Sky" by Dani and Lizzy.

Later, I got a tour of the property and thought of you, so I mentioned you to one of the owners, who knew where Rhame was located, as she had grown up just over the border in South Dakota.

July 11, 2025:

Watched your photo montage and still cried.

July 12, 2025:

During my morning nap, I started with a close-up of a rod and reel, then down the pole, and ended up sitting in a boat on a mountain lake, surrounded by tall mountains and a partly sunny sky. Then it turned into looking out across rolling hills and land from a covered front porch. The porch and overhang were dark brown.

Then I started running through faces again. I saw two different versions of Fred flip by. When I see him, he usually comes across as himself standing there, but I ruin it by concentrating, and the picture disappears into someone else's face.

Recently, I noticed that visions appear almost like inverted X-rays, then fill out into normal-colored scenes/images. They are also short and in bursts, rather than long like they were a few months ago. I'm taking that as a sign that I really need to slow my brain down. I've also found that if I try to concentrate on something rather than simply viewing it, the vision disappears.

I watched a YouTube video regarding *Planetary Magick of Saturn*: Mind blown on this video regarding binding commitment and Saturn, which Fred brought up a couple of months ago. Also, it speaks of a guardian angel working with Saturn.

July 13, 2025:

Eyes open at 5:17 a.m. "Killing Me Softly With His Song" is playing in my head. I see and hear 123, 123—instantly think of the only picture I have of him and myself from the 2023 New Year's Eve event. Then I see a balding man in his forties or fifties, wearing shorts and an Izod, walking toward me on a desolate paved road while looking at his phone (not sure what that last vision means).

July 14, 2025:

I woke up at 5:17 a.m. again. The first song was Amy Weinstein's "I'm Trouble"; then I heard Sade's "The Sweetest Taboo," and it has been stuck in my head all day long. I spent the evening talking with Fred.

July 21, 2025:

Woke up this morning with the idea of not thinking about you today—see if I could do it. Failed miserably since the moment I said your name. I started thinking about you. Oh well.

Sade's "No Ordinary Love" began playing in my mind, and stuck around for the majority of the day.

Took a nap this evening, and my mind showed me many pictures of you, then morphed into other pictures that looked like you but in different periods' wear. Were you trying to show me different looks you've had over the years? Also channeled a song, The Weeknd's "Blinding Lights"—haven't heard it in a while.

August 5, 2025:

I took a quick nap, twenty minutes tops. I didn't sleep much. Finally fell deeply into the mattress and fell asleep, and saw a couple engaged in a deep kiss on a *Little House on the Prairie*-type porch. Got in closer to see, and it was a slight variation of Fred and me. Then it jumped to the present day, and we were in our forties and still going at it. Hot and heavy—good grief, he's a good kisser!*

It turned into something slightly older with different locations/situations, but then I started questioning it, and it was gone. Wondering if that was live or fiction? Never had that thought before—not so directly.

He showed up, he initiated, he kept it going, with his different smiles. Huh…

Darn near every morning, I'm picking up feathers at Sturgis—all mourning doves—one of my favorites. I put them all in my mandala.

August 8, 2025:

An antlered buck showed up as I was falling asleep. Looked at me, then disappeared.

---

*I'll point out that Fred and I were never physically intimate, nor have I ever in the last fifty-six years before writing this book had a sexually-charged dream about anyone. Dull, I know, but I have other pressing matters to think about. Plus, before Fred's death, I rarely dreamed—and if I did, I rarely (and I mean, rarely) remembered them. Everyone who suggested I keep a "dream journal," I would laugh at them. There was never anything to write. My sleep was blanking out in a dark void.

August 9, 2025:

"Think I'm in Love With You" (Chris Stapleton) popped up on my music streaming service, and later, I went for a walk around what was left open at The Buffalo Chip. I was going to take a different route to the bar, but my intuition told me to go the usual route, across the grass and then up the pavement. Walking up to the end booth, I heard the same song, and no matter how far I got past the booth—up to fifty feet (?), I could still hear the song at the same level as if I were standing right next to it, so I walked back and listened to the rest of "Think I'm in Love With You."

Rhame, ND - Fred's property

August 11, 2025:

Before leaving Belle Fourche, SD, I asked Fred if he would send me either Moby or Chris Stapleton before getting to his house. I pulled onto Hwy 12 heading toward Rhame, and as I was making that left-hand turn, Moby's "Porcelain" came on. He came through. I was impressed and in tears as I headed west toward the "Ouzo Capital of North Dakota," as Fred claimed it to be.

Turned into Rhame, and two mourning doves flew in front of me and landed on the railroad tracks off to the side. Welcome to Rhame.

I spoke with Fred's neighbor for the better part of an hour. He gave me some petrified wood, and I gave him that large chunk of milky quartz from Dome Rock, Quartzsite, AZ.

Spoke with the wife of the couple who bought Fred's property. Got permission to sleep in Fred's yard. I had to break out pictures to prove to her that I wasn't full of it, since she knew Fred to be a loner.

Had Ouzo at the Waterhole Bar, spoke to people who spoke highly of him.

I feel at home and very safe in his yard. Very comfortable.

10:15 p.m. - My internet just cut out. I was going to watch *Clueless*, and then nothing. Was it bedtime in Fred's yard? The timing would track for what he told me was his schedule when he was employed.

August 12, 2025:

Spent some time in his yard looking at the variety of flora and the bunnies hopping around out there. Peeked in the windows and did a short video of my visit. It reminded me a lot of my house in New York Mills, and I really didn't want to leave. I was very comfortable out there. *(video)*

Mt. Pleasant, MT

August 13, 2025:

Saw Fred's doppelganger at a truck stop in Mt. Pleasant, MT. Blown away and took countless pictures. I spoke with this couple (his wife was with him), and I showed them pictures of Fred, and they were blown away, too. Found out his surname is Olin. His grandfather, Fred Olin, married Dorothy Tower. Oscar Oberg was an uncle of theirs. Obergs lived south of Washburn, ND. (These older named relatives have since passed away, according to this person.)

Idaho Falls, ID - Harvest Host Location

August 15, 2025:

I asked Fred to talk to me or touch me.

Last night, around 3:00 a.m., while I was trying to get back to sleep, Fred hugged me. He showed up, smiled, sat beside me, and I could feel him by my side. We sat in silence, then he stood up, and I stood up, and I walked to him, and he pulled me to him and wrapped me in a full bear hug. After a bit, I wrapped my arms around him and hugged him, too. I could feel the hug and him. Then I fell into a deep sleep for two hours. It was lovely.

Arimo, ID - Hawkins Reservoir Campground (BLM)

August 16, 2025:

Took two gummies rather than sticking to one—had a lapse of reasoning and forgot how to do mathematical equations, and slept for a couple of days… Oops!

Bed at 10:00 p.m. on the sixteenth and now up at 10:00 a.m. on the eighteenth, Monday morning. Overall, I slept all night on the sixteenth, then for another twelve hours on the seventeenth, and nine hours on the eighteenth.

Had two experiences of shutdown—one while lying down and one while standing up—had so little oxygen in me that I was shaking uncontrollably. Both times, two bars of dark black and yellow thin rods of air shot through my RV—in by the driver's seat and diagonally toward me—and settled my heart long enough to breathe and stop shaking.

These bars also came in with a thunderous, incredibly loud, driving roar. It was a quick jab of air from these two prongs. The sound alone would wake you up. It was almost as if someone had increased the bass from someone shouting "NO!" over a long period of time.

Got packed up and out of there by noon. Moby's "Porcelain" was the third song playing as I left the Hawkins Reservoir, headed toward the 2025 Burning Man Festival.

August 24 - September 1, 2025:

Burning Man 2025—couldn't bring myself to go to the Temple. I wasn't going to say "goodbye" to you, so there was no reason for me to go. The magnetized 2025 pocket calendar, displaying March 2025, still sits over my stove. I hate that calendar.

Oddly enough, I didn't get any communication from him while at Burning Man. I felt his presence, but didn't get any messages or anything. (He did tell me in April 2026, through Kimberly, that he didn't like Burning Man and had nothing to say about it.)

Alamo, NV - Pahranagat National Wildlife Refuge

September 2, 2025:

Bird across the late afternoon sky.

Spent a while scrolling on the phone when I first got to the campsite, and my mind was niggling at me to go on a walk, but I ignored it while sitting at the picnic table. A strong gust of wind suddenly hit me, and I heard, "Go for a walk." So, I did, and collected two sticks and one chalk rock. *(video)*

Bullhead City, AZ - RV Park

September 3, 2025:

Morning: Before leaving the campsite just outside of Alamo, NV, (north of Las Vegas), there was a nice shot coming up, but I was going to drive by. My mind said to stop and take the picture, but, figuring I had enough pictures of mountains and lakes, I continued driving. Suddenly, my phone shuts off the music, and I hear "take the picture." So, I stopped, took the picture, turned the music back on, and continued driving out of the park.

6:30 p.m. - Listening to Billie Eilish, "Birds of a Feather." At the line "Until I die…' the song faded, and then the phone stopped streaming. When I turned it back on, the next song was "Strange Effect" by Unloved.

7:00 p.m. - Lots of dragonflies showed up this evening.

Phoenix, AZ - RV Resort

September 5, 2025:

Rather than heading to Quartzsite for the winter months (2025-2026 season), I had decided after he passed away that I needed a break from Quartzsite, so I signed on as a seasonal at the RV Resort I had visited in April/May. I intended to stay from September 2025 to May 2026.

Arrived at the resort and, while driving in, wondered where I could put Fred's bowl while parked for the winter—somewhere where it wouldn't get damaged but somewhere I could get to see it every day. The nightstand popped into my head. It looks great there. I joke with him about it, asking, "Did you ever think this bowl would be on a nightstand, in the back corner of an RV owned by someone you knew for less than fifteen months, parked at a resort in Phoenix when you made it?"

September 6, 2025:

Meltdown this afternoon and evening. Not horrible but not doing great, either.

September 7, 2025:

Vision this morning of a Spanish Villa on fire with a blue car (early to mid sixties) parked out front.

The line: It's a blessing to have been considered a friend by him rather than nothing at all—a variation of it.

September 9, 2025:

Coming up with titles for this writing: *An Unexpected Journey*

September 10, 2025:

Video for Moby's "Porcelain" showed up—I've never seen this one— nature shots. Lots of angel numbers were spotted between September 8th and September 11th.

September 11. 2025:

Video for "I Think I'm in Love With You" by Chris Stapleton popped up.

September 12, 2025:

Six months today.

Sade's "No Ordinary Love" started off the day.

Fred stopped by this evening while getting to sleep. Today was very sad, lots of weepiness.

Rather than going numb to begin with, my body felt as if it were shrinking and withering like a dried-up branch, and then my consciousness expanded. Hard to explain, but my mind/awareness expanded past my physical self. It was weird. Interesting but odd.

Then Fred showed up in a stark white room, smiling, wearing his shoes, jeans, a brown plaid shirt, and a cap. I told him that I had hoped I hadn't overstepped any boundaries with visits, that he was doing well, and that I had asked for a hug and gotten one, but it wasn't as intense as the one I had gotten a few weeks prior. I thanked him for his companionship—and told him I appreciated it.

September 13, 2025:

The more I think about it—and it randomly pops into my head at the oddest times—the vulture I saw out at the Cactus Forest was probably Fred. I locked eyes with it—honed right in on it and only it, much like what I did with Fred when I first met him. Shortly after that, Kimberly told me about the soaring black bird, which might be a vulture.

I locked eyes with it for a smattering of seconds, then looked down and then back up, and it was gone. Because it keeps coming to mind, I tend to believe there was something to it all.

Saw a couple of big black birds flying on the thermals today while sunbathing. One even went over enough to cast a shadow on me.

Every day out at the pool, there's always a little breeze when I need it. Maybe?

September 14, 2025:

Seeing lots of birds on thermals and casting shadows. One even managed to get a shadow on the bottom of the storage unit over the bed. My RV is backed up against a wall of oleander. (Explain the physics on how that happened. ???)

September 15, 2025:

I woke up talking to Fred, and after half an hour or so, he visited me with full-body tingles. I have become more in tune with him being nearby or about to go into tingle mode when my chest and stomach sink, and then my body goes numb… then it waves into tingles, normally starting in the legs, though he has entered around the neck before, too.

When it happens, I'm so happy that all I can mumble is thank you, miss you, love you, and appreciate you. After all of that, this morning, I apologized for being so damn tongue-tied. You smiled. This vision of you is the 2023/24 desert look.

You appeared in a bright white light. I got rather mopey for a second, and it went to a dark matte brown. I apologized, tried to be happy again, and the white light returned.

I did ask how you enjoyed Sturgis and Burning Man, though. I am still waiting for a report on those questions.

During the afternoon, out at the pool, slight wisps of a breeze and two noisier-than-average mourning doves flew over the pool, about twelve feet off the top of my head. (On account of the mourning doves, I don't feel I'm grasping here.)

September 16, 2025:

Waking up, my mind went back to its favorite subject: What did I do wrong to make you run on November 18, 2024, besides the obvious result? To make you ignore me? The answer I came up with this morning was that the doctors probably gave you a "less than a year to live" diagnosis, and you came down to sew up loose ends and spend your last winter in the desert. I'm going to guess when you and I started making plans for future events, stretching into spring—for example, the boat races (and now looking back, you did get silent with that short conversation)—you knew you weren't going to be around; that spring wasn't promised. I bet that's when you decided to cut and run. I understand that now, but I wish that had all been divulged last November and you hadn't cut me out of your life.

Thinking about it, the lack of oxygen I experienced in Idaho is the same as no oxygen with COVID. (I'm sorry, Fred—it was not my intention.)

Revelation Facebook entry:

```
It only took six months and a few days to figure
out/put the final pieces together of why/when
he decided to ghost me the last four months of
his life.

   It was when we settled into our usual banter
around the campfire on 11/18/24. He brought
up our winter calendar of activities, and I
confirmed that I was already scouting and had a
list. He promptly took out his phone and start-
ed looking up events, locations, and dates.
Some of those event dates stretched into the
spring of '25.

   Put a pin in that thought. ^^^

   In the winter of '23/'24, he was not feeling
well but kept up as well as he could, when he
could. On his good days, when we were camping
together, we'd do things. On his not-so-good
days, he slept in his rig, and I worked in mine.
```

May of '24, when he finally got back to North Dakota, it was determined that his heart was only putting out twenty to twenty-five percent of oxygen with each pump. In essence, he needed a heart transplant, which was brought up in the summer of '23 at that doctor's appointment. He went in every six months.

While texting over the summer of '24, he told me he wouldn't be returning to Arizona because of his health issues. I told him that, obviously, I was bummed out, but I understood.

He was the type of person who not only held his cards close to his chest but also enjoyed surprising people, which he did with me quite often. He loved the happiness shown when giving, and I didn't disappoint with my reactions during those times. (I'll add, most of the time it was pure kindness, little gestures—those are really what mean the most.) In this vein, he told me in September 2024 that he wasn't coming down, but at the beginning of November 2024, he began posting pictures of his next adventure with little to no description. I knew his standard route to and from Arizona, and holy hell, Fred was coming to Arizona!!! Hot damn! (That line, for me, blows past any other good and happy lines I've ever heard in my life, that's for sure; besides the health of my kids—standard disclaimer.)

The doctors must have figured out his meds, and he got the "all-clear" to travel, and hot damn! As I said, he wasn't typing in many captions, if any. But each day, he posted another picture of his travels, and I could pinpoint each one. I could track his ETA—dependent on how long he'd stay in Overton, NV—not that I was stalking him in any capacity... (insert whistling and eye averting)—he stalked me, too! Gah!

Anyway, he spent only three days in Overton, whereas he normally spent two to three weeks (he basically moved every three weeks or whenever he had to empty his tanks). He reiterated that to me in November. He said the weather and the wind were dictating it, but one weather system wouldn't last three weeks. I knew better.

Then he arrived in Quartzsite, and the universe went into full synchronicity mode, including having us cross paths a handful of times over three days, in addition to the times we planned to meet up. It was getting funny. Oddly weird and funny.

He came over on the eighteenth. We had a campfire, started talking and making plans, and I saw him shift, then go a bit silent. He wrapped up the campfire after ninety minutes (our campfires usually last four to six hours), and literally drove away out of my life. The universe had us bump into each other one more time before it was established that I was never going to hear from him again. He ignored me and pretended not to see me. He didn't return any more texts or phone messages. What in the hell had I done?

Seriously, what had I done?

In reality, I've been wondering about this question since about November twenty-first, when he stopped returning texts. Then the twenty-third, when our paths crossed and he blatantly ignored me, and then the twenty-fifth, when I laid it all out on the line—bared my heart and soul, which I'm sure was pretty obvious to anyone; even waitstaff would ask us how long we had been married—it was ridiculous. He wrote back the next day, telling me that if it weren't for his pacemaker, he would have died during the summer of '24 (and I remember seeing one of his Facebook videos—end of July—where he looked unwell, ashen gray, skinnier than a few weeks prior—he'd been through the health ringer.) He told me I was spot on with some of my observations and way off base with others (which I had incorrectly surmised and ruined my chance of spending time with him even more—clearly a mortal mistake that I kick myself over every day.)

But I will never regret baring my soul and stating the obvious. You'd have to be an inanimate object hidden away in a dark box in a dark closet not to have noticed what an idiot, blubbering, doe-eyed, hearts-aflutterin', nim-witted, tripping-over-myself, fool I was when he was nearby. But I will say, I thought I did a damn good job covering up my true feelings when he wasn't near me—I easily reverted into "hard-ass, stay away from me, Kiersten." It's a comfortable feeling for me. I do it well.

But if I were anywhere near Fred, it would revert to the embarrassment described above. (My gawd, Kiersten actually *does* have emotions. Huh...)

Anyway, going back to the info in the first two paragraphs, I believe he came down to Arizona for winter rather than sitting in North Dakota (he clearly still had his mental faculties to make that decision), and he came down for the sunsets, the warmth, the relaxation, for friends… and for me.

I only wish that I had known the inside secret of his limited lifespan. I found out after the fact that he didn't want me to remember him from his last few months, but rather when he and I were hanging out, and we both wished we had met earlier in life—one of our many conversations in the desert. Since he was in North Dakota and I was in Minnesota, we knew about a lot of the same things and places.

There was more I was going to add, but my mind just blanked. It's gone. Well, if I remember, I'll add it. If not, whatever. It was the explanation of another question/situation I worked through, but I can't recall it now. It's associated with this whole mess, but I can't remember.

In April of '24, he saw one of my videos about antelope and told me ranchers refer to them as "speed goats." I think that's a funny term; it makes me giggle. Don't know why, just does. I had been telling him about all the times "speed goats" had made me laugh throughout the summer. Not always appropriate times to have the giggles, either.

This, I believe, was his formal notice to me that he was heading south, if I hadn't figured it out prior.

I'll add, I'm not making stuff up/grasping, either. This is actually a good percentage of how we communicated; sure, we talked with words, but the conversation was peppered with curiosity and discovery. It was a unique and fascinating way to converse—a heck of a lot more interesting than mundane chatter.

I remember what the last thing was: I have figured out what makes me the saddest, besides him being by himself and having to decide at the age of sixty-two to shut down the party because of his body. The sadness for me is knowing that there was an opportunity for a deep, meaningful, and mind-blowing relationship, but that it would never be entertained seriously. Stunted before anything could ever happen. A chance down the shitter. Not just for me, but also him, and us—the "current" us and the "what-could-have-been" us.[*]

---

[*]Regarding the picture I had pinned on the Facebook post and its caption: He was in southern Wyoming for the shot, and the remark was directed to me about "speed goat" anything. (It was an empty mug of "Speed Goat Ale" at a bar in Green River, WY.)

September 17, 2025:

First morning since November 2024, when I didn't wake up crying about this whole situation and wondering what I did to make you leave and never talk to me again. Refreshing, to say the least. I'm glad I figured it out. Sad it took so long, but it all makes sense now.

I thanked Fred again for sticking with me, communicating with me, giving me wondrous gifts of time and shared experiences, and telling me that he loves me. I can't begin to tell you how much that means to me.

This evening, I sat down and watched several of Fred's videos from Facebook. Shared some to my Facebook page with commentary. Spent a good one and a half hours doing this. When I shut it down to move on to something else, the little desk fan that had been keeping me cool the entire time shut off. I checked the Bluetti, and it was still at seventy-six percent, but the D/C power button was no longer on. Who turned it off? I'm blaming Fred.

A lot of tarot spreads sound a lot like Fred again.

For some background, a few months prior, I had expanded on some concerns I had about a person I had met in May and asked for his opinion before going to sleep. I mentioned again that if I don't have enough clues that he's "approving" of this older-male-wannabe-suitor, by what this older-male-wannabe-suitor says, does, etc., then it's not happening. Not that I'm a needy, whiny, clingy person, but I believe Fred has good intentions for me, and I respect his opinion. (I was already unamused by this older-male-wannabe-suitor and was beginning to push him away. It's not a good sign at the beginning of a potential relationship to look forward to the other person going away, and feeling inconvenienced when that person wants to hang out every day.)

I'll add, this guy's son had invited him to live with their family in Texas, and while with me, he vacillated between staying in Arizona and going to Texas—he had even asked me to move to Texas with him. I shut that idea down and started lightly swaying him to see how good a move to Texas would be for him. I was pushing this guy out of my life, but wanted Fred's back-up to make sure I wasn't pushing out someone I shouldn't have been.

I really enjoyed seeing all of Fred's videos last night. Heals my heart, especially with my newfound revelation of how everything went down.

September 18, 2025:

Weepy at times, but for the most part, another Thursday.

Thursday evening, while walking from the pool to the hot tub, I noticed a person in my peripheral vision (I didn't see them directly; I just noticed an individual in the corner of the pool, similar to how one might notice a table in a corner). That person then appeared in the hot tub, and I talked with them and others. There were many similarities, but there was no attraction or connection. This is what I tell Fred: I need that connection and electricity. This person tried to be suave, offering compliments and engaging in conversation, but I didn't feel a connection. (I want a connection that I notice.)

September 19, 2025:

Early morning dreams/visions were intense: Slept a few more hours this morning and got to enjoy a heavy makeout session with Fred—felt sensation and everything—both directions. Good grief, he's a good kisser, among other things—if anything, my mind has exulted him to that level if that's not in fact the case.

This morning, talking with Fred, I told him that I need the connection with the next person—I need the *"full Fred experience."* If there isn't a connection, energy in the air, and with touch, the synchronicities, the everything, then I'm not interested. I'm stubborn, and my standards have increased exponentially since Fred. So… it's Fred's fault.

I also realized/shared that, from the moment I saw him get out of that truck, I equated everything about him with his face (obviously). My soul made that connection; my subconscious labeled him as "home" (comfort, safety, and somewhere I wanted to be), so that's why I stare at him all the time, memories or not. Looking up and seeing the rest of the world brings anxiety. Pictures and videos of Fred bring peace and tranquility, although there are a fair number of sad times, too, done by both of us—lack of communication and how it was handled.

10:03 a.m. - Right as I'm typing, after I said I needed lots of signs regarding this older-male-wannabe-suitor, this individual calls and tells me he's been staying with a female friend at another resort in California during his surgery and recovery. He'll be back here today, and she's coming with, staying for a couple of days, then flying out on Sunday afternoon. Talk about a "sign" of where that relationship is going! (I'm laughing) I asked if this was my "notice" to not expect or initiate anything physical upon his arrival? And he sputtered, "Well, not until after Sunday afternoon." Damn near had it to the exact time. LOL. Yeah, this older-male-wannabe-suitor is a good-time guy, and I don't blame him at his age. Why not? Don't get tied down—got it. I had already started urging him to move to Texas with his son. So, there you go.

September 20, 2025:

Knocking is a spirit touchpoint, and I know I've heard at least two succinct knocks over the course of the past few months.

The litmus test of one of Chris Stapleton's songs, "Think I'm In Love With You," failed greatly right before the dance tonight. I'm in tears.

Good? Anything negative with men, I simply think of Fred, and I'm good. It resets me.

September 21, 2025:

First morning thought: Was L.M. his "sidepiece" specifically for the rallies—a formal or informal arrangement? Would explain "loyalty." Otherwise single, but not really?

After breakfast, a nap gave me a straight-on instant multitude of faces/ bodies from different periods and situations. I got the feeling that I was seeing all of the "Freds" throughout time.

Willie Nelson—"Always on My Mind." Started from the first line and continued through. Listened to each line, intently—more than I ever have in the past. Tears.

And I really didn't remember this point until I clicked on a random video a bit ago, and the mention of Willie Nelson came up about 1985 Farm Aid. That's what jogged my brain, although I had promised myself that I would remember it from my bed to my office, and still forgot about it during that time.

I watched a tarot video tonight that I can only imagine probably matches Fred.

September 22, 2025:

"No Ordinary Love" by Sade started off the morning.

The radio came on when it was off while I was waiting for this older-male-wannabe-suitor, in his RV, to come back from the bathroom. He claimed he'd turned it off, but it flipped back on by itself: The first time it switched on by itself, and the second time—after I had turned down the volume, the volume turned back up by itself. I asked Fred if this was him and felt a strong "Yes."

I figured out the lesson Fred was here to teach me, besides absolute true love: I watched two videos while eating breakfast, and the second one made me cry so hard I had to stop. The result? Love myself as much as I love Fred and others. And this is true—I give to and love others—the chosen few—so much, but never show myself the same. I learned early on that my worth was always tied to something: what I could do for my family, others, work, etc. If I did nothing, or less than desired, I wasn't worth anything (hence, the overachiever in me). I also don't give myself things. I make myself happy with memories, second-hand, used, etc., and never do things for myself. I also (...one other thing I can't remember right now).

Who is Kiersten? Show Kiersten's authentic self. Choose you—elevate Kiersten. Build your own foundation (including financial), sage your space. Incense for calm. The final cards pulled: Fool and Chariot—Aquarius and Cancer. At around the twenty-minute mark, my computer briefly froze up, glitched, and didn't fully reset, causing the open pages to time out.

September 23, 2025:
Found a feather under this older-male-wannabe-suitor's lawn chair.

September 24, 2025:
Ran across Nass Auto in Phoenix—faintly remember Fred bringing this up. Exotic Sports Cars.

September 26, 2025:
Morning nap, Fred popped up vision-wise. I said "Hi," and a gust of wind hit the side of the RV. A montage of his faces, and then I fell asleep.

A song popped into my head, late sixties—what's the song?

September 28, 2025:
A large bird was flying out at the pool; it disappeared when I noticed it, then showed up about ten minutes later, after I had asked Fred to come back.

I noticed and watched a bird while listening to the "Boys of Summer" by Don Henley. Got wistful and weepy. I miss Fred.

Starlink Launch tonight—memories.

September 29, 2025:

A lot of angel numbers over this past week. I really started noticing them today. Is this Fred, the universe, or Spirit Goddess? Saw a tarot reading recently where angel numbers and synchronicities were mentioned—that there would be a lot of them.

September 30, 2025:

A gust of wind came across the pool area—I made mention of a front coming in, but there were no clouds, and only that one gust.

Later that evening, I realized the gust was probably Fred saying "Hi," and my heart was happy. I told him of my intentions with this older-male-wannabe-suitor and that I still very much like and love him (Fred). He's still my number one choice. Good grief, I miss him!

October 1, 2025:

The first song up on Pandora is Chris Stapleton's "Think I'm In Love with You."

A few songs in, Pandora quit. Everything was fine, but it just quit.

It stopped again, but the next song on was Chris Stapleton's "Without Your Love."

I think Fred is nearby.

Another thirty minutes, and "South Dakota" plays.

Every thirty minutes or so, another Chris Stapleton song plays—the last one is "Loving You on My Mind."

October 2 - 4, 2025:

Synchronicities, songs, angel numbers up the wahzoo. Not so much on visions, but I've been tired and not sleeping well.

October 5, 2025:

I was invited to a rock-crawling adventure. Went into the Mesa trailhead (burros) and as we were driving in, Fred's life montage song came on the radio, became louder (to me), so it drowned out the engine I was right in front of. Then I saw a large black bird fly overhead, running its shadow across the road in front of us. During the break, farther out into the back country, I was standing there, at a distance from the rest, and a gust of wind hit only me. I had a feeling he was along for the ride that day. *(videos)*

October 6, 2025:

I asked Kimberly to get a hold of you on the tenth. I'm looking forward to hearing from you.

October 9, 2025:

Moby—"Porcelain" came on within two songs of talking to Fred.

I thanked him for knocking on my roof—three knocks, followed by two, then nothing. Looked out the window, and there was nothing. Didn't hear anything above or below my rig.

Angel numbers up the wahzoo again—warms my heart. Before the knocking and hearing Moby, I had this overwhelming feeling that he was watching me wash the dishes. After I "outed" him, that's when Moby came on two songs later.

**Email from Kimberly Dawn,
who connected with Fred
on October 10, 2025:**

Automatic writing is proving to be a great way to communicate.

Everything in *"quotes"* is the direct message as I heard it. In parentheses are what he showed me. Otherwise, it's a description of what I felt/saw/knew. I truly hope these resonate!

Reading – October 10, 2025

"I'm having fun. In the breeze, crickets (showing me dry brush and donkeys and small birds flying). Knock knock, flickering lights, wind. All me."

STURGIS

"I was there. (showing me the gas station scene from before-apparently a symbol for Sturgis) I see it all.

Engines, the smell of the oil/exhaust. Packed diners, baskets with hamburgers and fries, beer, crowd noise, the smell of leather, music. Your smile. It's funny watching men come on to you. They don't stand a chance. Thanks for going, Babe."

BURNING MAN

NOTE: For this one, he didn't *"say"* much. It's like he doesn't want to talk about it. He's relaying what he sees and how he feels being there instead. He is showing me a bonfire in the dark, with trees nearby. I feel sort of like I'm in a clearing in a woodsy/camping area...not real deep in the forest though. He's conveying a feeling of this being a sort of peaceful, communal, sacred space. And, like being in a library, it'd be disrespectful to break the energy with voice. It seems that, for him, this is an experience you feel rather than verbally describe. There's a meditative quality. People sitting quietly and relaxed in a circle, swaying... maybe to music. He enjoys just being there–soaking up the vibe. Maybe this is an event he likes to immerse himself in and observe rather than participate in or be at the center of. Does that make sense?

ROCK CRAWLING

"Geesh." (He's showing me a rocky outcrop with boulders that sort of make a ridge, with a pretty view beyond. It's sunny, dry, but not oppressively hot.) I'm getting a *"I'm glad we did it, but never again"* feeling from him.

"You always lost your chips (he's showing me a Lays bag with a red clip on it.) *Put them in the same place each time."*

"I like seeing you adjusting to life – treasuring memories but moving forward. You still need to chill sometimes. Just be. Listen. You don't have to control everything. Let your guard down. You're safe. I won't let anything bad happen to you, my love. Buddies for life. (He's showing me your two chairs, on a throw rug with the table in between. Camper in the background.) *You can't get rid of me. Keep smiling and talking to me. I love it and will respond."*

    NOTE: I feel like, if you ask him, he'll leave you physical signs/symbols...like a feather, a stone, or something small – to confirm your connection.

"Tell her that she should follow through on the decision she's been pondering. It will be good for her in the long run. She doesn't need to hold back. Everything will be alright. I love her."

- Kimberly Dawn

Verifying what my friend saw/heard:

STURGIS

"I was there. (showing me the gas station scene from before—apparently a symbol for Sturgis) I see it all. Engines, the smell of the oil/exhaust. Packed diners, baskets with hamburgers and fries, beer, crowd noise, the smell of leather, music. Your smile. It's funny watching men come on to you. They don't stand a chance. Thanks for going, Babe."

Of this message, the biggest thing that stood out to me was his calling me "Babe." This term is something I use for every one of my kids and typically my significant other. As he's been hanging around with me, he's definitely heard that term when I've spoken to my kids on the phone or in person. And a couple of months ago, I documented a vision in which I stopped myself from calling him "Babe" when I was talking to him, then later admitted it to him, and he walked away, seeming to ponder what I just said. (This entry is written on June 3, 2025, in this book.)

BURNING MAN

NOTE: For this one, he didn't "*say*" much. It's like he doesn't want to talk about it. He's relaying what he sees and how he feels being there instead. He is showing me a bonfire in the dark, with trees nearby. I feel sort of like I'm in a clearing in a woodsy/camping area...not real deep in the forest though. He's conveying a feeling of this being a sort of peaceful, communal, sacred space. And, like being in a library, it'd be disre-

spectful to break the energy with voice. It seems that, for him, this is an experience you feel rather than verbally describe. There's a meditative quality. People sitting quietly and relaxed in a circle, swaying... maybe to music. He enjoys just being there—soaking up the vibe. Maybe this is an event he likes to immerse himself in and observe rather than participate in or be at the center of. Does that make sense?

He actually showed a Fourth of July camping trip I was on with some friends in Wisconsin. Burning Man is definitely not swaying to music in a forest... well, maybe swaying to music, but there's no forest to be seen.

*Between the events attended, the traveling, and the RV repairs, I can understand why he'd get confused. I get confused, too.**

ROCK CRAWLING

"Geesh." (He's showing me a rocky outcrop with boulders that sort of make a ridge, with a pretty view beyond. It's sunny, dry, but not oppressively hot.) I'm getting a *"I'm glad we did it, but never again"* feeling from him.

We had talked about rock-crawling/mudding while he was still alive, and how I would definitely go again, and how I should definitely have my own RZR—imagine how much fun I could have then! He was definitely along for the ride that day: Besides feeling his presence, his photo montage song blipped into the streaming music and darn near drowned out the engine noise; a large black bird flew overhead. And the video glitched while driving into the BLM area.

"You always lost your chips (he's showing me a Lays bag with a red clip on it.) *Put them in the same place each time."*

I asked Kimberly to ask him where I put my chip bag. I found it a day before and told Kimberly to hold off on asking, but he's still pointing out my (lack of) domestic organization skills in this message. By the way, the Lays bag is my Limon chips, and my chip clip is red.

---

*Found out on the April 21, 2026 connection, he didn't like Burning Man and has nothing to say about it.

NOTE: I feel like, if you ask him, he'll leave you physical signs/symbols... like a feather, a stone, or something small — to confirm your connection.
I have more feathers, rocks, and types of wood in this RV than I know what to do with. He definitely delivers.

"Tell her that she should follow through on the decision she's been pondering. It will be good for her in the long run. She doesn't need to hold back. Everything will be alright. I love her."
This message was in regard to cutting the older-male-wannabe-suitor loose and out of my life for good.

Driving around Anthem, AZ, Ronnie Milsap's "No Getting Over You" was on the radio when I flipped to that station. Although I knew he hadn't arranged it, I got the feeling he would still have sent it.

10:33 p.m. - Barry White—"Never, Never Gonna Give You Up" (Pandora)

October 12, 2025:
Got a couple of hard knocks on the RV this morning. Fred claims it's him.

October 13, 2025:
First video watched—MIND BLOWN. Well, then. Arcturus, Pluto, underworld, lesson, level up, etc. Covers the last six plus months, in my case, and this older-male-wannabe-suitor solidified my decision: Never the BS, only the real thing. Talk about a one-eighty between this older-male-wannabe-suitor and Fred. I also told Fred that he is the ONLY man I haven't blocked out of my life. And that I needed the two weeks with this older-male-wannabe-suitor to get a car and to "make nice" while he was here. (I only had an RV to drive around, and needed someone with a car to bring me to the car dealerships.)

October 14, 2025:
A couple of softer knocks around the RV.

October 15, 2025:

Visions of outboard boating on mountain lakes.

"No Ordinary Love" by Sade started off the day.

October 16, 2025:

I told Fred I was going to start referring to him as "Babe," too. He started it with the last Kimberly communique.

October 17, 2025:

Pandora streaming suddenly stopped. The birds were particularly loud and joyous in the trees. Light breeze out at the pool. Decision made to go to Palm Springs in a week, and finally take him on the aerial tram.

October 18, 2025:

"Communication with (Fred) was effortless, like it was something we were continuing from long ago." A true line taken from proofing someone else's book now.

October 19, 2025:

Stepped out of the RV today and found a perfectly pristine mourning dove feather right off my step. Out at the pool, the song "Passionate Kisses" by Lucinda Williams played (played yesterday, and I made a comment about it). Before it started, the birds were unusually loud and joyous in the tree; then they faded out, and the music began. At that point, a light but steady wind rippled across the top of my body (I was on the lounge chair)—lasted a couple of bars, then went still again. When I did get up, I focused on some nearby still flowers. I asked Fred if he could move them, and before I could finish my sentence, the flowers started moving, although there wasn't much of a breeze—I was sitting right next to them. After the one I was looking at started, the rest of the flower bed joined in. Still no wind. He is impressive. That's for sure.

October 22, 2025:

Knocks upon waking, otherwise it was a fairly quiet day, but all I did was work—didn't get out of the rig once. I like full hookups.

But... It's become a habit: I arrive in Quartzsite at this time of year, and I have space all around. My nearest neighbor is *wayyyyyyyyyyyyy over there*, not ten feet away.

But... then I think of all the places out there where I'd feel sad, and there's a group of people out there who made my first year miserable, and during my second year, Fred chose to spend time with them and suddenly ghosted me (later found out why, but it still hurts.)[*]

So then I think, *Never mind, I'll sit here this season and be happy, or as happy as I can be.* I'll definitely get a bit of work done since I'm the youngest single person here. (I'm thinking the median age at this park is late sixties or early seventies with a lot of eighties and a few nineties for seasonal and permanent residents.) Great people, and I have a few acquaintance-friends... At least we know each other's names and say "hi" when we pass. Younger couples, closer to my age, come in over the weekends, but whatever. I generally keep to myself.

But I *really* am missing the open desert. Really, really a lot. I'm planning to be back out there during the 2026/27 season, if the universe allows it, both mentally and physically.

Lastly, I'm going through Quartzsite on Friday, and then I'm planning to visit a couple of friends out there next Monday and stay the night with them. Maybe if I take it one step at a time, I'll be able to reacclimate myself to being out there. But last year really sucked. Up through November 18th was fine, then the "ignoring me thing" started. I was hoping I'd be able to meet up with him in Yuma or Holtville to get down to the bottom of why he was being an arse to me, but I didn't see him again until he posted his last video on March 12, 2025—a date I will forever hate. After that, I was scratching at the walls to get the hell out of there for the rest of March and into April, when I could finally leave for good (I was waiting on my kids' flight schedule to get my AWD car, which wasn't towable).

Just typing that last paragraph reminds me that I made the correct decision not to be out there full-time this year. Seriously, Fred made such a dent

---

[*]Fred told me why he did what he did last year with the whole ignoring me thing, and I understand his reasoning, but it still hurt me a lot, and I've shared this sentiment with him a couple of times since March. What's done is done—can't change it. But both of us finally know the score. Only, we both wish we had known each other longer and had better communication while he was still here, in physical form.

in my psyche that I can't even imagine spending any more time along the entire western edge of Arizona. I really like it out there, but the memories of my overwhelming sadness would literally kill me.

Seriously, the heart palpitations and debilitating sadness are starting to creep in by just typing all of this... and here come the tears. I'm going back to bed. I'll attempt a better "morning" when I wake up in another hour.

October 23, 2025:

Got up and chatted with Fred—can't remember about what at the moment. Then I saw a sunset picture in Quartzsite from a friend, and reposted it on Facebook and said I miss the sunsets, which I do. I can't commit to being out there full-time this year. Then, in the shower, the second song that played was Moby's "Porcelain." I thanked Fred and smiled.

October 25, 2025:

Fred was chuckling at this afternoon's situation—he could hear and see a man doing his best to flirt with me, and I wasn't having any of it. Fred gave me an afternoon of butterflies surrounding me as I sat around the pool. (I later found out from other park residents that this older gentleman, who couldn't remember what he was talking about and was asking somewhat offensive questions, had alcohol-related dementia. He was trying his best to have me find him interesting. It didn't work. I did find him annoying and disgusting, though, and finally left the area.)

October 26, 2025:

Drove to Palm Springs: Driving west today, I crested the hill overlooking Quartzsite, and a flood of "everything Quartzsite" rushed in. Uncomfortable, but manageable. But then the sign for Hwy 95, Parker and Yuma came up, and my breathing became labored, and the tears were just under the surface. I looked ahead at the California horizon and kept my mind on the road and traffic, but decided I hated the word "Yuma."

I'll be out in Quartzsite on the way back from California, though that's still tentative.

It sucks because I love it out there, and would much rather be out there. But, but, but... way too many memories. I'm going to try my best to cope, but I will give myself an out if I become a lump of goo on the desert floor, unable to breathe.

October 27, 2025:

Thinking of the Yuma thing, I remember driving into the LTVA area and seeing the word "Yuma" back in 2023 with a slightly sinking feeling of it being the "end of the road," a "dead end" feeling, and how many times since then I've looked at the word with a weird, indifferent feeling. A feeling of the last resort, the end of the world, indifferent but wrong. I didn't know then, but I am putting it together with the similar feeling I had in 2019, when I couldn't see too far into 2020. Was I predicting something that far out? With a few months left of 2019, I couldn't get past a feeling of "nothing" after February 2020, when I was busy arranging my book signings and presentations well into 2020. Then COVID happened, and that was the "nothingness" I was picking up on in October and November of 2019.

Sat out in the hot tub with my sister—lots of butterflies and dragonflies. Wasn't really thinking of going out—can get lost in work so easily, but the nudge of getting out to sit in the hot tub overtook me.

October 28, 2025:

Woke up singing Celine Dion's song, "For All The Love."

Looked up at the energetic outline of Fred sitting on my sister's couch while I was at the kitchen sink. Maybe imagination, but I had a pull to look at the corner of the couch and saw a faint signature of Fred looking between the TV and me. Short-cropped beard with a new haircut.

As I was falling asleep for the night, the brass handles on the nightstand jangled twice—no apparent reason. The side of the bed is six inches away from the nightstand.

October 29, 2025:

A late-night message came in around 11:00 p.m. While talking with Fred before bed, I remembered the hollowness of March 12th and the feeling of dread on March 11th. And the news from his cousin on March 5th that he was back in the hospital with COVID. And on March 4th, when my intuition told me to go back to Quartzsite and skip Yuma. Thinking of

Fred and his POV on how everything went down. At 11:51 p.m., the heart palpitations started.

While watching YouTube, the license plate shown in this video about *The Top 10 Signs You've Found Your Soulmate* was B228hm. What was Fred's plate?? Something similar. 239 BZP?

While watching this video, I get the feeling of Fred being behind me on my sister's couch. I'm sitting at the table with my back to the couch. Maybe imagination, but when I look, I can see him sitting in the corner of the couch—his head outline right above the back of the couch. (The dining room table is behind the couch, which is facing the other way toward the TV.)

Noticed shadows of birds flying over this afternoon—their shadow crossed the table, although I heard the flock fly over and away from the house. The birds were nowhere near an angle that would have cast shadows on a table six feet inside the door, which has a ten-foot veranda ceiling/overhang anchored to the house. I could see the patio, perhaps, at the edge of the covered veranda, but not sixteen feet into the house on the surface of the table.

Noted the purse pull in the evening and said thank you again for the kind gesture. It's been my lucky charm for nearly two years now.

Angel numbers all day—actually all week. I seem to only look at the clock when there are angel numbers. Tons of soulmate videos are popping up on my YouTube feed. Along with songs, Fred—I'm convinced—sends me various videos to watch on YouTube.

November 1, 2025:

I spoke with you while sitting out in my sister's backyard. I was watching the hummingbirds, all of the yellow butterflies, the hawks floating on the currents, and the dragonflies. Got dive-bombed by a butterfly—so close, I could feel the air displacement. Nice breezes every so often. I pulled up the chair for you to join, should you have been interested. At points, I could faintly see the outline of your legs crossed at the ankles. I did find a beat-up small white feather on my sister's patio. And it's now somewhere in the car, I know I have it.

I realized there was a vase of sunflowers in the corner of my room at my sister's house—had always been there, but I never took note of them. Finally seeing them brought me back to the April reading of sunflowers—seeing them as confirmation, besides sunflower decor at the RV resort.

November 3, 2025:

A tarot reading mentioned weekly masculine energy watching over, a maple leaf-shaped cloud* was mentioned, and more. Saw the blimp out at Chiracoa Summit. Same blimp I saw while in your campsite, after your passing. (random—something to remember.)

Later that evening while in Quartzsite—on the way back to Phoenix—I watched the sunset, and earlier, went into town for wings. Wound up talking with a guy who was sitting next to the corner, that Fred, then I sat at. Left and then I got this strong urge to go back in and get the guy's number. Texted thanks again, but haven't heard anything since. Which, in reality, is fine since I have much to do. Corn fed boy out of Waterloo, IA. Doubt I will, either. Too damn busy right now.

November 4, 2025:

Woke up briefly and went back to sleep at 4:52 a.m. At 4:54 a.m., I heard two distant but distinct, muffled knocks on the top of the car/driver's side. My eyes flew open, and I got a sense of "mission accomplished." I planned to note it in the morning, but I'm getting it down now. After writing it, it seemed distant, so I asked Fred, "Was that you? Did you do two knocks?" And I heard, "Yes."

Got up at 6:29 a.m. and started taking pictures of the sunrise.

7:30 a.m. - I drove to the spot where we met and had an overwhelming urge (made a U-turn) to sit outside and eat my Danish and drink my water. Then I started noticing rocks and collected a few. I had an urge to walk around the car the other way, which caused me to spot the motherlode of quartz rocks. And a spine vertebrae. Collected them up in a bag and brought them home.

Drove home and picked up "Birds of a Feather" clearly on the radio, and "I Think I'm in Love With You" past Salome, on the way to Wickenburg, doing its best to stay out of the crackles.

---

*The evening Fred passed away, a maple leaf-shaped cloud formed from the NNW over the desert and my RV.

November 5, 2025:

Just realized Fred and I have damn near identical cover photos on Facebook. Both pictures are of his favorite cacti, but from different angles.

November 6, 2025:

Had an early morning of heart palpitations, then tingling in the legs and stomach. Body detached. Not as strong as it has been in the past, but definitely something compared to the last couple of months of nothing.

November 7, 2025:

Thinking of how well a GoPro would have documented all interactions with Fred.

November 8, 2025:

Crying mess over missing Fred.

November 9, 2025:

Put words to missing the opportunity of something good found, fifty-four years into this life. Realizing soulmates was not actually just a tagline.

November 10, 2025:

Flickering lights in the bathroom, loud birds, including one really loud crow (made me want to go outside to look, but I was busy working), coyotes, and a quail??? Noisy this morning. Noted the number of feathers in my mandala. Just noticed "Fred" is all next to each other on the keyboard. "F," "R," "E," "D." Clever, I thought.

November 11, 2025:

I took a selfie this evening. Had the urge to do so, posted it, and wrote that every selfie was for him. And they were.

November 12, 2025:

I teared up while driving to Walmart over Fred's ignoring me last year. I asked for an apology/at least an acknowledgment of what he meant by leaving a feather for me, and I would be looking for it. Did he, or does he now, know how hurtful it was to be ignored, knowing that he was spending time with people who couldn't/didn't give a shit about him, while a friend was sitting across the highway being ignored? I'm sure he knew it wasn't nice since he tracked me on Facebook—he was still curious. But the pain about that whole situation; I'm not a needy, whiny, or clingy person, but I was, and I still am, hurt. Always go back to—there's not much that can be done now. What's said is said, and what's done is done.

I also get the feeling he'd like to have me back in Quartzsite. I'm sure he's already attending the various activities out there and stuff, and traveling everywhere else, including Saturn. It would be hard for me to be there, especially in November and December.

November 13, 2025:

While falling asleep, I witnessed a sunset over the mountains—full color with haze, standing next to a black horse with a Mexican rug over its back, and Fred sitting atop with a black hat on. Didn't see a saddle.

November 14, 2025:

Got a couple of Chris Stapleton songs on my disco channel this morning. Tears, of course. "Loving You On My Mind," "South Dakota," and "Without Your Love."

5:37 p.m. - Just got onto Pandora to get the earlier song titles, and Chris Stapleton popped on first with "I Was Wrong."

6:10 p.m. - "Starting Over"—Chris Stapleton.

6:50 p.m. - "Devil Always Made Me Think Twice"—Chris Stapleton.

Got back into the RV and could see/hear Fred laughing over the "Resort Romeo" thing—another guy who was playing the hopeful suitor.

By the way, I felt him watching me get dressed this morning. My back was facing him—I was facing the back window, and he was in the office area.

Tingles on the bottom half of the body at bedtime.

November 15, 2025:

Woke up this morning singing April Wine's "Just Between You and Me."

Instant astral travel, dark path winding, then floating, tumbling, flying, all views in color with lines of ultraviolet on plants. Flew up to space, went through the sun, and came out as a glowing being. Not on fire, but aglow and intact. Then I fell asleep.

November 16, 2025:

Tingly feeling in the lower half of my body only, upon waking.

November 17, 2025:

Woke up singing "Joy Of My Life" by Chris Stapleton as well as "Luckiest Man Alive."

November 18, 2025:

In childhood, I learned strength, resilience, and courage.

My ex-husband reinforced my independence and helped me have my kids. (Yes, I wrote "my" kids. A whole different story with all of that.)

The relationship between 2014 and 2019 clarified what I will and will not put up with, cementing my personal respect.

Fred showed me true love.

The hopeful suitor at the resort confirmed that I wasn't interested in playing sloppy seconds, second fiddle, or someone on hold waiting for another person to become available again. He was narrow-minded, pretentious, and in some cases, utterly delusional.

Posthumously, Fred—over time—has shared with me: He has shown, clarified, and confirmed other "suspicions" I've had about existence, humankind, purpose, cycles of life, etc.

November 22, 2025:

Coming back to Phoenix from Mexico, just short of Buckeye, April Wine's "Just Between You and Me" came on. His song had popped into my mind a week ago, and I told Fred I remembered him telling me he had taken a date to see the band in Fargo in the early eighties. I recognized the song immediately. Have no idea why it popped into my head a week ago—one of those morning songs on November 15, 2025.

November 23, 2025:

Going to see blues live music this afternoon. Woke up singing "You Should Probably Leave" by Chris Stapleton.

November 25, 2025:

Found two pennies, heads up on the ground at night, walking into the potluck.

November 26, 2025:

Before waking up, I saw a blue-highlighted letter or word. Touched on that, and I woke up.

November 27, 2025:

Got a side/front hug from Fred while sitting on a couch, right before falling asleep. We were both sitting on this couch in this lucid dream—short hug.

November 29, 2025:

I haven't been talkative for a couple of days. Fred is probably thanking his lucky stars for the peace and quiet. I really have nothing to talk about. He sees that not much is going on.

I do tell him about my restlessness from missing Quartzsite sunsets.

When getting the silverware and fixings out for dinner, I felt as if I were looking through his eyes, putting stuff on the table—a strange feeling.

Watching the making of the movie *Ghost*—popped up on my YouTube Feed.

I told him I appreciated the days when we would just sit. Sometimes I'm good with sitting like this this weekend.

November 30, 2025:

I woke up from lucid dreaming this morning. A situation of what if Fred and I had remained together and he didn't die, but an illness still wracked his body. I wasn't necessarily taking care of him, but I was hanging out with him 24/7 (he had nursing care). His body had begun wasting away, but he was still there in mind and soul. It was real, and then the alarm went off. I remembered it throughout the entire day.

December 2, 2025:

There was something, and I mentioned it to my mom yesterday, but I have since forgotten. (The memories slip in and slip out that fast. Sometimes they come back, but other times, no.)

December 3, 2025:

Light knock (one tap/knock over bathroom). Baby Bash's "Suga Suga" was the wake-up song.

December 4, 2025:

Received a heavy comfort of "it will be okay" this morning after stating my worries upon waking.

Put on my disco channel an hour after telling my mom this. And again, Chris Stapleton's "South Dakota" came on as the first song, and then "Let's Get It On" with Marvin Gaye.

10:45 p.m. - Another wannabe suitor was over against my will—he was going to drop off tacos and instead stayed for four plus hours—good cripes almighty. All he did was talk, and Fred and I hung out in my mind. Personally, I get the feeling Fred is truly amused by the various ways wannabe suitors approach me. ((Fred did it the right way.))

December 5, 2025:

3:22 a.m. - Heart palpitations started while laughing with Fred about the prior evening. Then asked him about his presence, and the heart palpitations subsided, but didn't completely go away.

I was humming Joe Bonamassa's "Southbound" before dozing off, and felt a prick on my thumb, and then a force of energy slammed into me. No longer relaxed but now on full alert.

3:30 a.m. - Then a cool, light breeze in my face while still lying in bed.

December 6, 2025:

During my shower with the disco station, I made the joke out loud of betting that a Chris Stapleton song would come on by the third song. Sure enough, the second song was "Loving You on My Mind."

Wrote to his cousin about the random fact of December 6, 2023. Didn't hear back, but I'm sure his family is hoping I'll disappear. I'm sure they don't know what to say to me, and/or if it seems like I'm a weirdo looking for something. Oh, well. I'm being straightforward, and I understand the weirdness factor, too. (Who is she? And what does she want?)

December 12, 2025:

Nine months since his passing.

Woke up to "No Ordinary Love" by Sade.

I shopped at Walmart, and when I picked up the cart, I had a random thought of how people hold the handle - do most use just the plastic? Or hold it as I do, with the width of my shoulders? Random stupid thought.

Halfway through the store, as I passed the electronics section, my body temperature rose. By the dairy case, I started getting electrical shocks from the cart (has never happened before—like, ever). I moved my hands to the plastic handle and continued to get electric shocks through it. I finally asked Fred if that was him. Came up in my mind to ask. How weird. I moved to pushing the cart with balled up fists, then just my fingers. The heat subsided by the registers, and shocks stopped.

December 13, 2025:

Researching the shocks from the day prior, and "Traveler" by Stapleton started playing in my head.

December 14, 2025:

I think what it boils down to is that someone entered my life whom I expected would go really well, but instead the universe said, "Psych! You don't get to be that lucky." We never had the opportunity to hang out more, to communicate, to argue, to laugh, to hug, or to do anything. All of it was cut short, and that seriously pisses me off. Yes, I might find someone else (who had better be just like Fred, remind me of him, and meet my astronomically high standards), but I see it as taking fifty-four years to find Fred. I know I won't be here in another fifty-four years, and with my limited amount of social life, I'm not holding my breath.

December 15, 2025:

Early in the morning hours, I told him that until someone crosses my path who reminds me of him and doesn't piss me off, he's stuck with me, and he may as well go with it. I'm a stubborn cuss.

December 16, 2025:

Lots of birds in the morning and the evening. Aware of coyotes howling every so often through the evening, beginning with the sunset and lasting through until morning. Lots of birds and butterflies near the pools.

Half the time, I wonder if I'm imagining things, but… Lots of taps on the roof yesterday, unless I have a squirrel or a heavy bird jumping around up there, I don't know…

Got into bed, lights out, then after tucking myself in, I felt a very obvious "impression" of the mattress behind me indenting. My eyes sprang open again. Like someone stuck their hand in the mattress behind my shoulders, and pressed down. Because of that indent, my body slightly rolled toward that indentation.

Afterward, I felt a steady, cool breeze specifically on my face, not just in the general area. Lying in bed.

4:44 a.m. - Little spoon to Fred, and he was hugging me. Heart palpitations began again.

December 18, 2025:

Woke up to Dolly Parton and Kenny Rogers' "Islands in the Stream."

December 22, 2025:

Started getting sepsis videos popping up on my YouTube feed.

December 23, 2025:

An understanding that I have stuff to do in my life before I take on another person; that he wasn't on my radar when I came to Arizona. Not closed off to it, but also not actively searching for another person.

NDE videos are showing up on my feed now.

December 25, 2025:

Questions cleared up—Matt Fraser popped up on my feed. Confirmations.

December 27, 2025:

Dreams/visions:

I found a long feather on the ground—about two feet long—a little muddy and wet, but definitely of a good size. Maybe five inches across at its widest. (I found this feather on April 12, 2026.)

December 29, 2025, Facebook entry:

```
I have come up with a good explanation of how
I feel:
    It's as if I were walking along the Earth's
surface, and the ground opened up which I fell
into for fifteen months of fun, magick, the "being
at home" feeling of pure connection and respect,
followed by confusion, sadness, and, lastly,
the debilitating, soul-crushing somberness.
    Then the Earth spat me back up to the surface
and closed that rip in time. When I look back,
there's nothing except scrub brush and swirl-
ing miniature eddies of sand, except for the
one picture I have pinned to my Facebook page.
I have a couple of videos from our adventures
where I either caught a glimpse of him or heard
him talking, or the pictures/videos he took
during the '23/'24 season, where I am either
heard or seen. I purposely didn't catch him
on video or in pictures because I didn't want
to presume he'd be okay with being in my video
productions, and I thought he had a girlfriend,
so I didn't want to cause any ruffled feathers.
It's also why I minded my manners.
    The only people who could vouch for us hang-
ing out are those in Quartzite (La Posa South,
```

Beer Belly's, Tyson Wash, Dollar General), Yuma, Pilot Knob, Holtville, El Centro, and Calexico. The many waitstaff who asked us how long we'd been married (and I would tell them we had only known of each other for thirty days, to be met with their answers of us seeming like we'd been together for a long time; the "energy" between us), the people who took our movie tickets and served us our concessions, the tourist attraction people who took our pictures and/or spoke with us, the gas station attendants who would see us come in together and talk throughout the store, the people in the various grocery stores, the Yuma and El Centro Walmarts, the Yuma Marketplace, the Yuma Harbor Freight, the Cocopah Racetrack, and the patrons who wandered into the Whiskey Road Saloon every Monday night in January '24 for the Monday Night Music Bingo game which I usually won and would give the drink tokens to Fred for his red beers.

Early on, we had mastered the ability to give the other one the "look" of agreement in a situation to "wrap up and move on" with whatever we were doing or wherever we were; that unspoken look of agreement that long-term couples can give each other, and know they are on the same wavelength and respond accordingly. We didn't have to speak, nor did we have to be together to know what was being "said" and shared; it was always a well-timed mutual glance, a slight nod, and the next course of action we both silently agreed upon.

It is a relationship that was never a "relationship" but, at the same time, was/is one of the most significant relationships either of us has ever had and still has.

Only because I can't shut up about him, does everyone know my absolute devotion to him—not only physically, but everything about him. He managed to make this cynical, jaded, grouchy person realize that the term "soulmate" is not just a Hallmark greeting-card tagline. (I'm not being funny here—that's truly what I thought, and I've said that very line so many times, it still easily rolls off my tongue. But now I know there is something so much more possible between two people than what I could have ever imagined.) It only took damn near fifty-five years to learn that someone could be so utterly connected to someone else. Again, I thought it was all BS; life is *not* a Hallmark movie—act accordingly.

I cry because I miss his physical presence here in this realm; his company. We had the best conversations (he was incredibly intelligent and curious), and, equally, the best hours of quiet contentment, sitting next to each other. Sure, there would be a stray comment here and there, but we could easily sit next to each other for hours, staring at the Imperial Sand Dunes on the horizon, for example, in quiet solitude, and we were both thrilled to be there. (If you've ever been to the Pilot Knob LTVA, you know there's not a g.d. thing to do there, so the company has got to be pretty darn special to be absolutely content out there for the majority of a day.)

I'm pissed that the timing was off. He even said it himself this past March, after the fact. Had he not been sick and dying, I know we could have given a relationship a good shot. If it didn't pan out, at least we tried. But for the massive amount of energy we shared just by sitting next to each other in lawn chairs, let alone talking, going places, and doing things, etc., I think we could have had a long time together. And the mere fact that it took fifty-five years to find this person, only for him to disappear fifteen months later... Seriously, WTF?

Given that the timing was off and our "relationship" was not observed by people close to either of us, it feels as if history has chosen to dismiss the time we had together; seriously, a rip in time. A smatter of minutes in all of history that only I and one other person experienced, and only I'm here to talk about it. If I were anyone other than myself, I would think I've lost my marbles. Carrying on about a person who was so monumental (not a word I would use loosely) in my life, and I have nothing to prove that I'm not making this stuff up. I can't sit around a campfire with anyone we mutually knew, and shoot the sh!t about how great he was, or do the "remember that one time he/we did this" stories. It's very lonely, and then compound that loneliness with him not being here, physically.

Lastly, my over-analytical brain tells my heart to get over it. My heart and soul are telling my brain to f*ck off. I'm experiencing and witnessing (all at once) an inner turmoil that flips between practicality and my version of "real" life with my experiences, and the acknowledgment that someone managed to prove to me that the term "soulmate" is more than a tagline, and that you can be oh so comfortable with someone, so quickly, so... unexplainable. It was literally freakin' magick.

And *ALL* of the above is my experience with him based on my belief that he had a S.O., and he didn't correct me because he knew his days were limited. Could you imagine what more it would have been if he had come clean with me and corrected my assumption of him being a "taken" man? If two adults actually "communicated???" (I do chew his arse on this point... just because he is no longer here doesn't mean he gets a free pass out of this faux pas.)

There is so much more, and it will all be in my future writings. I'll finish that book this spring. Most of it is already written—just need to put it together. Not sure I'll list it for sale, though. More of a collection of memories for me. If my workload allows…

December 30, 2025:

12:03 a.m. - I woke up from a dream right after I went to sleep of a semi-truck crashing into a curb along a narrow street, causing the trailer to jack-knife, slamming into/through the building. I was standing across the street, and the semi came in from the right and slammed into the building, jumping the curb at the corner.

1:11 p.m. - I looked up the dream I had the night before and it actually happened somewhere in Nebraska—about the time I woke up and jotted it down on my phone.

4:30 p.m. - I was doing the dishes and requested the possibility of Moby on one of my Pandora channels.

At 5:30 p.m. - The stream paused, and then Moby began. I smiled and said thank you.

Fred showed and clarified things for me more than teaching me. Showed love and thought. Clarified belief and spiritual things. I asked him for the third time (that night) whether he had finally gone to Spiritual Pathways, just south of Lead, SD, and I felt satisfied that he had. (I had been bringing this up to him for the last handful of months—that he should go visit. Finally, tonight, I got the feeling that he did.)

December 31, 2025:

Promised Fred I would turn off the waterworks as a new resolution. Made it to January 14, 2026, when Lisa channeled him.

Getting ready to go out for the evening, I had asked Fred for Moby. It took nearly an hour, but after a long pause, "Porcelain" showed up. I smiled and thanked him. (I will add that sometimes I ask him for certain songs within my thoughts, too; testing if my phone is listening to me rather than having him send me songs. So far, even when I request a song from him in my thoughts, that song shows up.)

Asked Fred about his day, then fell asleep.

January 1, 2026:

Going to sleep last night (December 31, 2025), I saw oversized vegetation glowing under a blacklight. I walked down the path and fell asleep. Before that vision, an owl started, then coyotes, and a few raindrops. Got a video of it on Facebook. Also, on December 31, 2025, the clock showed: 1:11, 2:22, 3:33, 4:44, and 5:55.

January 2, 2026:

Morning nap: A couple of voices came in to say "Hi." A couple of those voices said my name. Fred was sitting higher than me to my right. He was looking over his left shoulder, down towards me, smiling.

Damn near every day, okay, every day, I'm seeing angel numbers all over the place. Always on clocks.

I had a past life regression done to see if I could pinpoint more details on the information Fred gave to me on the first message through Kimberly back in March 2025, six days after he passed away. I had found someone who specialized in this in Scottsdale, AZ. Here are the results (and some of them don't surprise me as I've had visions of these in the past):

```
Hello Kiersten -


I enjoyed our time together and exploring some of the
many past lives you have led! A kindred old soul!
    I have included the notes I took down during our ses-
sion, and then at the bottom, I intuited some on the
card that you drew at the end of the session—Seven of
Cups—which was encouraging us to look across some of
these lives to identify themes, and in particular, emo-
tional themes. As a reminder, your intention was to find
out how many past lives you have had. Since we jumped
around to no fewer than eight and you told me about oth-
ers you explored prior to our session, I would say there
are a multitude.
    Here we go!


Life One - Life on the Prairie:
You were a woman in her forties to sixties (late in life
```

for that time) by yourself in a cottage surrounded by wheat fields and mountains in the distance (perhaps Montana). You could sense that you had grown children and were an empty nester, living there alone. In this life, you felt contentedly solitary and "present" with what you were doing.

Life Two - European Seaside:

You were a woman in your twenties or thirties in a large marble-and-granite town square, in front of a church with a tall metal roof that rose to the steeple. It was near the ocean, with choppy water, and you were in a black dress. You seemed to be the only one there, like it was a ghost town. You noted how beautiful the sun on the horizon was, with clouds rimmed in silver and gold, its rays shining through them. Your feelings in this life were somber and, again, seemed solitary.

Life Three - Beach Life:

You were a woman in her fifties on a spit of an island in the Bahamas, no shoes, cold drink in hand—like you were in a commercial. You described palm trees and beautiful, sunny weather. Your feelings in this life were delighted, satiated, and "just enjoying the view."

Life Four - Jungle:

You were a woman doctor in her forties going through a jungle (like the Amazon), and your job was to document plants. You felt like an early-1900s explorer, helped by the indigenous people of the area as you trekked through. You were left-handed and had a notepad and a pen to document the plants. It was a hot, steamy environment, and you were dressed in a net over your face to keep the bugs from biting. You felt a sense of urgency to see and document as much as possible.

Life Five - Bring Back the Fish:

You were a woman in your twenties dressed in Inuit gear, and you felt like an Inuit. You were ice fishing in the cold while watching the Northern Lights, with a low sun on the horizon. You have a family, and you cannot come back to the village without the fish. You somehow know the process for preserving the fish you catch. Your feelings in this life were of wonderment and contentment.

Life Six - Pioneer Woman:
You were a woman in her thirties, with a husband and several children (some of whom had passed), and a dog, in a covered wagon in the southwest US (AZ/NM). You were looking for a new place to homestead to get out of the bad weather in the Midwest, maybe part of a gold rush, and didn't seem to be part of a wagon train, but you had cattle with you. You had a feeling of faith that everything was going to turn out okay.

We took the opportunity of another soul being in this scene to ask some questions. When you looked at your husband, you thought it might be Fred's soul. You described him as having kind eyes and a kind face, and feeling like home. He said that you have been in many past lives together—17, 71, 717—some combination of 7s and 1s. Your purpose or lesson in this life was—what is beyond? Your husband's message to you was about insatiable curiosity and to just keep going.

Life Seven - Ready to Go:
You were a woman in her late seventies or early eighties in Romania, standing near ornate buildings on a gloomy, cold day. You wore a long, thin dress, a white-lace bonnet, and a black skirt. Your feelings were of drabness—life is drab. You looked at your hands and said, "Damn, I got old." You were ready to leave that life and were bored with it.

Life Eight - Riverboat to NOLA:
You were a woman in her late twenties, dressed to the nines in a bustier dress, high-buttoned boots, and carrying an intricate parasol. You had a gentleman next to you who seemed to be a fiancé or a husband, someone who could have been another life with Fred in it. He had dark eyes and dark, short hair. Your feelings about the

trip were about having fun and being satiated, as if you had just had breakfast. In this life, you had way too much money.

When we went to the in-between, we talked about contracts with your mom, your ex-husband, the man you dated from 2014 to 2019, and Fred. No agreements or contracts were changed or altered.

At the end of our session, you asked the cards what you were to take from this experience, and you drew the Seven of Cups (emotion). My interpretation is that you got to see a lot of different lives, as you asked to do, and now, looking across them to identify the emotions, may be helpful. You identified one of these early on, saying you know how to be alone and don't mind being alone/solitary. I would also suggest that you have lived many adventures. In many of these scenes, you mentioned not wearing makeup and being somewhat androgynous, which probably allowed you to move through society largely unnoticed.

My question to you is whether you are using those abilities picked up in your past lives to your benefit in this life? It sounds like you are an adventurous nomad who makes her home in the world wherever she lands. Is your preference to be solitary, or is it just where you "end up being/becoming?"

The affirmation for the Seven of Cups is: My wildest imagination is a tool that I can use to inform my future in a down-to-earth way. As I mentioned, traditionally, it is read as having many paths to choose from. In this case, I think it is asking you to look across the lives we have explored and bring forward some of the lessons we have learned to carry with you on the path forward in this life, to inform your future.

What was the feeling in your gut as you were in these lives? What was the feeling in your heart center? I wonder if there is an embodiment of the experiences that you can bring forth that provides you with some guardrails. You were bored and done with one life, so not too far over there on that spectrum. In which life were you the happiest? In many of them, you said that you were

content—is that enough for this life you are living now?
I am not suggesting that you rate this life based on
other lives you have lived, but is there something from
those lives and experiences that can be re-utilized here
to make this go-round even better?

Best,
Amy

January 5, 2026:

3:13 a.m. - I woke up and fell asleep. Then again at 5:25 a.m.

I started reading Matt Fraser, listened to the owl, and popped into my head the refrain for Chris Stapleton's "I Was Wrong."

6:25 a.m. - I got out of bed to get the phone to find the song (also his birthdate).

Four and a half days into not getting weepy.

January 6, 2026:

Did I think of a song this morning? I think it was by either Styx or Kansas. I know the song, but I forgot right away before I had a chance to write it down.

Sitting at the table/desk this morning, I thought of something—putting two and two together and had a realization. I laughed, looked up, and asked Fred about it, but as fast as it came in, it was gone. But did state that it had been six plus days of no crying.

January 7, 2026:

Fred showed up at Kimberly's last connection in October, wearing a red T-shirt and jeans, grinning from ear to ear. I'm going to take that as being genuinely happy in the moment. (This was the same outfit he was wearing on November 16, 2024, when he hopped out of his truck, grinning ear-to-ear, at the Ranger's Station at the beginning of the 2024/25 season.)

January, 10, 2026:

I was working a tradeshow in Phoenix, and when I looked up, I saw Fred walking around the corner of the aisle I was in, perusing—a grey t-shirt, blue jeans, and signature brown hiking shoes.

Talking to you in bed tonight, I see you standing there smiling at me, then sitting to my right and looking over your left shoulder at me with your sneaky smile. I'm laughing and smiling myself.

January 12, 2026:

Various tarot readings on YouTube are ringing true—not so much with what might happen in the future, but definitely with situations that happened in the past.

January 13, 2026:

I asked Fred to remind me about the bridge in Wickenburg the next morning—a low clearance railroad bridge to avoid.

YouTube Channel Tarot Readings were popping up in my feed, stating that the person on my mind would be coming in this week in some way. I ignored all of them with the sentiment of "whatever," then the fourteenth (below) happened: Lisa channeled Fred in the car.

Quartzsite, AZ - Tyson Wash LTVA (BLM)... I couldn't stay away.

January 14, 2026:

Streaming music stopped at the Wickenburg intersection, where I was waiting to turn right to bypass the bridge. I got it turned back on before turning, and it worked fine all the way into Quartzsite. (Fred had cut the music and the speaker to remind me of the train bridge.)

On the west side of Wickenburg, after thanking Fred for sending me a reminder for the train bridge, I asked him to send me either a Chris Stapleton song of his choice or Moby's "Porcelain." I told him he had eighty-four miles in which to do it. At the end of the exit ramp, right before I came to a complete stop at the top of the exit to turn right on Riggles Road, the lull between the songs coming in paused a little longer than usual, and then Moby's "Porcelain" came on. He did it within those eighty-four miles.*

Driving Lisa back to Phoenix, my entire conversation with her became much more interesting when she channeled Fred directly on the western side of Wickenburg, and he remained with her on the way to the resort and while we sat in the car, talking outside her fifth wheel.

From the conversation in the car: Lisa channeled Fred, and he wants me to write the book. The book is the key. I'll meet the guy that Fred is sending to me at a book signing. Lisa tells me he is everything I want in a man: intelligent, caring, independent, and so on. The book will be a bestseller, and there will be a sequel. I'll know instantly of this connection, and something about him will remind me of Fred. I'll know instantly. This is why Fred was in my life, to show me this connection so I would recognize when it happens with someone who (doesn't have health issues this time around)—someone to spend the older years with. Bittersweet.

Fred also says he doesn't often show himself to me or do the tingle thing because I wouldn't be able to handle it.

Lisa channeled him through a power surge that rose from her feet and charged her body. She could see his face in front of hers. She said she was beginning to fall asleep, blinking, when a surge of power ran through her feet, her body buzzing. Then she heard and saw Fred.

I told Lisa during the channeling that I didn't want Fred to think I was trying to make money off of him and our story. She said Fred wants me to write the book. He says that's the key, and he's sending me someone I've never met before. He showed this person to Lisa, who described him as tall, very handsome, and the perfect person for me - that Fred said I would know instantly that this was the person he was sending me, because I would have the same connection with him that I had with Fred. She told me that he said the book would be a bestseller and that there would be a sequel. I'd be meeting this person at a book signing, with my hair up in a style, and gave me other specifics about that particular day.

---

*To set the stage: I needed help moving my two vehicles out to the desert. My friend Lisa (one of whom wrote a Foreword for this book) offered to drive my car out behind me, while I drove the RV. Then once the RV was in the desert, I would drive her back to Phoenix in the car. I will also add that she had never told me she had had past experiences with channeling spirits and such. This conversation never came up between us in the three plus months we had known each other.

She told me he was coming back to me. He told her he was coming back, that the book was the key, and that I would know the minute I saw this person.

I then asked her how he was coming back in this lifetime? And she said, she didn't know, but was only conveying what *he* said, which was that he was coming back in this lifetime.

Fred remained right in front of her throughout the car ride and showed up to her with a neatly trimmed beard, white hair, a leather jacket, sunglasses, and riding chaps. When we got back to the resort, I showed her the picture she described, and she was speechless. He kept his presence known in the car while we talked a bit more before I got back on the road.

While driving back, I chatted with him all the way to Quartzsite. I told him that I was working the Big Tent Show from the seventeenth through the twenty-fifth, that I would need the twenty-sixth to get organized, and that I would start working on the book on January 27th. I felt satisfaction with my scheduling commitments.

January 15, 2026:

One music stop—can't remember if it was attached to anything. I had been talking to him, though, all morning.

Lisa said she will try to channel him again this evening. Didn't have a chance last night.

January 17, 2026:

Started working at the RV show and could "see" Fred wandering around.

January 18, 2026:

WATCHING EVERY SUNSET—WONDERFUL TO SEE AGAIN. (Missed the previous sunsets because a mountain was in the way.)

Lisa told me a couple of days later that she was sitting outside, talking with another friend of ours, when a strong gust of wind slammed into both of them out of nowhere. It wasn't windy at all that day, and she instantly had the feeling it was Fred.

January 19, 2026:

One guy walked by with the same gait and height as Fred, with a similar profile. Then, in the parking lot, another guy drove by me who looked like Fred with his arm set on the car door of the truck.

Light knock while getting into bed this evening. I'm feeling lazy (overwhelmed) with the book. I have little time to get it done, and it must be perfect.

January 20, 2026:

One knock on RV.

January 21, 2026:

Woke up from sleep thinking I had a dream about trancing out.

Up at 2:22 a.m. for the bathroom, and 3:33 a.m., the coyotes were howling and running through the wash.

7:13 a.m. - I woke up and heard a slight tap on the roof (no tree cover in the desert).

January 22, 2026:

A relationship that was but wasn't, is but isn't, always. (line popped into my head).

January 24, 2026:

A few knocks throughout the afternoon and evening.

January 25, 2026:

Earlier today, I confirmed that the bird I saw in Marana was a black vulture. I still have that haunting vision in my mind of when the bird and I locked eyes, just like I did with Fred on December 6, 2023. Every so often, I think about that bird and how it hopped into sight, we looked at each other, I looked down briefly, and then the bird was gone. Hunched over on the ground, it was huge and probably forty feet in front of me. Heavy overcast, and dusk was setting in.

January 26, 2026:

Knocks and taps while I was falling asleep.

January 27, 2026:

Woke up to knocks and taps. No wind and no trees covering my roof. I don't hear them during the day, generally. Or at least more at night when I'm in bed.

It occurred to me that when Lisa repeated the name of the book while channeling Fred, she said the book title slowly as if she were savoring every word, then in a different tone (her voice just slightly changed, she dropped the pitch ever so slightly) with conviction said slowly—drawing out each word as if mulling over the conviction one more time while verbally expressing approval, *"An... Unexpected... Journey... I like it."* Would that have been Fred talking through her?

11:11 a.m. - A video popped up in my feed about the correlation between a couple of things that happened to me in the past.

11:49 a.m. - This morning, while dinking around and not being very productive, I had a YouTube video going and was playing a game on my phone at the same time. While looking at my phone, the computer, which was plugged in and charging, blanked out. It didn't totally shut off or reset, but blacked out and made two four-noted "bling" noises I'd never heard before, probably five-ish seconds between the noises, which caught my attention. I moved the mouse, entered my PIN, and nothing was amiss. I've never heard those chimes on any computer I've ever owned, but when they caught my attention, an inner voice told me to get to work and stop screwing around.

Started outlining this evening.

Released and viewed on this day: A video of the integration between two things that have happened. Made sense.

The first two hours awake, I charged the Bluetti with my solar panels to one hundred percent full—took a little over an hour. I then brought it inside and started charging the computer, the phone, and the indoor solar light. After forty-five minutes to an hour of that, I had seventy-eight percent of a charge left, then took the Bluetti out of the RV and into the backseat of my car to inflate the tire. In those twenty feet—a couple of seconds, I lost seventy-eight percent of a charge to an absolute zero percent charge. Well, shit! I plugged the solar panels back in and, with a two-percent charge, ran the air compressor on my back tire so I could leave. I left twenty-five minutes later than I had originally planned. About an hour later at the tire place, the thought of being saved from a possible accident popped into my head. Again, Fred does things with electricity. And more importantly, did he save me from a possible car accident by delaying me?

January 28, 2026:

Last night, I remembered there were videos from a couple of months ago suggesting my soulmate wanted to go into business together. I thought that was a load of crap until I got Fred's directions to write the damn book. OHHHH!!!

Went to a community campfire and remembered when Fred would tell me he enjoys sitting around fires and would generally never have one if he were by himself.

January 29, 2026:

I woke up with a clearer thought than what I've come up with over the past handful of days. I believe Fred was obviously on his own soul journey, dealing with things he needed to learn, but to take care of me, he made sure he entered my life before his ended, so I would recognize what to look for in the man he sends me in the future. (Typing that is causing me to tear up.) He knew he would have an illness and pass away at an early age, but still needed to be in my life briefly to teach me what true love is and what it feels like, so he could send me someone when he wasn't here in this physical realm.

Interestingly, when he died and before I knew any of this, I told him he was going to have to send me someone since my track record for recognizing anything in the game of love was null and void and viewed with a cynical and jaded eye.

I also apologized to him for being a challenging pain in his proverbial butt.

February 1, 2026:

Something right before sleep, didn't write it down, and forgot by the next morning.

February 2, 2026:

Remembered the thing from the night before, but figured I'd remember what it was, then I forgot by the next morning.

February 3, 2026:

Outside for four hours this afternoon: entertained by one fat chipmunk, two yellow butterflies, seven quail, and one barn swallow.

February 4, 2026:

4:30 a.m. - I woke up and remembered sleep-talking and having a cotton-mouth during that event. I was talking about hiking or moving, and pulled two strands of hair out of my mouth. I was thinking that I could use a shower.

4:44 a.m. - Realized it took forever to charge the Bluetti yesterday with full direct sun, whereas on other days it's done in no time.

I remembered another dream about having my travel trailer delivered to Wyatt's Campground in Belle Fourche. ??? (I don't have a travel trailer in Belle Fourche, but I've camped at Wyatt's before.)

After that, I received a message to keep jotting things down rather than relying on my memory, because that'll let other things come in and be remembered.

5:11 a.m. - An urge to check the call time to Chelsea on March 12, 2025, when I got back into the rig after the wind hit the RV—correlating that with the death time in Yuma. I remember my tunnel vision in the direction of Yuma—quiet, warm, still…

Going back to sleep, I remembered that on the ride back to Phoenix, I told Lisa that Fred was shy to begin with, and then added that, when he was comfortable with you, he would carry the conversation. She emphatically nodded her head while stating, word-for-word, the tail end of that sentence along with me. I knew I was talking with Fred then.

I spoke with Lisa on the phone while she was looking at Fred's Green River, WY picture from November 2024 - on his way to Arizona, and she said the photo kept changing as she looked at it. She also said that he is being impatient with this book and wants it written ASAP.

February 5, 2026:

Got chewed out by two killdeer while refilling my water tank—I've noticed I'm more acutely aware of birdsong since last March.

Going to sleep—I told him that my version of talking sexy was measurements, spatial issues, charts and graphs, and science and space, not flowers and shit.

Then I apologized to him again for being annoying, but then followed up with, "That's it! I'm your consolation prize for successfully spending sixty-two years on Earth, this go-round. And because of that success, you get your very own Kiersten."

February 6, 2026:

Early this morning, a video about choosing your destination before birth popped up in my YouTube feed.

Spoke with Lisa for nearly three hours. Along with various everyday stuff, I shared some ideas about how people who were meant to be in your life for a purpose look different to you than those who come in and go out.

Also, the quality of people. Likening it all to a pinball machine.

Just finishing typing that last line and remembering my conversation, I came up with another title for a book and the overview of the contents, or at least the beginning of a new manuscript if not the sequel I'm being told I'll write.

February 7, 2026:

Spent the day writing on Fred's book. Stopped due to lack of light, and I am at the point of January 1, 2024. I was conserving battery.

I walked around outside for a bit, checking out a new spot that had opened, then I came back in and started typing this note. The solar light next to me popped on, and I smiled.*

February 8, 2026:

Sat outside for the sunset and was visited by one gray moth, a chipmunk, doves, sparrows, and quail.

February 9, 2026:

Dove, quail, hummingbirds, and spider webs for this evening's sunset.

---

*You have to touch it for it to pop on. After half a minute, it turned off by itself, too. I smiled again. Then I turned it on myself, and after fourteen seconds, it turned off on its own. *(video)*

February 10, 2026:

Checked Facebook friend list and your name was missing. Freaked out. Restarted the computer, and your name appeared for the rest of the day.

February 11, 2026:

Name was missing again—since 8:30 a.m.!!! Have checked periodically. Nothing yet. Have yet to restart the computer. I'm getting the feeling, though, if I got back to work, your name would reappear. The "get to work" schtick.

February 12, 2026:

"You Should Probably Leave" was playing at the Chevron next to London Bridge.

The light switched off twice this evening.

Remembered Lutes Casino—the last place we had dinner together. I thanked him for bringing me, and apologized for complaining about the cheese sauce on the nachos and the greasy meat that particular night.

February 13, 2026:

Lisa called to let me know another wind burst hit her while she watched her husband play pickleball. The first thing out of her mouth was, "Knock it off, Fred." The fact that her first thought was him… he's sticking around.

Fred wasn't on my Facebook list this morning—showed up briefly in the afternoon, which I got a screenshot of—and then was gone again in the evening.

Just finished watching this video at 11:11 a.m., realizing he once again described Fred. The different phrases: "here to teach you things" and "has lived many lives," etc.

The movie *Serendipity* (2001) struck me a day ago, and although I didn't say anything, the movie showed up on YouTube today. Naturally, I watched it, and this movie has one of my all-time favorite movie lines. To avoid copyright issues, I'm not going to quote the line in this book, but if you enjoy romcoms, I suggest you watch it. And if you've already seen it, I suggest watching it again, and listening closely to the part where the main character's obituary-writing friend reads him a letter while walking through Central Park. It's the line about the "sublime plan."

Early in the morning, there was a knock on the back corner of the rig. Most of these knocks are so quiet, but loud at the same time. Quiet because they are, but loud in my head since I instantly recognize it as a distant knock. It's weird. My eyes usually spring open or suddenly look up/around. It's an involuntary movement.

February 14, 2026:

8:58 a.m. - I started singing "Believe" by Cher.

9:11 a.m. - I began singing Al Green's "How Can You Mend a Broken Heart?"

Looked up the two videos about business with love. Didn't pay much attention to those before January 14th. Now it makes a bit more sense.

1:11 p.m. - Editing an author's third novel. Talking about two characters considering marriage, and I think to myself how foreign that would be. Would that be something I could even do? Then thoughts slide over to Fred, briefly - would that have even happened if we had met earlier?

Something thought of:

Age seventeen: This was the first transition in life to adulthood (1986).

Age thirty-four: The second switch began with the divorce (2003).

Age fifty-one: I was single and preparing to leave Minnesota (2020).

Age sixty-eight: ? (2037).

Life changes around every seventeen years for me.

3:14 p.m. - I'm editing someone's third novel, and realize out loud—I tell Fred about it—that I'm subconsciously inserting my life and Fred's into these storylines, thinking what could have been. Maybe. But as he put it, this go-round, the timing was off. Right after this thought, the spoken "Earth Angel" refrain starts in my head. I'm now smiling because I now know where all of these songs are coming from—Fred and I played Music Bingo on those Monday nights in Yuma. Face palm on that realization—a commonality.

Fred was missing from Facebook all day today.

February 15, 2026:

Every so often, I think about walking into the Whiskey Road Saloon and coming up from behind him while he sat at the high-top table waiting for me. He was looking at something on his phone on the right side. I came up on that side, happened to glance at what he was doing, and saw his phone. I blurted out, "What are you looking at?" and he quickly shut down his phone with an embarrassed look. I won't say anything more, but it was pretty funny. I didn't say anything more to him—the look on his face—you could tell he was mortified. I was laughing.

February 16, 2026:

I started singing "Hooked on a Feeling" for the better part of my trip to Palm Springs.

February 17, 2026:

One of the overhead lights in my sister's dining room flickered once while I was working at the dining room table.

February 18, 2026:

I don't know if Fred helped at all, but my computer hasn't charged at all today or last night, either, and it's still on after sixteen hours, holding at a steady thirty-one percent charge. (The charger needs to be replaced.) I said thank you to him in case that was what happened.

February 22, 2026:

Going to sleep that night, I heard in my right ear, "I really miss you, too."

February 23, 2026:

Morning taps/pops.

That afternoon, a voice told me to get over to the neighbor's twice to introduce myself. (probably nothing to do with Fred) ??? These days, though, I never know for sure about things that aren't directly tied to him.

February 26, 2026:

Had the right-before-sleeping run-through of faces. I finally asked, *Who are these people? Connections from the other side? Are these people wanting me to channel them? Soul connections?* There are hundreds and hundreds, thousands, of faces of everyone, and in the mix, I saw Fred in the crowd.

I followed him, losing sight of him occasionally. Followed him to a train platform, and he got on one and sped away.

February 28, 2026:

Fred was at the top of my Facebook list, finally reappearing after a week and a half of not being there. He showed up this morning as a reminder that I promised him I'd start typing again this afternoon and throughout the weekend, then wrapping up at the end of next week and into the next—getting it done sooner than later in March, edit in April, proof in May, release in June. Has he been missing for the past ten days?

I talk with you morning and night, and all day long—my "Morning Fred Fix" and the evening chill, and the daily shooting the shit. The photo montage serves as my daily litmus test—I talk with you every day, and I think of you damn near every minute.

March 3, 2026:

Cool breezes usually blow around my legs when I'm sitting at my desk—they come in constant waves. Nothing moving, no ventilation on, can be hot as hell in here, and the cool breezes will be ice cold around my shins—typically below my knees. Has been happening since Fall 2025, when I first noticed. Not sure I documented it, though. When it started, I freaked out, thinking I had a hole in my flooring somewhere. Tore this place apart looking for where this breeze was coming from. I found nothing. Now, I'm guessing it's Fred's presence.

March 11, 2026:

Working on a contract, and a voice said to go for a walk. I protested because I was working, and I got another request. I suggested I'd go after I finished the project, and a third time: "GO ON A WALK!"

"FINE! I'll go on a walk!"

I made a thirty-minute YouTube video of my thoughts, and at the end, two barn swallows dive-bombed me just like they did on March 18, 2025. This time, though, they screeched as they flew over within a foot of the top of my head. I ducked. *(video)*

Then my YouTube and Facebook went out at 10:15 p.m., when I had promised I would start writing at 10:00 p.m. Fifteen minutes passed, and those two channels wouldn't work for me, although the hotspot was still transmitting, and I could still get Google Docs to save. Four bars of 4G—

restarting my phone and computer and resyncing—no go. Spent two hours of the night writing this book.

March 12, 2026:

Butterflies in the morning.

Posted this on his Facebook page with the picture of the cacti from his spot at La Posa South:

Kiersten Hall>Fred Nass

```
Me and your favorite cacti are missing you today
and always.
```

Lunch with Lisa and Nancy in Wickenburg, AZ.

Promise of the book schedule in the car on the way home from lunch.

6:16 p.m. - I looked at Fred's Facebook page on the computer; it showed him as being on ten hours ago across his picture. (Facebook policy—the timestamps only go up to three hours of being offline, and then no longer display)—ten hours prior would be close to the time I posted on his Facebook page for his one-year "missing him." I took a screenshot of this.

Recorded the sunset.

The internet stayed on until 8:00 p.m., and then the internet went out for about two minutes, and then came back on —proving he was there and watching me keep my promise.

I have been typing since 8:45 p.m. - it's now 11:12 p.m.

March 13, 2026:

Typing at 11:22 a.m. about the burst of wind that hit my RV on March 12, 2025, a burst of wind just hit my rig again, moving it when there really isn't any wind outside. Again, nothing is moving.

I'll add that Fred wasn't on my Facebook friend list this morning.

I did look at his Facebook this morning, and no one else posted anything on his page. I couldn't care less if anyone appreciates my post, but where was everyone else? Well, everyone has their reasons, opinions—it was just sad to see that everyone went on with their lives and forgot/didn't bother to post something for him on the one-year anniversary of his death.

March 14, 2026:

I worked on the book.

He wasn't on Facebook today.

As I was getting into bed tonight, I got a message from Fred. He clarified his earlier statement that I was unable to handle channeling him fully. It's not that I couldn't handle it. It's that I can't now because of emotions on both sides. His energy would be stronger with me because of our shared strong emotions.

Heart palpitations were strong, and my brain popped this up out of nowhere. Once written, heart palpitations are gone. Breathing back to normal, and my heart is relaxed.

Besides the above message, it also occurred to me that when a message is coming in, my body's physiology changes; my heart races, I heat up, if I'm sitting or lying down, my body will detach from my consciousness, etc., and it can stretch from a couple of seconds to a couple of minutes.

March 15, 2026:

I worked on the book.

Filmed the last sunset in Quartzsite for the season. Stopped out at Fred's spot while driving around.

March 16, 2026:

Moving to a new location in Arizona to escape the heatwave coming into Quartzsite over the next couple of weeks.

A large black bird hovered over me, my RV, and my car as I was taking the last video of Quartzsite before hitting the road.

A crow was talking to me in the Bluewater Casino parking lot.

Went out to watch the SpaceX launch that didn't happen, but made me remember the one that I filmed and Fred used on Facebook.

A lot of "he likes you" videos are popping up on YouTube.

March 17, 2026:

Woke up to magpies hopping around and chattering on the roof of the RV.

Upon waking and before opening my eyes, I was looking at the face of a mourning dove. In color, looking around and at me. Then I heard the magpies and their songs.

Got on the road, asked for Moby, and the third song (of "Porcelain") came in after an extended pause. Once I heard that, I immediately felt comfortable knowing that Fred was on the road with me.

Another large crow in the truck stop parking lot is hopping around and occasionally talking.

A swarm of bees showed up, stayed for maybe twenty minutes, and then left. Encompassed my entire RV. I was in Seligman, AZ.

Thinking about the bees, The Beekeeper just popped into my head. I did look up the spiritual meaning—interesting and pertinent info of being divine messengers between this world and other realms.

March 18, 2026:

Decided to call the RV "The Magickal Mystery Tour."

Got to my next spot that afternoon, with a beautiful sunset. The Navajo Nation practically surrounds the location. I was told that it's a magickal land. Very energetic.

March 19, 2026:

If this was anything, I've opened the hood of my car before, but I stopped at a gas station to fill my coolant, and for the life of me, could not find the latch under the lip of the hood. So, I drove over to a car service place, the guy found it instantly and took the cap off slowly—reminding me that I need to be careful (which I know—but realized had I done it myself—I would have forgotten, being I was in a hurry this day—I would have been burned since the coolant was already boiling.) He's always keeping me safe—much like the Bluetti situation in January.

March 20, 2026:

If I work on other things or watch a YouTube video for a break, Fred doesn't appear in my Facebook friends' online sidebar. But if I work on his book and quickly check Facebook, there he is, listed among the top three online. It happened five times today. I'm also hearing knocks and at times, really loud, noticeable birdsong. (Nothing like pressure.)

March 21, 2026:

Video of Fred moving the cord—caught the tail end of the movement. *(video)*

Then, for half an hour, cool breezes wafted around my uncovered shins.

He's in the house and wants to make sure I stay on task for this book.

1:00 p.m. - my phone just bleeped and spat up an app that I have had in a deep sleep for the past year.

2:34 p.m. - Spoke to Chelsea, showed her the video of the cord moving, and said something else about Fred; she voiced her concern that I was in an unhealthy situation and that it was an obsession. I assured her that I was fine and Fred and I had it all figured out. She found the video odd.

Last night, unexpectedly thinking about how Fred said he was coming back via Lisa in January, the question: "Can the two people who are twin flames fall in love with the same soulmate?" The answer is "yes" from the Google rabbit holes I researched.

Saturn crossed my feeds, thoughts, etc., again, and I looked it up—binding souls and a karmic commitment.

March 22, 2026:

8:33 a.m. - Abrupt snap into the mid-1960s with scrolling wrought-iron plant stands, astro turf, stepping out of a trailer, sliding glass door. Sixties "railroad conductor" cap, long brown hair, midriff halter top with colorful patched pants. Walking out and leaving fast. I heard a sharp "Kiersten" from an older female—a grating voice trying to catch me as I left. Full color in the blink of an eye. In this vision, this "Kiersten" walked out the door and turned right past me to her right and to my left. I was facing her, and she was looking down. My heart rate spiked noticeably, and when the vision ended, it began to subside. As a side note, I've often wondered whether I had another life that ended before this one and whether I reincarnated immediately. Was this scene one of the last moments of my existence before this current lifecycle?

Taps on the inner walls of the RV.

Ravens in the juniper on either side of me.

Sounds of metal bars scraping together.

Note to self: Look up Krogher with an umlaut (???) or some variation. (Had this vision—will need to follow up on this.)

As soon as something happens, I must write it down immediately rather than thinking I'm going to remember it. I get the feeling of trying to remember and visualize, but it seems to disappear and sink back into the depths of my subconscious before I can write it down if I wait past a minute. It literally pops up and then disappears within a minute, or less.

Earlier, I remembered childhood bullies in the neighborhood and being able to look forward and protect myself. Saw bullies conspiring in the neighbor's backyard. I protected myself with visions then and still do today.

Got a couple of tingles and buzzing this morning with some astral travel. Body numbing out.

After the 1960s burst, I was looking at a concrete slab sitting on a bench next to Fred. I saw his left foot on the ground with his sneakers, and his right leg crossed over his left, and he was wearing jeans and a dark plaid shirt. Solid legs, neck, and head, but no outline of the torso. He was looking slightly off to the left while I was sitting on his right. I saw most of his profile with his scruffy look and wind in his hair. The rest of him would have probably filled in if my mind had stopped racing and I had stopped over-analyzing.

The landowner said on the first night that the land has a lot of energy, and you'll either enjoy it or it will drive you insane.

I just realized the Navajo Nation and the magick and energy involved literally surround me.

Have always been interested in New Mexico for some reason, and when I went there in 2018, I was energized.

I'm finally understanding the "let go" advice. It's not so much about letting go of the stress as about letting go of the constructs.

I've always felt that I've been riding the cusp of something more—something I'm supposed to be doing. Bigger, better, expansive. I'm getting it.

The previous tarot read said the end of March would be very magickal. I didn't believe that a couple of days ago, but I do now.

An idea popped into my head—*Go out and meditate at sunset.*

I guess that I reincarnated in 1969, from the mid sixties. I have had that thought for the longest time.

I'm following up on the "sequel" suggestion. Would that be the twin flame coming in as a future relationship, as Fred suggested in January, through Lisa?

I watched a tarot reading on YouTube, and it ended with a Two of Cups, and the King and Queen of Wands. I wrote on this content creator's wall: You've nailed it with this reading. I have been promised "my person" is coming back to me, but through another person, since he passed away over a year ago. I'm thinking it's his twin flame, since he said I would recognize him. That last part popped into my head last night; I had been wondering since this past January how all that would work in this physical realm and in this time. At the moment, that possibility is the top contender in my over-analytical, scientific, Aquarian brain.

March 23, 2026:

Another memory popped through into my consciousness: One of those evenings around the campfire, Fred and I had been talking about travel, driving to and from wherever, and I wondered out loud what the time difference from one place in Arizona, for example, is (really) compared to another location in Arizona, although it's all in one timezone? For example, the eastern side of Arizona will experience sunset earlier than the western side; however, the entire state is in one time zone. He immediately replied that twelve and a half miles equaled one minute of solar time. Not only did he impress me with his knowledge, but oh, did I find that intelligence sexy. He knew the answer immediately, and that was swoonworthy. (I'm a huge nerd.)

I learned quite a bit from him, enjoyed listening to him, and watching how his mind worked. He was a fascinating guy (still is), with random and expert knowledge. Extremely interesting to talk to. Again, the crown jewel was our conversations, generally around campfires.

March 24, 2026:

Woke up by hearing someone gasp/scream. Female voice, older, maybe?

6:00 p.m.: Talking with a neighbor and a friend from Palm Springs about how our lives crossed and put us both in our current, positive situation. I was telling her stories from my travels to her hometown, and she brought up how weird it was that we might have unknowingly crossed paths in the eighties, but didn't meet until February 2026, when we could help each other. (Has nothing to do with Fred, but these days, maybe it does?)

I told her that I often wondered if Fred and I had ever crossed paths. And then I told Fred that I would have Kimberly ask the next time they connected.

Additionally, while talking to her, I looked over her shoulder and saw a "UFO." Later, when I took a picture of the moon and the night sky, the "evidence" was still where I had seen the UFO earlier. I have a picture of the exhaust trail/cut through the atmosphere. I filed a report with a UFO website.

9:46 p.m. - Fred decided I needed more light near my keyboard, so he flipped the desk lamp on for me.

10:10 p.m. - A couple of heavier taps on top of the rig.

March 25, 2026:

I remembered the "Yelp Review" I wrote for him after leaving for Quartzsite to pick up my RV. I didn't put any identifiers on it or tag him. I told him I'd leave him a "Review" before I left Old Fogey Hot Springs. He didn't believe me until I posted it on Facebook, which garnered several likes and comments. I didn't hear anything from him, and I thought maybe I had gotten "too weird" for him. I wasn't being malicious; it was from the heart, about what a great person he was, and about camping with someone. I do not write reviews for everyone I meet, nor do I give them five plus stars or stellar praise.

I had a premonition of how Fred may come back to me in this lifetime, as Lisa said he would. Actually, there are two ways that could happen, which led me down a rabbit hole of quantum physics. Again, I didn't start this day thinking about all of this. This stuff pops into my head, and sometimes the information is "on fire" rather than being a lukewarm passing thought. These two possibilities were "on fire" and very "front and center" in my thoughts. I felt "clarity" opening up, and I felt great as I considered these possibilities. (Note: I do not have the time or the fortitude to examine items that don't fit my task, schedule, or interest level. If something comes in "lukewarm," I might make a note of it, but most often, I treat it as a passing thought that wisps by. When they are "on fire" though, I stand at attention and take note. When I thought of these two methods, it felt like I was finally seeing past a wall of static, into clarity and possibilities.

March 26, 2026:

First song up on Pandora disco station was "You Should Probably Leave" by Chris Stapleton. The third song was "South Dakota," and the fifth was "Joy of My Life." Over on YouTube, the first song that popped up in my feed was "Think I'm in Love With You."

March 27, 2026:

I went shopping today and picked up bananas, which reminded me of the trivial fact that both Fred and I searched for the perfect bananas. Both of us liked them green right on the cusp of turning yellow. From there, I remembered he loved cucumbers and would drink Cucumber Gatorade (it sounds weird, but it's not bad), and he loved garlic. He despised yogurt and green olives. Loved red beers. Was a consummate "foodie," and I even remember seeing a video of him doing a shot of something with a mummified toe at a bar in Alaska. (I have a palate for varied cuisine, but that's most likely where I would draw the line.)

Halfway through the store, it popped into my mind that once, while shopping in Anthem, my shopping cart started shocking me. I laughed it off, and not ten steps later, the cart handle shocked me, and then a couple of cans on the shelves shocked me. I thought the first shock was odd, but when it continued, I told Fred I didn't want to be shocked throughout the store and asked him to please stop. And the shocks stopped.

April Wine's "Just Between You and Me" keeps popping up; I finally looked up the lyrics. The phrase, "A love that seemed strong was not meant to be," hits.

This song has been playing in my head, on and off, for weeks now.

Earlier today, I was wondering whether I'd get back up to Sturgis this year, given rising gas prices. Then I remembered when we first met, I told him I had never been on a motorcycle before. I never did get an invitation. The only time we talked about it was when I thought I'd gotten a nice picture of his bike's silhouette against the sunset, but instead, all he saw were the bug guts on the windshield. He had told me he had laid his bike down once, and it took him and two other guys to pick it up because it weighed 850 pounds. He later told me about his medical conditions. I figured that either he wasn't in good health to give a newbie a safe ride, or didn't want to since he saved what he referred to as the "sissy seat" for a significant other, as in the woman he could never bring himself to talk about with me, and/or the phrase I've heard before of "No one rides for free; it's either gas, grass, or ass." I would have paid for the gas, believing he was a taken man, and I didn't have any available grass on me. Then that led me to thinking of Sturgis again, and I even went in 2025, and STILL did not get a ride!

Lastly, thinking of him at Sturgis again, I remember when he told me of him and his friend at a saloon in Deadwood. I had been telling him about the South Dakota Book Festival, how it is held in Deadwood every other year, and how I had never yet had a chance to see one of the "shootouts on Main Street" followed by the Court House Trial. He told me about himself and his friend at this bar, and Kevin Costner came up from behind them, slapped both of them on opposite shoulders, leaned in between them, and asked, "What are we drinking, boys?"

Apparently, the three guys sat around that evening, sharing drinks and stories. If I remember correctly, he said it was after *Dances with Wolves*, and Kevin was in town for some event having to do with the movie—from memory: a museum, or fundraiser, or something along those lines.

And the Pinball Hall of Fame in Las Vegas just popped into my head, too. He enjoyed his visit there and wanted to make sure I had a chance to go after I told him how much I love pinball machines.

March 28, 2026:

Remembering the information Fred gave me through Lisa and Kimberly, and then delving deeper into his comment about coming back to me during this lifetime, I hypothesize that he is telling me I will have a long and happy life. Which means… even with all of the turmoil on this planet, right now, the Earth keeps spinning, and life will get better—at least for me. But even if that doesn't happen, personally, I'm happy to know that "this too shall pass" and eventually, we will all crawl out of the quagmire that is currently making humankind suffer.

This is an example of the random stuff that floats through my gray matter each day.

9:30 a.m. - While working on the story part of this book, I was going back through his Facebook posts to clarify when something happened and whether it was a photo or a video. I will note that whenever I do look through his Facebook page—when I get up to his last video of him in the hospital, hours before his death—I look away. I physically turn my head and scroll through that section as fast as possible. I will not watch that video again. Ever.

But as I scrolled back to late 2023 and early 2024, I noticed that my posts were now visible on his page. Before his death, anything I tagged him on, which wasn't much since I didn't want to embarrass him or have his family or friends ask him questions, which would have put him in an awkward position, would never pop up on his page. He had my tags blocked, and yes, that hurt me, but it wasn't my place to dictate what he did and didn't have on his page. And in reality, the best part was spending time with him.

This morning, while scrolling back to a particular date, I noticed my posts were now appearing on his page. All of them. He must have unblocked my tags before he died. (Or did he unblock my tags after his death being he is good with manipulating energy/electricity?)

And let the tears commence.

Not that it makes a difference in the big picture, but to have the "proof" that I'm not just pulling this entire memoir out of my arse is huge. I've already written about my posts being blocked earlier in the book, and I'm not going to go back and change it; that was my known reality when I wrote it, and today, over a year since his passing, I learned a new tidbit.

For a break, I watched the movie *Jules* on YouTube while eating dinner. At the end of the movie, the alien needed cats to power the repair equipment to fix his ship. I saw what happened and remembered the red/pink stone Kimberly saw in one of her readings. Then, of course, the cats. I'm laughing.

March 29, 2026:

Lots of knocks over the past week or so. And I was haranguing you about something as I was working on this book, and I heard a faint, "Yeah, yeah, yeah." I then laughed and told you not to give me that line, and I felt a warm smile and heard one last "Yeah."

March 30, 2026:

Damn near every other song or two was Chris Stapleton on the disco station while working on the book.

And after a better part of a week, I told Fred he was missing on my Facebook page. Within an hour, he was back on the list.

I cut the music to tell him about the shot of the two lawn chairs out at Pilot Knob in the moonlight—how much I wanted to say the truth, but I didn't want to overstep any bounds.

Spent a good fourteen hours working on this book today.

As I fell asleep, my body dropped and numbed out. Third eye opened, running through a variety of random visions. Couldn't make sense of it, except that I hadn't had many visions lately. Maybe I was playing "catch-up?"

March 31, 2026:

5:00 p.m. - A cooking pot, stacked inside another cooking pot for the day, "settled," moved as if being pushed further into the bottom pot. Made me jump. No wind, nothing moving, I was sitting here typing. Moved by itself. Probably a reminder to wash my dishes—I've only been telling him that for the past few days that I have spent working on his book.

Darn near every other song while streaming music is by Chris Stapleton. No complaints.

6:00 p.m. - Introduced the book cover to social media and the website. I asked what Fred thought. And the next song played was Moby's "Porcelain." I think he approves.

8:58 p.m. - One song ended on Pandora, and then another started, but it only played a bar or two, glitched out, and then popped into "Sweet Home Chicago," Blues Brothers. Now "So Afraid of the Darkness" by Walter Trout is playing. Interesting lyrics.

Before going to bed, I realized the date. Two years ago, we were at the Texas Roadhouse in Yuma with the waiter who didn't believe that we hadn't been married for years. He's the one who brought us two bags each of those peanuts with our check. I believe he got a good tip. March 31, 2024, was the first day of the best bonus week I could have asked for. Thanks for still being in Arizona and at the Pilot Knob LTVA when I arrived.

Epilogue

Written on March 31, 2026
before Kimberly's connection with Fred
on April 21, 2026

It has been said that Quartzsite gives you what you need—not necessarily what you want. In Fred's case, Quartzsite gave me both what I wanted and needed, but with the proverbial "fine print."

I'll add another familiar adage: "Hindsight is 20/20." As I've mentioned several times throughout this book, I really never knew where I stood with him. I had a strong underlying idea, and there were clear high points, but at other times, I did not know.

Since he began connecting with Kimberly on my behalf, I've learned what really happened and why everything happened the way it did. Each day, I get a bit more "comfortable" with what went down between us. The unknown and the inability to get a good handle on it were frustrating to me. The confusion of being absolutely ignored, and the devastation of learning of his impending death from his last Facebook Live video (just typing that has the tears coming again, full bore) gutted me completely. Those ingredients make up the toxic mix that had me on the edge of calling it quits myself. When something so wonderful enters the picture and is then taken away, leaving so many unanswered questions and no communication—as I said earlier, I understand *why* now, but at the time and throughout, I was utterly distraught and inconsolable.

And I can only imagine what it was like for him. He tried to figure me out and was a polite gentleman who (I'm sure) picked up that I liked him, too, after I finally figured it out. But because I never followed up on any obvious opportunities (because I believed he had a significant other in some capacity), I caused him self-doubt, similar to what his mixed messages were causing me. We got along fantastically—we certainly had the platonic friend thing going full-tilt, but kicking it over the fence into something more never happened. We could talk about anything except the nature of our relationship; whether it was anything beyond friendship was never spoken of or resolved.

Along with my presumption that he had a current relationship (which he never clarified either way), I knew he wasn't doing well healthwise, so I followed his lead on any activities we planned. I had no problem hanging out with him and was perfectly happy to sit next to him for long stretches, which I'm sure he thought was odd. And quite frankly, as fast as I flitter about from one thing to the next, I found it rather odd, too. But because of that, I knew that my heart and soul were all in, even if my over-analytical brain wasn't one hundred percent onboard.

In reality, he couldn't get rid of me if he tried—and he did—even when we were hanging out together; between the hot and cold, the suggestions of other men I might be interested in, the attempts to tell me about L.M., his insistence that he wasn't smart and couldn't talk right, and his occasional silence that he could never pull off for very long since the two of us could not stay quiet when we were near each other. He tried—he really did, but I wouldn't go away. And even now, I apparently still won't go away, and the two of us still banter on.

But I can see why he did what he did. He was a sixty-two-year-old bachelor who, although he had friends and family, I would imagine did most of his personal things by himself, including dying. And I'd probably do the same if I'd been doing things by myself for over sixty-two years. You're already busy with more important matters, such as health issues, countless doctor appointments, hoping you'll live to see another day, and getting your affairs in order. There is limited (if any at all) mental and physical space to allow a new person in and cultivate something when you know there is a finite amount of time. Even to me, that sounds like a real hassle; you're wrapping up all of life's loose ends, and then a strong pull towards a potential love interest enters your world, but life's clock is literally (and loudly) ticking. As he said after the fact, the timing was off, and I completely understand now.

I will admit that I was jealous of L.M.—but again, I was nowhere in his life until that fateful day in December 2023 when he showed up to watch the movie *Elf* on a bed sheet hung over the side of a renovated shuttle bus out in the Sonoran Desert. But I am glad that he had someone to hang out with for a good portion of his life, leading up to his death. I wish he had expanded on his relationship with his "Very Good Friend, L.M.," but again, who needs more potential hassles with that loud ticking clock following you? It was best that he left it as it was. He had me as a friend in Arizona—someone who would spend time with him and wouldn't be put off with simply sitting around a fire and staring into the vast openness of the night sky. Someone who apparently was very content to sit with him and enjoy his quiet company. He played it well, and I'm sure if I were in his situation, I would have done the same.

Since March 12, 2025, I thank him each day for entering my life and am getting a smidgen more comfortable with this entire situation. I let him know that I truly appreciate and love him very much. I say "comfortable" because our relationship was and still is something I have never experienced. I'm sure others have experienced this or something similar, but such situations are rarely discussed. In reality, I was keeping my notes but never planned to put them out there for all to see until he insisted I tell our story.

I know he made a concerted effort to come back down to the desert one more time for the 2024/25 season to see me, as well as soak in the warmth and sun, and knock a few more things off that bucket list of his. I'm happy that he kept "living" and didn't succumb to sitting in bed waiting for his "expiration date" to arrive.

However, I've often tried to pinpoint when he decided to cut me off cold turkey. With the beaming smile on his face, the morning after he arrived in Quartzsite in November 2024, I knew he was all in on that day. If it was the end of that day, after that evening's drum circle, that he was going to cut me off (because he was very quiet that night), I flubbed up his plans by listening to the universe tell me the next day to go look for coffee at the new Dollar General on the east side of town. He was rather surprised and agreed under pressure when Captain Crunch and I held him hostage in the grocery store with the pointed invitation to a campfire the next evening. I know he went out to Beer Belly's that afternoon for live music and a few beers. Was it that afternoon he made the promise to himself to cut me off?

As usual, though, he fell right back into the familiar, compatible rhythm we had always had around a campfire/simply being together, and he started bringing up ideas for things we could do that season, and I responded accordingly. During our conversation, he once again interjected that his heart couldn't handle a lot of stress and bumping around, to which I nodded, but that line still didn't make me run for the hills. I would imagine to him that I was either really dense and not picking up what he was trying to say, or I didn't care and really liked him, and the latter possibility is what really scared him. He didn't want or need that hassle.

In less than two hours around that campfire, and after I told him I really missed our traditional morning soaks in the sun, his vibe instantly changed. The smile on his face disappeared. He called it for the evening, blaming it on the wind and cold, said goodbye, put his lawn chair in the back of his truck, and drove out of my life. I knew when I watched his taillights disappear down the driveway of La Posa South, across the highway, that something was not right. Something was very wrong, and it all went downhill after that. As I mentioned earlier in this book, his Facebook posts were few and far between after that date, and his videos were not as chipper as they once were. He was tired and sad. And across the highway, I was tired, sad, and confused.

But now I understand what happened, and I feel so bad for him. I feel bad for myself. I feel bad for us and for what could have been if the timing hadn't been off this time around. There are several things a reader can glean from this book, but the most important is *communication*. Everything else can be worked out, but please don't leave your loved ones (family, friends, or a potential partner) in the dark when they care about you. That circumstance really rips the heart and soul out of people who love and care for you.

As counterintuitive as it is to say, I am relieved he is no longer here in the body that once plagued him with a myriad of health issues. But I am forever thankful and grateful that I get to talk with him each day, and to see/hear/feel, and even smell his cologne every so often, and it's more frequent than not. With his body issues out of the way, I spend each and every day with him, and I feel so loved and comfortable. I value (more than anyone could possibly imagine) his existence in my life, as unconventional as it may be viewed in today's society. I am also not swayed by those who feel it's their place to dictate to me what I can and cannot believe based on their presumed convictions, especially when I know full well what I'm experiencing every day and, recently, what my friends have been experiencing with me.

Lastly, I know I mentioned I was only going to document up until March 31, 2026, but Fred has begun making his presence known to others beyond Kimberly and Lisa when they connect with him. When I'm talking about him, which is more often than not, Fred has begun showing up in some manner for others to witness be it the flickering lights, interrupted music streams/radio play, electronics timing out but still functioning with appropriate power levels, temperature changes, blasts of wind, objects moving, and most recently, a car stereo flipping on at a high volume level. Fred is not gone at all. He's still here with us, and he loves to have people talk to/ with him. He is still his wonderful, sometimes cheeky self, who likes to be sneaky and playful. And I am so happy that Fred and I have finally opened all our lines of communication.

Journal Entries

I know I said I'd finish documenting on March 31, 2026. However, Fred has shared additional messages and revelations during the final editing and design of this book, which I believe should be included.

April 1, 2026:

Fred is missing from the Facebook line-up. He was on the past two days, though.

I'm getting a strong scent of Tide pods—started ten minutes ago, I suppose. I know Fred used those. Mine are sitting in a sealed container behind a wall, ten feet away from me. I'm not wearing clean clothes right now, and I haven't had a shower in six days. Not that we all need to know that…

11:19 a.m. - Working on this book and ran past the rune breakdown of your name. Decision made: stars on neck, and Fred's sigil on my lower back. I'll do that this summer.

11:57 a.m. - Sade's "The Sweetest Taboo" came on, and the sinking feeling showed up in my chest, starting the heart palpitations—usually when Fred is around. (I've experienced heart palpitations throughout life— usually with a lot of coffee, but I haven't had coffee in…. In a long time.)

I was watching one of my favorite content creators on YouTube when the comments about lucid dreaming and astral projection came up. I then asked Fred if he had ever known that I had visited him via astral travel in the last six weeks of 2024. Probably four times. I described it to him. It'll be interesting if I get a response of some type or interesting dreams. I'll have to have Kimberly ask him if he ever knew, or ever felt me there, or dreamed of me?

11:11 p.m. - The light went out.

11:17 p.m. - The light came back on.

The light stayed on while I worked, between 1:30 a.m. and 3:30 a.m. But when I finally got to bed, it would flip off, and if I ignored it, it would flip on again about ten minutes later. Or it would flip off, and if I needed it, I would turn it back on, only for it to flip back off within five minutes. Uh huh… Someone was being "cheeky" again.

April 3, 2026:

A lot of solar lamp flickering and not on Facebook.

April 4, 2026:

A lot of solar lamp flickering and not on Facebook.

April 5, 2026:

A lot of solar lamp flickering and not on Facebook.

April 6, 2026:

One of the Fox Pointe authors passed away on April 5, 2026, and she popped into my mind before I opened my eyes—just woke up though. She was smiling at me, with a skinnier face and a gray short-sleeved shirt, a spotlight of sunshine on the top left of her head. As soon as I recognized her and said, "Hi," she disappeared. I got up and ordered her flower arrangement for her funeral service.

April 7, 2026:

Called Lisa to find out if she was done with her Foreword. While talking with her (the best way to describe it), Fred pushed off the RV (like pushing off a wall while swimming) and was at her place within two minutes, kicking up the wind on an otherwise windless day.

A lot of solar lamp flickering and not on Facebook.

April 8, 2026:

A lot of solar lamp flickering and not on Facebook.

Felt a pinprick on my right thumb while sitting at the dinette table—remembered the pinprick feeling from last year.

April 9, 2026:

A lot of solar lamp flickering and not on Facebook.

April 10, 2026:

Left for Lisa's in Phoenix.

That night, while Lisa was cooking dinner and I was sitting in a recliner on the opposite side of the rig, the RV ever so slightly shook from side to side. This made Lisa spin around and ask if I felt it, and I said, "Yes." Then it happened again. Keeping in mind, there is no way to wiggle that RV side to side since it's packed in between two other RVs, lengthwise. Fred was "in the house."

The overhead light flickered.

April 11, 2026:

Sitting with Lisa in her living room, we both witnessed Fred playing with the hallway light, which neither of us was near.

Later, I showed Lisa how to do energy work by using both telekinesis and electrokinesis: energy balls, pushing negative energy toward her, the paperclip-and-staple trick, casting a circle around her, and then taking it down so she could feel the temperature differences.

April 12, 2026:

Lisa, Nancy, I, and another friend went to an Ostrich Ranch in Marana, AZ, where I found the two-foot feather I envisioned on December 27, 2025.

Later that evening, I suggested we watch the movie *Contact* (after I brought up the VLA). After all these years of watching that movie, I had the urge to look up any correlation between Vega and Arcturus (mind blown).

April 14, 2026:

I woke up to Linda Ronstadt's "Blue Bayou" playing in my head.

Blinking solar light—with an urge to get to work—lots of writing.

April 15, 2026:

Blinking solar lamp all day—with an urge to get to work—lots of writing.

Two white butterflies at this newest spot.

April 16, 2026:

Blinking solar lamp all day—with an urge to get to work—lots of writing.

I was adding the "Everyone has their own kink" paragraph and noting that Fred nearly fell off his chair from all the fidgeting he was doing. I heard the wind coming in across the field across the street, but was busy writing, and as it grew louder, I looked up and out the screen door to see a big gust of red sand headed my way. Most of it went under the RV, but he was telling me he was embarrassed, I'm sure.

April 17, 2026:

Blinking solar lamp all day—with an urge to get to work—lots of writing. (sent out ARCs).

Texted Lisa about the Foreword, and then asked Fred to light a fire under her butt. Wind pushed off the RV again, and within a handful of minutes, her online gin rummy game seized up on her phone, and it didn't matter what she did; nothing worked until she emailed me the Foreword, and her phone unlocked. (Thanks, Fred.)

When I sent out the ARCs, I got one huge gust against the RV on an otherwise windless day.

April 18, 2026:

Allowed me to film him messing with the solar lamp. *(video)*

April 19, 2026:

I told him this morning that if we didn't continue carrying on this way after his death, he was still very much appreciated when he was here in the physical realm, and yes, loved. What we have now is the cherry on top, the bonus of it all, and such a blessing. Something I look forward to every day. Very happy he's here with me. I enjoy his presence.

I caught him in the act of changing my computer clock. *(video)*

You're still not on Facebook.

Bought a turquoise necklace from a twelve-year-old named Carmella today in Winslow, AZ. There's a feather on it. (Feather = good luck, according to her.)

The two white butterflies showed up again this afternoon.

I've realized that when he wants me to see certain videos, they pop up in my feed: Marfan's, sepsis, heart, planetary, tarot readings, science stuff, Arcturus info, etc.

Light came on this evening when it was getting dark, and when I needed the light, it went off—he's having fun.

11:43 p.m. - I just noticed that there was light static in my ear, and my right ear just showed up with a solid noise signal. After wondering about it, it went away. (Fred used to have that water static sound in his ears, too.)

April 20, 2026:

Three plus hours of driving—not much, but I did get Moby's "Porcelain" before turning onto Hwy 602 with all of the potholes. Concentrated more on those than the song. But thanked him, as well.

Got to the hotel, and once again, my computer thought it was on Eastern time.

April 21, 2026:

Please read the last chapter, entitled "Fred's Thoughts on April 21, 2026."

Ears with a water rushing sound, then a one-note sound, for a short amount of time.

April 22, 2026:

Got a single note in my ears for a few miles of driving.

That night, I closed my eyes to sleep and instantly saw a wooden board with lettering on it. All caps, three rows, but I was passing to the right of it and missed whatever message was on it. I remember seeing the letters "B U S," but there was more to that word than "bus." Perhaps I'll dream of it again.

April 23, 2026:

Driving this morning, I got another one-note tone in my ears for a short amount of time.

I was plugging batteries in, and behind me, a lantern came on. It wasn't on when I sat down. I thanked Fred and figured out how to shut it off.

April 24, 2026:

Quiet.

April 25, 2026:

Called Lisa to ask her to please write more—don't hold back. On the phone for 1:07:00. At the end of the conversation, she began channeling Fred again. I think Fred is going to help her rewrite the full Foreword.

This afternoon, one of the bike's spoke decorations started blinking on the floor.

April 26, 2026:

Facebook post: I took my "morning nap" and, while still groggy but waking up, "I Was Made for Loving You" (be it Kiss or Yungblud) started playing in my head, and then my heart began racing. The electrical tingling hit my shins and feet for a few seconds, and I welcomed him in, but those subsided. My heart kept racing, and I listened to this video, which was automatically followed by Chris Stapleton's "South Dakota."

I told him last night that he is a pure romantic and I always feel loved. I told him this morning—something he's heard me say many times, that I'm the pickiest SOB when it comes to who I spend my time with, and it's hard as hell to impress me, but he brings the game every time.

These lyrics hit. Pure, unfiltered, and literal.

He keeps me sane by loving me, and I fully reciprocate.

April 27, 2026:

I had to run to Cedar City, UT, today. It's about a one and a half hour drive, one-way, from where I am out in the "boonies." The radio reception isn't the greatest out here, so I loaded up my speaker and my Bluetti for the drive. I pulled up my disco channel on Pandora and started driving.

Around four or five songs in, I'm at about nine thousand feet, and my stream cuts out halfway through a song. I figure I'm out of range, which is weird since I get great service damn near everywhere I go, but I figure it'll pop back on eventually.

After the better part of two minutes, Chris Stapleton's "I Think I'm in Love With You" comes on (keep in mind I was listening to KC and the Sunshine Band—but Fred has been known to slip in Chris Stapleton songs and Moby's "Porcelain" on whatever channel I'm listening to whenever he wants—and he'll cut a song off to send me a specific song, too.) He sends me songs all the time.

I smiled and thanked him, and yes, a tear or two fell. But then another blues song came on, and I thought *okay*, and then another... so I asked him, "Did you switch the channel/station?" And I heard a "Yes."

Sure enough, I got to Cedar City, opened my phone, and the screen quickly switched from what was originally playing (KC screenshot from when the phone screen originally went into standby) to Eric Clapton's screenshot on my Stevie Ray Vaughn station.

I didn't so much introduce him to the blues, but that genre and that station became the "go-to" for every campfire we had, and every time we spent an afternoon soaking up some Vitamin D. And of course, I listen to that station damn near every time I travel—it's great traveling music. Who doesn't want to fly down the highway with Muddy Waters, George Thorogood, and Johnny Lang?

So, note to self: My traveling companion prefers the blues (or his classic rock, which I also like.)

PS. I'll add, he sent me:

- "I Think I'm in Love With You"
- "You Should Probably Leave"
- "I Was Wrong"
- "Without Your Love"
- "Loving You on My Mind"
- "Joy of My Life"
- "Bad As I Used to Be"
- "Tennessee Whiskey"

Eight songs over the course of the last hour of driving. He really is quite the romantic.

April 28, 2026:

I realized this afternoon that for the last couple of days, the "friends online" sidebar has been missing.

Got the single note/tone in my ear for a few minutes earlier this evening.

9:55 p.m. - Slight drafts of ice-cold air floating past me on the desk—between me and the computer screen.

10:23 p.m. - Just heard a faint "I love you."

April 29, 2026:

Got a few Chris Stapletons on streaming today, otherwise quiet so far.

I did ask him if, when he comes back to me through a new person in this lifetime, we will still have this connection? I sure hope so.

It also occurred to me that maybe my Facebook posts were not unblocked before he passed away; maybe that's something he did after the fact, much like the way he already manipulates electricity/electronics, etc.

9:48 p.m. - Case in point with the electronics: My friend just sent me a message on Facebook two minutes ago, yet it says it was sent twenty-three hours ago, and she was supposedly last online twelve hours ago. I just sent her the screenshots, and she has agreed that he's having fun with the electronics again.

10:10 p.m. - Wrapping up the last of the proofing, and gentle wafts of very cool air are "breathing" onto my face. He's in front of me.

April 30, 2026:

Well, it has been established. Long road trips are when the blues are to be played, and really no other genre. Again this morning, I ran another errand, turned on my disco channel, and it played half of an Al Green song before it glitched. There was an extended lag, then Chris Stapleton's "Traveler" came on, followed by other blues songs. When I got to my destination and looked, the same thing from Monday: turned on the phone screen, it jumped from the original screenshot of Al Green's album cover to one of Eric Clapton's album covers playing on the blues station. I've received and understood the message.

Fred's Thoughts

Email from Kimberly Dawn,
who connected with Fred
on April 21, 2026

Well, Kiersten,

If I hadn't lived it, I might not have believed it. As of
late, I've been noticing a shift in my reception, from
clair-based experiences to flat-out channeled messages.
Like having a verbal conversation in my mind. I didn't
see it coming, but it all makes sense. He wrote the
ending to your book. Take a look.

 I will preface by saying that when I sat down to open
up, I saw a dragon gently flying over clouds... purples
and fuchsia colors. And on this dragon was Fred... which
was a sight, let me tell you. He dismounted the dragon
and walked directly toward me (very tall) until he was
out of my periphery, then sat down in the same chair
with me. I took this to be an opportunity to channel,
so I opened the door to him, and this is what happened.
He wants the channeled message to be the bow that wraps
up the package.

Kiersten, this isn't going to be the reading you expect-
ed. You're used to me showing Kim memories, pictures,
scenes, and signs. Not this time. Both you and she have

grown, and you're ready for this channeled message. In Kim's mind, I arrived on a purple dragon, gliding over rolling purple clouds. Imagine me, in denim, a leather jacket, and shades, riding a purple dragon like a Harley! I hopped off, walked towards Kim, and asked her to convey through her. I'm sitting with her now. Everything from here on is my words directly to you.

I am so glad you found the strength and courage to write this book. Ours is a beautiful story. It began lifetimes ago, and here in the desert, we meet again to fulfill and continue that love, a love that transcends time and space. It is multidimensional. And while that is hard for many to grasp, you and I know that it is as real as anything you can see, smell, or touch. Imagine if I had remained in the 3D. Would we have found the same connection? Probably not. The process of finding each other across dimensions involves far more than meets the eye. Openness, forgiveness, growth, integration, and the willingness to accept and believe in something beyond what humans are taught as acceptable. Thank you for taking that chance. Thank you for being the one to stick your neck out; to take a chance on me and on love.

This book is not just about the connection that you and I share. It's a testament to the fact that there's more beyond what humans are led to understand. We are so much more. Capable of so much more. Much of our lives are spent trying to catch a glimpse of what that is. Even the smallest glimpse can be a touching memory that lasts a lifetime. And, for some, a lifetime of small moments begins to add up. How could they be imagined? We all share a common desire for something more. This internal feeling that there must be something more. The "why am I here" and "what's this all for?" It's for each and every one of us to learn, experience, remember, and find our way back to Center. The Center of all that is.

Kiersten, you think you're writing this book for you and to honor us. It's also part of the now. The rising of Earth's frequency, connection to Source, growing, and awakening. Eyes are opening, hearts are warming, and lights are beginning to glow—similar to the one on your table. (chuckle) And so it goes, soul after soul reconnects with self, and collectively we light up the world.

Up until now, this story has been based on two people. You and me. Love and connection. But in truth, it reaches much further than that. It's a beacon, a ray of light and hope for those who, in their heart of hearts, know there is something more to this existence but are afraid to embrace it. Afraid to defy what they've been taught, afraid of the isolation or ridicule that can come with defying the norm, afraid of the unknown, and what they might find around the corner. But imagine if Kim hadn't been moved to reach out to you. Imagine if you hadn't accepted her offer and the resulting message. The list of intersections is infinite. The synchronicities are not random. Never before has there been such a perfect opportunity to embrace and integrate all that is. In a world full of distraction and chaos, focus on the light.

When one light glows near another, the radiance grows. On and on. And, light never shines brighter than in darkness. So, my love, let our love be the first flame in the path to lighting up the world.

I love you,
Fred

I also had Kimberly ask about my flickering lights:

"I'm not going to lie, I'm enjoying this dimension. Toying with K's light is a fun way to let her know I'm here. And, yes, I'll communicate with it if she asks."

My thoughts on Fred's message from today:

Well then!

He'd be right—I wasn't expecting this message. But I'm also not surprised.

Have you ever thought, "Is this it? Is this all there is?" Sure, you can get excited about your favorite team winning, getting a new car, being proud of yourself for a job well done, buying a new outfit, or whatever. But in the big picture, is that all there is? I know I've had that thought a gazillion times.

Since my single digits, I've always had an inkling that there is something more; that the story we are all spoonfed from "Day 1" is a false narrative. Or, at the very least, not the complete story.

When I was five years old, I started asking questions, and when I did and got the standard three-ring-binder, one-size-fits-all answers from those who didn't want to bother with an inquisitive child, I realized that if I wanted the answers, it was up to me to find them.

Fast forward to my teenage years, and I was in bookstores and libraries looking for answers that made sense to me. Seriously, how can a school's science class teach you one thing, but society and outside influences tell (and threaten) you to believe something else lest you be cast from the "modern-day" world?

I kept up this curious nature into adulthood, and with the accessibility of the internet, I fell down fascinating "rabbit holes" into various topics that started sculpting the narrative of the information I already had, along with the beliefs I had researched and hold to this day.

Upon meeting Fred, my thoughts regarding him were limited to everything you've read so far in this book. However, after his death and the closer connection we formed—especially after he emerged from the limited human brain and concepts/beliefs learned over sixty-two years, he unknowingly (or maybe knowingly) started stitching everything together for me. All of the things that made sense to me—all of the personal research I had done and continue to do. This most recent message from Fred puts it all together for me, then asks/begs me to keep filling in any blank spaces and to learn even more.

Earlier in this book, I mentioned that the best way to "woo" me (probably with different wording) is to talk to me in scientific terms. Give me facts, teach me something, and give me the opportunity to teach you something; reciprocal learning and discovery, if you will. With this message, he has certainly done that: what I've figured out over all of these decades has been confirmed. Then, with this new information, my curiosity is piqued once again. I have a new research project! (This is exciting to me.)

I do understand what he's talking about in this message, and I have asked him to send me more material to learn from on YouTube or to share different thoughts and ideas to research. One of my favorite things to do is learn, and it's even more fun (and fulfilling) when someone confirms everything up to the current moment and then gives you more to think about. More mysteries to unravel. More rabbit holes to explore. I know that not everything on the internet is true, but it's a great place to start and expand on for your own research.

From what he's shown me so far and continues to convey, I have a clearer, deeper understanding of death and the "simulation" we're all taking part in. Pure and simple, all living things—including humans—are balls of energy. Since energy is constantly regenerating, we never die. People just shed their "human body" when it's time to clock out; our true selves (souls) are having a "human experience." We are here to learn and help our souls ascend, and we choose to return to school (this planet) to continue our growth journeys.

Acknowledgments

First off, thank you to everyone who has ever crossed my path and heard me talk about Fred ad nauseam. Those kind people who let me speak until I could speak no more, which probably meant hours out of their lives listening to me rave on about a guy they may never have met and/or would never have the chance to meet in this lifetime.

Of course, a huge thank you to my friend Kimberly Dawn, who came into my life nearly six years ago for something entirely different, and, unknowingly at the time, would literally save my heart from shriveling and dissolving into dust in March of 2025 with her gift of mediumship. I am so happy that she felt comfortable enough to offer her help and share her insight and understanding with me. I honestly don't know where I would be today if she hadn't offered to connect with him six days after his body gave out in that hospital bed.

As for Lisa Anne, I had the pleasure of meeting her and forming a fast friendship on October 4, 2025—a mere six months ago, as I write this. We clicked as "sisters from another mother," but I had no idea she also had a deep sense of mediumship. I didn't find that out until she fully channeled Fred on the drive back to Phoenix on January 14, 2026, which allowed me not only to learn additional information but also to speak to Fred directly, and he responded. It was another opportunity for conversation; granted, it wasn't as long, but it still counts to me.

My daughter, Chelsea, also has a stake in this unexpected journey. She is the person who did the cover design, editing, and formatting, as she has done for my first six books. She is talented beyond belief, and I'm so happy that she is my co-publisher for Fox Pointe Publishing, LLP. She does her mom proud with everything she touches and has surpassed every expectation I've ever had. Chelsea is also great company when I'm down in the dumps, especially in situations like this. I love her very much, and she is awesome!

Last but definitely not least, a loving thank you to Fred, who didn't give up on me when I couldn't figure out why he was talking to me and kept coming around. His kindness and politeness finally made my mind click, and my heart engage—picture slow-grinding gears spitting out copious amounts of dust. I thank him every day for the time he gave me, even when he wasn't feeling good. And even though he claims he wasn't able to show me love, he did so every day and continues to do so even though his human body is no longer walking this Earth. This book wouldn't exist without him in my life. Furthermore, I would still be cynical and jaded about matters of the heart had I not met him in December 2023, which allowed our souls to recognize each other. But for him to remain in my life past March 12, 2025, I am more than relieved/pleased/honored that he has; I would have been an absolute shell of a human had that not been the case.

About the Author

Kiersten Hall is a thirty-year speaker/presenter, thirty-five-year comedienne-in-hiding, thirty-six-year entrepreneur, forty-two-year salesperson, and lifelong, self-proclaimed hippie. In 2023, she became an empty-nester after thirty-one years of children in the house and now lives as a full-time nomad/RV'er, constantly searching for a perpetual summer with no snowbanks or inclement weather in sight. Kiersten still writes and gives author visits, school readings, literary events, etc., across the United States, all designed to keep her busy (and out of trouble).

To date, Kiersten has published six books, with *An Unexpected Journey* being her seventh. Much like her varied interests, she tends to write about whatever piques her curiosity, allowing her to share her stories with all ages across several genres.

Published Books

"I Do"—Fifteen Years of Wedding Misadventures
memoir and bridal planner

Corner Confessions
hybrid fiction/non-fiction novel, first in series

The Lies We Live
hybrid fiction/non-fiction novel, second in series

JELLYBEANS
children's picture book with an emphasis on inclusivity and kindness

The Blue Frog
children's picture book with a "whodunnit" flair

Scout
children's picture book about a newly adopted puppy

An Unexpected Journey
memoir and "love letter" to my soulmate